Maternal Pedagogies
In and Outside the Classroom

Maternal Pedagogies
In and Outside the Classroom

Edited by
Deborah Lea Byrd and Fiona Joy Green

DEMETER

DEMETER PRESS

Published by:
Demeter Press
c/o Motherhood Initiative for Research and
Community Involvement (MIRCI)
140 Holland St. West, P.O. 13022
Bradford, ON, L3Z 2Y5
Telephone: 905.775.9089
Email: info@demeterpress.org
Website: www.demeterpress.org

Demeter Press logo based on Skulptur "Demeter" by Maria-Luise Bodirsky
<www.keramik-atelier.bodirsky.edu>

Cover Design/Interior Design: Luciana Ricciutelli

Printed and Bound in Canada

Library and Archives Canada Cataloguing in Publication

Maternal pedagogies : in and outside the classroom / edited by Deborah Lea Byrd and Fiona Joy Green.

Includes bibliographical references and index.
ISBN 978-0-9866671-6-9

1. Teacher-student relationships. 2. Motherhood.
3. Critical pedagogy. 4. Feminism and education.
I. Byrd, Deborah Lea, 1953- II. Green, Fiona J.

LB1033.M38 2011 371.102'3 C2011-905663-1

Debbie dedicates this book to…

Derek Leland Byrd,
who teaches me in so many ways how to be a better person and mother
and to
Elizabeth Louise Machen Byrd,
who taught me to treasure honesty, integrity, and friendship.

Fiona dedicates this book to…

Liam Seth Edginton-Green, my son who, from the first moment
our eyes met, has graced my life with his teachings of patience,
kindness, insight, and an unstoppable love of life
and to
Keith Louise Fulton
my mentor and friend who, with the upmost respect, care, support
and compassion, guided me through my early years of teaching and
encouraged me as a young scholar to follow my interest in
exploring the realities of feminist mothering.

Table of Contents

Acknowledgements

We are most grateful to Dr. Andrea O'Reilly, who over the last decade has created, nurtured, and sustained a feminist and international community of scholars, artists, social service providers, and activists who share a desire to pay tribute to motherwork, to support those who engage in it, and to critically examine—and from a variety of cultural locations—all aspects of (other)mothering and motherhood. Andrea O'Reilly is the founder of the Motherhood Initiative for Research and Community Involvement (MIRCI), previously the Association for Research on Mothering (ARM), the *Journal of the Motherhood Initiative for Research and Community Involvement* (JMI), formerly the *Journal of the Association for Research on Mothering* (JARM), and Demeter Press, the first press in the field of Motherhood Studies.

We also would like to thank the spirited Renée Knapp, Coordinator of MIRCI and Publishing Coordinator at Demeter Press, who works tirelessly behind the scenes to organize conferences and to assist those who are publishing in JMI or with Demeter Press.

May the four of us continue to learn from one another and enjoy each other's company for years to come.

Introduction

Maternal Pedagogies: In and Outside the Classroom

DEBORAH LEA BYRD AND FIONA JOY GREEN

WHAT IS THE RELATIONSHIP BETWEEN mothering and teaching, especially as conceptualized by feminists? Are there "maternal" ways of constructing and transmitting knowledge and if so, how do these vary according to such factors as race, class, gender, ethnicity, sexual identity, nationality, and/or (dis)ability? What kinds of teacher-student relationships characterize the interactions of a given group of mothers and the children they're rearing, and are these dynamics stable or do they change over time? Is it empowering to attach the label "maternal" to a specific set of pedagogical strategies and goals or to use the adjective "maternal" to describe specific teacher-student dynamics that occur in the classroom and other public settings? Or is doing so limiting—tantamount to re-inscribing patriarchal and racist notions of "proper" female behavior, endorsing heteronormativity, and/or perpetuating essentialist notions of mothers and mothering?

These are some of the questions addressed in the essays that follow, essays that build upon an extensive, interdisciplinary body of anti-oppression scholarship. Many of our contributors draw upon research and theory in the fields of critical pedagogy and feminist ethics and philosophy, extending the arguments of such scholars as Paulo Friere, Nel Noddings, Lisa Delpit, Mary Belenky, Gail Sloan Cannella, Karey Harwood, Gunilla Dahlberg, Peter Moss, Vivyan Adair, and Margie Mayfield. Some essays contribute in new ways to scholarship on indigenous, Afro-centric, post-colonial, and anti-racist mothering and pedagogy, using in fresh contexts theories articulated by bell hooks, Beverly Daniel Tatum, Mary Washington, Frantz Fanon, Peggy McIntosh, Johanne Archibald, Njoki Wane, Beverly-Jean Daniel, and Susan Bernheimer. Other essays explore the relationship between mothering, teaching, and learning within the context of disability studies, queer studies, or ecofeminism, and several chapters draw upon scholarship in the field of feminist pedagogy and activism, citing articles in journals like *Feminist Teacher, Radical Teacher, Signs,* and *Women's Studies Quarterly* as well building upon the work of Frances Maher, Mary Kay Tetrault, Berenice Fisher, Nancy Naples, and Charlotte Bunch. Last but not least, many of our contributors creatively deploy and critically examine such concepts as attentive love, maternal thinking, othermothering, and intensive mothering, drawing upon a rich body of feminist scholarship on mothering and motherhood, especially the writings of Adrienne Rich, Sara Ruddick, Andrea O'Reilly, and Patricia Hill Collins.

Given the anti-oppression "parentage" of the essays in this collection, it is perhaps no surprise that this text articulates the co-editors' conviction that any meaningful examination of the relationship between mothering, teaching, and learning must be based on an intersectional approach to the topic; it is essential that we talk about maternal pedagog*ies*, not *a* maternal pedagogy. Not only do definitions and assessments of the "maternal" vary over time and from individual to individual and culture to culture, but maternal pedagogies are always in flux, always performative, always processes embedded in specific contexts and employed by individuals and groups whose positionality, values, goals, and strategies are ever-shifting, as are those of the children/students in the teaching and learning situation.

In some ways, the contributors to this collection are a homogeneous group. All are Canadian or U.S. residents affiliated with educational institutions, and most (if not all) implicitly or explicitly write from a feminist point of view. In other respects, however, the contributors are a diverse group. Some are rearing children; some are not. Some examine the topic of maternal pedagogies from the perspective of a teacher and/or researcher, some from the perspective of a child/student, still others from the point of view of someone who is simultaneously a practitioner and a recipient of maternal pedagogies. Some authors describe ways in which individuals and groups who do not occupy positions of unearned privilege and power use maternal pedagogies to resist oppressive ideologies and practices of the dominant culture; other authors reflect on how belonging to one or more privileged groups can affect one's pedagogical views and experiences. Some writers focus on the teaching and learning that occurs when parents interact with their children; some turn their attention to teacher-student or teacher-parent dynamics in educational institutions and other public settings; still others examine ways in which pedagogical engagements with one's children inform or differ from interactions with other kinds of students. Some contributors foreground ways in which works of fiction perpetuate and/or challenge prevailing paradigms of mothers and mothering; others examine ways in which public policies and institutions shape or are shaped by maternal pedagogies.

A number of issues, arguments, and concerns surface repeatedly in this collection. Many of the essays remind us that dominant ideologies about mothers and mothering are socially constructed and thus culturally and temporally variable. These essays urge us to resist viewing anything associated with the maternal as "natural" and to reject all totalizing, essentializing definitions of "good" or "normal"—whether these adjectives are applied to mothers and mothering, to children and students, or to teachers and the processes of teaching and learning. A number of our contributors critique the modern, patriarchal, Eurocentric belief that to mother effectively, one must be emotionally demonstrative, constantly available, and always willing to put the needs of one's child/student before one's own. At the same time, many of these writers want to celebrate maternal pedagogies that are based on what is variously referred to as attentive love, an ethics of care, and a deep concern for the student's socio-emotional as well as intellectual growth. In other words, these authors want to pay tribute to some of the values, goals, and behaviors that Western patriarchy generally (and often dismissively) labels "maternal," and they share Sara Ruddick's conviction that mothering is important and empowering intellectual work. But they do *not* want to suggest that the teacher-student dynamics that *they* deem maternal are the "best" or "correct" way to construct and transmit knowledge. Most of our writers also emphasize the importance of disassociating mothering from the female body and the reproductive process. The practitioners of maternal pedagogies who appear in this collection are a diverse group: they include people of both sexes, people who are and who are not parents, people who are and who are not biologically related to the children in their homes.

Another theme that runs throughout this collection is the importance of situating discussions of maternal pedagogies in a context that acknowledges the role that systemic oppression, cultural imperialism, and issues of unearned power and privilege play in all teaching and learning situations. Some of our contributors examine the varying ways in which power dynamics inform pedagogical relationships between mothers and their children, between teachers and students, or between school officials and those who teach the children outside of school hours. Several authors cast a critical eye on mainstream educational institutions in the U.S. and Canada, arguing that these institutions often promulgate the cult of individualism, legitimize oppressive norms, pressure students to dismiss the dominant teachings of their community or indigenous culture, and produce citizens who for the most part are unaware of or indifferent to the systemic oppression of various marginalized groups. However, some of our contributors note that educational institutions can be sites of empowerment—places that resist cultural hegemony, that blur traditional boundaries between insiders and outsiders, and that provide members of oppressed groups with the knowledge and self-confidence to navigate a society that does not welcome—perhaps is even hostile to—their success.

Another idea that crops up over and over again in this collection is that maternal pedagogies are an effective way to promote various forms of agency, advocacy, and activism. Several of our contributors suggest that practitioners of maternal pedagogies tend to view all engaged in the process of knowledge construction as both teachers and students; as a result, the learning process becomes empowering for all parties, perhaps especially so for those who traditionally are positioned as recipients rather than transmitters of knowledge. Other contributors describe maternal pedagogies that are based on a desire to perform and model (not just discuss) a critique of capitalistic, patriarchal, and heteronormative ways of seeing and being. Still others describe pedagogical strategies that give students practice combating oppression or that could help equity-seeking groups collaborate more effectively.

Finally, many of our contributors commit themselves to bravely breaking the silence about taboo subjects: the families and sexual lives of queer individuals, the personal and political consequences of failed pregnancy outcomes, the belief that one is an inadequate or "bad" mother, the fear of dying, the shame at one's own or a loved one's ignorance, the pain and anger of being negatively stereotyped, ostracized, or discriminated against. As this list suggests, many of our authors—and many of the people our writers interview—share with readers highly personal, intimate details of their lives. Through their anecdotes and stories, they personalize the political and politicize the personal in moving and intellectually provocative ways. And they do so from a variety of cultural locations—but especially from the margins. If our culture's idea of a "normal" mother is a white, heterosexual, middle-class, "fully abled" woman with a husband, a couple of biological kids, and a dog, relatively few of the practitioners of maternal pedagogies who speak (or who are spoken about) in this collection are "normal." That is something that delights us.

When finalizing our work on this collection, we had great difficulty deciding upon the order of the essays because the texts are in dialogue with one another in so many complex and multifaceted ways. At times one hears echoes: similarities in viewpoint, experience, or argument. At other times one hears discord, as one contributor's perspective or claims clash with those of another writer. In the paragraphs that follow we explain why we decided to present the essays in the order we did. But feel free to chart your own way through this text, reading first those essays that sound most engaging, challenging or alluring to *you*. And of course we hope that you will revisit the collection as you face new learning situations, pleasures, and dilemmas.

*****

As the title "Maternal Pedagogies: Not Just for the Female and Fertile" suggests, we have chosen to open this collection with three essays that warn both of the danger of uncritically valorizing behaviors that patriarchal/ racist/ heterosexist cultures deem motherly, and the danger of always and exclusively associating things maternal with women, especially women who have borne or who are rearing children. In "Queer Pedagogies and the Specter of the Maternal," Jane Ward notes that an essentialized and highly gendered mother/father binary continues to prevail in the U.S. and that as a result, most students expect female teachers—whether or not they are mothers—to interact with them in "maternal" ways. Students generally expect female teachers to be openly nurturing, flexible, accessible, and forgiving, whereas they expect male teachers (again, whether or not they have children) to have "fatherly" relational styles: to be more aloof and emotionally reserved, more strict and demanding, more authoritarian—which gives male teachers the freedom to occasionally interact with their children/students as a "buddy" or fellow "dude." But as Ward points out, students' tendency to conflate pedagogical and parenting styles in highly gendered and heteronormative ways is disrupted by openly queer teachers, especially by those (like butch lesbians) who most dramatically violate students' expectations. Whatever their appearance, queer teachers who out themselves as parents or who talk about families in which there are male mothers and female fathers destabilize the maternal: they help students understand that "Mother" and "Father" are "performative categories that can be taken up by anyone who feels drawn to them, regardless of biological sex." As Ward notes, queer pedagogies are liberating, for they make "the broadest range of ways of relating to students (and children, more generally) available to female-bodied people, including what we might call 'fatherly' approaches, just as 'the maternal' must be extended to male-bodied people."

Ward argues that creating classroom space for critically examining queer sexuality and queer families, including her own, allows her to complicate and expand definitions of the maternal more effectively than if she were to remain silent on these subjects. Rebecca Upton makes a similar point in the essay that follows, arguing that open discussions of her own and other women's pregnancy attempts and outcomes allows her to foreground in fresh and powerful ways the need to challenge theories of the maternal that reify a reproductive norm. In "Pedagogy of the Obsessed: Infertility, IVF and How the Search for Maternity Affects Teaching, Learning and a Feminist Self," Upton first discusses two (in)fertility exercises she uses in an Anthropology course to show students that in patriarchal cultures, all women (but not all men) tend to be viewed and valued as potential reproducers; as a result, those women who cannot or who choose not to give birth to a child tend to be viewed as deviant, abnormal, pathetic, and/or disabled. Upton then illustrates the value of examining issues related to maternity and (in)fertility from a cross-cultural perspective. Such an approach demonstrates that fertility and infertility are constructed, defined, and function in different ways in different cultures. For example, proving that one is fertile by becoming pregnant as an unmarried teenager is socially acceptable and "normal" female behavior in Botswana but not in the contemporary U.S. or China. Upton also notes that in one country, being unable to lay claim to biological maternity can prevent or decrease a woman's access to valuable social and medical services, whereas in other countries, cultural attitudes or public policies relating to maternity may result in a woman disparaging her female children or bearing more children than she can afford. In short, Upton argues that fertility studies and maternity outcomes should be at the center of discussions of mothering and pedagogy because such topics can foreground in thought-provoking ways some of the cultural ideologies and practices that undergird sexism, racism, and other kinds of oppression.

The last article in Section One, like a number of essays that appear later in the collection, reveals that white Eurocentric cultures could benefit a great deal from understanding and emulating the maternal pedagogies practiced by women and men generally relegated to the dominant cultures' margins. In "Reclaiming Maternal Pedagogies in a British Columbia Aboriginal Head Start Program," Margaret MacDonald argues that most traditional Eurocentric educational institutions aid in the development of citizens who are uncritical of and thus quite willing to participate in a capitalist/ racist/ sexist/ homophobic society. Often these institutions (whether wittingly or unwittingly) pressure members of marginalized groups to forget or devalue the teachings of the communities to which they belong (in the case of the Stó:lō, through decades of forced residential schooling). And they generally do not welcome family participation in the formal educational process. But as MacDonald recounts, the Stó:lō people of British Columbia have developed a Head Start program informed by Stó:lō ways of knowing and designed to nurture the socio-emotional as well as cognitive growth of young Stó:lō children. Stó:lō Elders and other adults, especially mothers and grandmothers, share with Head Start teachers the responsibility of transmitting to young Stó:lō children indigenous beliefs and traditions, many of which could be labeled "maternal." For example, Stó:lō culture places a high value on familial relationships, on respecting and caring for the earth and its creatures, on learning through stories, and on communal and collaborative rather than individualistic endeavors. As MacDonald explains, the BC Aboriginal Head Start program not only incorporates such teachings and teaching practices into the curriculum, but twice a week brings Elders and other community members into the classroom to educate Stó:lō pre-schoolers about the values—and value—of their heritage.

The essays in Section Two, "Being a Recipient of Maternal Pedagogies: The Child/Student's Point of View," primarily, though not exclusively, recount and analyze the experience of being the *recipient* of maternal pedagogies. In "Re-searching Mommy: Narrating My Inquiry of Maternal Pedagogies," Jennifer Watt shares her ongoing struggle to conceptualize the term "maternal pedagogies" in ways that do not perpetuate oppressive ideologies like "intensive mothering" and that make it possible for men—and for women who are not mothers—to "identify with and invest in the concepts the term embodies." As she reflects on the mothering she has received from a graduate school professor who also is her doctoral thesis advisor, Watt aligns the man's pedagogical demeanor, goals, and strategies with definitions of intentional, empowered, and feminist mothering developed by theorists like Adrienne Rich, Sara Ruddick, Andrea O'Reilly, and Fiona Green. Among the qualities Watt labels "maternal" are the man's warm, gentle, nurturing way of interacting with his students; his desire to foster their self-confidence and self-reliance; his establishment of a learning environment in which knowledge is collaboratively constructed; his desire to teach critical thinking and methodological approaches rather than a set body of knowledge; and his belief in the value of recording, pondering, politicizing, and theorizing about the personal. Watt concludes her essay by reminding us of the impossibility (and undesirability) of ever stabilizing or "fixing" the meaning of the phrase "maternal pedagogies"; instead, she argues, we should relish the insights into power, privilege, and oppression that result when people of varied backgrounds and interests reflect on the countless ways in which mothering, teaching, and learning are connected.

In "African Maternal Pedagogies: Sociological and Educational Implications," Adwoa Ntozake Onuora simultaneously describes, celebrates and performs the maternal pedagogies employed not only by her own mothers, but by many other women (and some men) of African descent. Like Margaret Auguste in a later chapter, Onuora notes that "othermothering" is indigenous to African culture; relatives, neighbors, and members of the larger community play a central role in nurturing, protecting, and educating children. Onuora notes that although men can and do engage in such mothering, the majority of mother work, including the task of transmitting indigenous knowledges and ways of knowing, is performed by women. Like Watt, Onuora tells the story of her "growing understanding of, appreciation for, and commitment to engaging in" maternal pedagogies. And as in a later essay by Heidi Hutner, what prompts Onuora to re-discover, think critically about, and make constructive use of her family history is becoming pregnant and reflecting on the responsibilities that will soon be hers as a mother. As Onuora re-enters (and takes us back to) her childhood in Jamaica, she identifies two features of African maternal pedagogy that she is especially desirous of preserving and transmitting: "the notion that many lessons must be learned through experience and as one matures," and the belief that "metaphor, proverbs, and narrative… [are] effective vehicles for the transmission of knowledge." Onuora so treasures these cultural knowings that she is committed to enacting and sharing them with her readers as well as her daughter; interweaving traditional scholarly discourse with creative non-fiction, she invites us to discover for ourselves the pleasures of learning through Afro-centric stories and metaphors. Onuora concludes, however, by reminding us that many women of color living in the diaspora have little time, energy, or support for engaging in the maternal pedagogies indigenous to their cultures. She urges us to ensure that analyses of cultural imperialism and systemic oppression inform all discussions of maternal pedagogies "so we can begin to develop new strategies for praxis on educational transformation that will not only benefit Afro-indigenous women but will also validate the cultural knowledges of all racialized women."

The final essay in Section Two, "'If I Had a Normal Job, I Couldn't Do This': Exploring the Economics of Disability Advocacy Motherhood and Inclusive Education," also calls for an approach to maternal pedagogies that takes into account systems of unearned power and privilege—in this case, privileges based on family income, cultural capital, and physical and mental "ability"/ "normalcy." Samantha Walsh and Elisabeth Harrison express deep gratitude towards their mothers, who worked tirelessly to ensure that the educational system met most of the needs of their daughters with disabilities. However, the authors note that their mothers' success was due in large part to having access to resources not available to the parents of many children with disabilities. One mother did not need to work outside the home; the other worked in a family-owned business and had control over her work schedule. Both mothers had done well in and were knowledgeable about the workings of educational institutions, and both were white women whose first language was English. Both mothers were articulate and confident, and both owned—and could count on the support of many people who wore—"power suits." Walsh and Harrison do not fault their mothers for making use of the professional support networks and "cultural capital that was theirs"; however, they are distressed by their mothers' inability to acknowledge their class privilege—by the women's assumption that any "good" mother can find a way to be an effective advocate for a child with disabilities.

But even more disturbing to the authors are the ideological underpinnings of the pedagogical strategies their mothers employed as they sought to educate teachers and school administrators about the nature of their daughter's disabilities. Essentially, Walsh and Harrison argue, their mothers attempted to erase or downplay their children's disabilities by stressing that the daughter was "barely" disabled or by proclaiming that she was "really smart" and basically "just like everyone else except her legs don't work." Rather than arguing that disabilities and people with them deserve to be acknowledged, valued, and respected (the belief informing the advocacy of the mothers of children with AD(H)D that are discussed in the essay by Case and Proulx-Schirduan), Walsh and Harrison's mothers unwittingly perpetuated the notion that people with disabilities are deviant, abnormal, and bizarre, either pathetic or frighteningly dangerous. As an alternative to an individualistic "normalizing" approach to advocacy that maintains an oppressive status quo, Walsh and Harrison advocate activist and pedagogical strategies in which equity-seeking groups build coalitions to insist that we see and value human difference and guarantee equal rights to all.

Whereas the essays in Section Two primarily examine maternal pedagogies from the perspective of daughters/students, the essays in Section Three foreground ways in which specific women teach and learn from their children. In "The Baffled Mother: Maternal Puzzlement in Narrative, in Pedagogy, in Academia," Martha Satz examines her own and three fictional feminist mothers' complex relationships with their adult children—children whose behavior and values the mothers often find confusing and disturbingly non-feminist. Through their struggles to understand and support their daughters, these mothers are forcefully reminded—as they might not have been had their daughters been less "troubling"—that as feminists, they should be striving to form egalitarian relationships with their children, should be letting go of some of the power and authority that mothers inevitably have over their children, especially when the children are young. The baffling daughters in this essay teach their mothers the value of what Adrienne Rich calls "attentive love": the value of listening to, empathizing with, and trying to view life from the perspective of the child. And they teach their mothers a perhaps more difficult lesson: that when she succeeds in transmitting to her daughter some of her feminist values and knowledge, a feminist mother almost invariably will have reared a child independent and self-confident enough to choose a path that in some ways—maybe even in major ways—differs from the path chosen by her mother. Satz concludes her piece by suggesting that insights gained by these four mothers might be useful to feminist teachers dealing with students who don't eagerly embrace feminist ideas and values.

If Tabitha R. Holmes and Lynne A. Bond were to examine the interaction between the mother-daughter pairs in Satz's essay, most likely they would argue that the four feminist mothers develop (or re-commit themselves to) the pedagogical styles and strategies that tend to characterize a "constructed knowing" epistemological perspective. In "Maternal Pedagogies as a Function of Mothers' Ways of Knowing," Holmes and Bond build on earlier research in which they found that the pedagogical approaches used by mothers of preschoolers reflect the mother's ways of knowing and her particular understanding of the nature of truth and knowledge. In their latest work, which focuses on women who are parenting teenagers (children who can be as "baffling" as the young adults in Satz's essay), Holmes and Bond find a similar relationship between the mothers' epistemological beliefs and their teaching practices. Mothers with "Received" perspectives tended to employ "didactic strategies in which advice was dispensed and enforced," whereas "Procedural" and "Transitional" mothers "described pedagogies that required adolescents to actively engage in knowledge construction and collaboration." The sixty-two U.S. mothers who participated in Holmes and Bond's study vary widely in age, race, income level, and family size and structure. However, Holmes and Bond remind us that the epistemological schema they utilize (and especially the ranking of epistemological perspectives, with "constructed knowing" being regarded as the most complex or developed) are "undoubtedly culture bound," reflecting the world view of "majority cultures in Western technological societies."

In the conclusion of their essay, Holmes and Bond suggest that just as a mother's ways of knowing tend to shape her pedagogical interactions with her child(ren), so it is likely that a mother's parenting experiences will influence her ideas about the nature of knowledge and learning. Certainly this seems to be the case with the mothers who are interviewed in the next essay. In "Crossing Bridges: Maternal Pedagogies for the AD(H)D Child," Karen I. Case and Victoria Proulx-Schirduan describe how mothers of children with Attention Deficit Disorder and Attention Deficit Hyperactivity Disorder learn not only to understand and accept, but to treasure and celebrate the ways in which their children discover, process, and make use of information. Learning to let go of "feelings of guilt, inadequacy and self-blame," the mothers begin to savor rather than lament their children's "wildness," to be awed by the "energy, drive and intellectual gifts of these learners." Convinced that it is "not the learned mother who is most competent to instruct her children but the mother who understands them," the mothers of these children with AD(H)D engage in attentive love, then use their empathetic understanding of their children's cognitive processes to develop child-centric pedagogical strategies. One woman, for example, describes how she dealt with a young daughter who strayed from her side in a mall; instead of chastising the child, the mother used this moment to embrace her daughter's intellectual curiosity, sitting down on the floor with her to investigate the workings of security devices attached to clothing. The mothers in Case and Proulx-Schirduan's study also use what they learn from their children to advocate for them in formal educational settings; not only do they try to teach teachers and school administrators that children with AD(H)D aren't "bad" children or "slow learners," but they do all they can to ensure that the needs of their untraditional learners are acknowledged and met. Although the maternal pedagogies these mothers employ as activists don't *always* work, on many occasions they do convince teachers to make use of instructional strategies they have developed through daily, loving engagement with their children, strategies that "change potentially negative situations into positive joint learnings."

Section Four turns our attention from the teaching and learning that occurs when mothers interact with their own children to the pedagogical strategies that various sorts of "othermothers" use to nurture and empower their "students." Margaret Auguste's "The African-American Teacher as Othermother: 1863 to the Present" explicitly builds upon the work of Patricia Hill Collins and other scholars who have demonstrated that nurturing and empowering others' children has long been a common practice—indeed, an essential survival strategy—in African-American communities. Part of this essay focuses on the maternal pedagogies of earlier, little-known African-American educators: Lily Ann Granderson, Charlotte Forten, and the many unnamed female and male teachers of the 1950s who, regarding themselves as "Negroes first and teachers second," tried to prepare their students for the challenges of living in a white supremacist society that was gradually—and quite reluctantly—undergoing integration. Auguste also quotes from interviews she has conducted with contemporary African-American teachers, teachers who proudly and self-consciously continue the tradition of developing close personal relationships with their students and doing a great deal of mentoring outside of class time. Perhaps most importantly, Auguste's essay reminds us that intensive mothering is not necessarily problematic in all circumstances and in all cultures. Indeed, instead of pitying or critiquing self-sacrificing mothers who place their children's needs before their own, groups that are oppressed may regard as heroic those othermothers (including teachers) who are willing to risk a great deal—perhaps even their own lives—to advance the cause of their children/people.

In "Mothering Student Activists: Reflections on Maternal/Feminist Service-Learning Pedagogy," Deborah Lea Byrd identifies as the most important component of her particular brand of maternal pedagogy a desire to place her son and her students in environments where they can test, apply, and enact the feminist theories and practices that she has tried to inculcate. Most of her essay examines the pedagogical othermothering that occurs in an undergraduate Women's and Gender Studies service-learning seminar entitled "Single Motherhood in the Contemporary U.S.: Myths and Realities." In this course, undergraduates interact regularly with—and importantly, learn *from*—teenage and low-income single mothers. Then they must use their text-based and experiential knowledge to implement activist projects designed to support and empower these women. Through quotations from students' reflective journal entries and an analysis of a "before" and "after" survey designed to measure shifts in students' knowledge and attitudes, Byrd shows that a maternal/feminist service-learning pedagogy can be an effective way to undermine "the myth of meritocracy"; dispel false and demeaning stereotypes about teenage and low-income single mothers; and further students' understanding of the racist, sexist, and classist underpinnings of the U.S. welfare and criminal justice systems. These outcomes assessment instruments also suggest that asking one's surrogate children to engage in community-based learning and research can make them more appreciative of the wisdom and resourcefulness of marginalized and oppressed individuals, as well as strengthen their desire to "do feminism," not just read and talk about it.

Like Byrd, Heidi Hutner connects her personal experiences of mothering with the othermothering she engages in as a teacher, scholar, and activist. In "Mothering and Cancer: The Awakening of an Ecofeminist," Hutner powerfully recounts how her own and her family's battles with cancer led her first to fear that she would not be able to fulfill her passionate desire to become pregnant and bear a child, then caused her to feel guilty about being pregnant; after all, she might pass her cancer genes on to her child . . . or die at any moment. But just as mothers of children with AD(H)D learn to fault unjust educational institutions rather than themselves for the discrimination their children experience, so the experience of mothering teaches Hutner that her "polluted" body results not from personal failings, but from a "capitalistic and patriarchal system based on economic greed, domination, and the exploitation of nature (and many human beings) by a privileged few." This ecological "awakening" during her pregnancy profoundly altered Hutner's professional as well as her personal life, inspiring her to commit herself to an environmental othermothering in which she seeks to nurture and protect not only her students, but all living creatures and the earth itself. In addition to creating and teaching courses on ecofeminism, Hutner also adopted new pedagogical strategies. Like many of the contributors to this collection, she now engages her students in a collaborative construction of meaning in which the sharing of her own and her students' stories is an important part of the learning and relational experience. And like Byrd, she now requires her students to "do feminism," to design and implement environmental activist projects.

The final section of this collection, "Motherlines," stresses the importance of recording and preserving for future generations the pedagogical experiences, goals, strategies and theories of those who (1) believe that mothers and othermothers have valuable insights into the teaching and learning processes, and (2) believe that educators can teach about and perform/deconstruct "the maternal" in ways that are intellectually, politically, and ethically valuable. In "Reading Our Foremothers: Victorian and Eighteenth-Century Literary Mothers and Millennial Readers," Katherine Ellison and Cynthia Huff contrast the association of motherhood with irrationality and emotional instability that prevailed in eighteenth-century England with the characterization of mothers as moral saviors of home and homeland that was dominant in that country a century later. Whereas Upton takes a synchronic, cross-cultural approach to showing that ideas about motherhood are socially constructed, Ellison and Huff demonstrate that a given culture's views on mothers and mothering can change dramatically over time. Once students begin to realize that their own definitions of "good" mothers and mothering are not "natural" or universal, they can subject their own paradigms and expectations to critical scrutiny; when they do so, many realize that they have inherited and are unwittingly perpetuating the dominant Victorian expectation that mothers (but not fathers) be endlessly nurturing, self-sacrificing, and accessible. Analyzing novels about our foremothers also helps Ellison and Huff's students to realize that ideas about motherhood can be so central to a society that they can influence the structure and evolution of literary genres. Finally, Ellison and Huff's diachronic approach to eighteenth- and nineteenth-century British fiction teaches students that dominant ideologies about "things maternal" are constantly being contested, complicated and challenged; with this knowledge, students can potentially recognize and resist the limiting and patriarchal narratives that abound in their own society.

The notion that mothering has a history that needs to be recorded and transmitted to the next generation is developed in a different way in Marlene Pomrenke's essay entitled "Aboriginal Single Mother Students: Teaching the Next Generation(s) by Example." Pomrenke interviewed twenty Aboriginal single mothers pursuing post-secondary education in Manitoba to discover what motivated them to attend college, how they handle the challenges of being student-mothers, and what pedagogical goals and strategies they employ to encourage their children to follow in their footsteps. Like MacDonald, Pomrenke notes that to fully understand the maternal pedagogies being developed and deployed by today's First Nations people, we must be aware that Canada's indigenous population continues to experience systemic racism. High rates of unemployment and poverty, social discrimination, lack of preparation for post-secondary education, and feelings of isolation result in many Aboriginal people (and especially lone moms) being unable to enroll or stay in college. Moreover, the long history of forced residential schooling, through which the white majority attempted to destroy Aboriginal students' knowledge of and attachment to their culture, makes some contemporary First Nations people wary of educational institutions, which continue (though more subtly) to pressure marginalized groups to assimilate to the dominant culture.

What initially motivated the women in Pomrenke's study to overcome these obstacles was their desire, as mothers, to make both short- and long-term improvements in their children's lives—though gradually these women began to celebrate ways they themselves were benefiting from higher education. Pomrenke attributes the resilience and success of these student-mothers to their ability to identify and access a variety of external and internal resources; particularly key, according to these women, are Aboriginal student centers, support groups, Elders, ceremonies, and spiritual beliefs. As practitioners of maternal pedagogies, these single mothers employ two strategies. First, they teach by example, showing their children that doing well in college is desirable and possible. Secondly, and just as importantly, these Aboriginal single mothers talk openly and honestly with their children about the difficulties of meeting the ambitious educational goals they've set for themselves; they make sure their children know about the resources (mainstream as well as Aboriginal) that they've found useful in overcoming the systemic and institutional racism that Canada's First Nations peoples continue to wrestle with.

The final essay in our collection is Fiona Joy Green's "Feminist Maternal Pedagogies: Inside and Outside the Classroom." This essay, like Pomrenke's, focuses on a group of women who in very self-conscious ways try to educate their children about the nature of oppression and effective means of resisting it. And as with the Aboriginal mothers in Pomrenke's study, the Winnipeg mothers Green interviewed use a two-pronged approach: they strive to embody as well as analytically discuss with their children the principles they hold most dear. The primary pedagogical goals of Green's self-identified feminist mothers (which closely resemble those of many feminist teachers, whether they be mothers or not) are (1) to teach their children how to recognize various kinds of oppression, especially systemic oppression, (2) to convince their children that structural change is both needed and possible, (3) to urge their children to embrace the idea that power, property, and opportunities should be more equitably shared, and (4) to help their children realize that widespread cultural change depends upon collective organizing. And like many feminists teaching in classroom settings, these mothers try to inculcate a feminist world view by engaging in the collaborative construction of knowledge and by interacting with their children (as much as is possible) in egalitarian ways. Green's essay concludes with her admission that in her previous research, she had not sufficiently recognized the importance that love, affection, and compassion might play in the maternal pedagogies practiced by some feminists. Like many contributors to this collection, she urges those enacting maternal pedagogies (whether in the classroom, the home, or other settings) to engage the whole student, though not necessarily by performing those "feminine/motherly" roles that are valorized by contemporary patriarchal, Eurocentric cultures.

*****

Motherhood Studies is a relatively new but vibrant and growing field of academic enquiry, one to which we hope this collection makes a significant contribution. If we want to promote mothering and othermothering as intellectual and emotional work of great value, we need to examine how mothering might function in a wide variety of pedagogical situations and cultural contexts. This book initiates a dialogue among a diverse group of people interested in the relationship between mothering, teaching, and learning, and begins to explore the meanings and the potential usefulness and limitations of the term "maternal pedagogies." We hope that this collection will inspire others to join in such a conversation, especially those whose voices and concerns are not represented in any of our essays. For example, with a couple of exceptions, these essays focus on maternal pedagogies in various cultures that exist in the contemporary U.S. and Canada. And none of them address in a central way the role that spiritual beliefs or religious institutions and practices might play in the transmission of ideas about motherhood or in particular instances of pedagogical (other)mothering. We hope that some of our readers will choose to address these (and many other gaps) in our collection in the coming years.

I. Maternal Pedagogies

Not Just for the Female and Fertile

Queer Pedagogies and the Specter of the Maternal

JANE WARD

IN 2008 I PUBLISHED AN ethnographic book about queer activism in Los Angeles. Towards the end of the editorial process, my editor asked me to write a few more paragraphs in which I would reflect more precisely on what I meant in my introduction when I suggested that my ethnographic *method* was queer. More than simply a matter of researching queer subjects, I elaborated that queer methodology is oriented toward especially intimate (and sometimes even sexual) connections with participants, as well as greater comfort with the presence of sexuality—including the sexuality of the researcher—in the presumably asexual realm of research (Ward). Though I tend to view these methodological transgressions through a queer lens, I note here that they also resemble some of the unconventional methods taken up by feminist ethnographers. Feminist scholars, along with queer scholars, have problematized the researcher/subject dichotomy and have engaged in research methods that reflect their critique of scientific distance and objectivity, especially in the context of studying gendered and sexual practices. Such an approach has led feminist scholars into a variety of intimate relationships with those they seek to study (see Behar and Gordon).

Yet feminist and queer methods arguably reach a point of departure when it comes to the role that sexual reflexivity should play in our *teaching*. For good reasons, namely the sexual objectification and harassment that women teachers encounter all too often, feminist pedagogy typically places emphasis on supporting women teachers to establish a desexualized classroom persona. During my graduate training in feminist studies, women faculty and graduate students spent many hours discussing the ways in which we were sexualized by male students and colleagues, with most of these discussions ending with an affirmation of our right to preserve our sexual privacy and boundaries, especially in the classroom. We built consensus around the understanding that students were not entitled to any information about our personal lives or sexual identities. Experience told many of us that the benefits of being transparent about our sexuality—either our sexual identities or the fact that we were sexual at all—were outweighed by the cost of being subjected to male students' sexual gaze, a gaze so frequently accompanied by a lack of respect for our authority and/or the feminist content of our courses. We believed that women students, too, benefitted from being in a desexualized environment in which they could safely explore ideas without the looming presence of sexual objectification.

Instead of revealing information about our sexualities, we offered students other points of access to our humanity. We told jokes, made allusions to popular culture (our favorite music, TV shows, etc.), and in some cases, we shared stories about our families, thereby coming out not as sexual per se, but as someone embedded in familiar relations of caring and intimacy with parents, siblings, partners and/or children. Yet making oneself relatable by revealing our locatedness within families is a privilege in its own right, and has its limits for queer teachers. Given homosexuality's longstanding association with isolation, promiscuity, singlehood, childlessness, and various other "threats" to the institution of family, heterosexual students typically view queer families with suspicion or curiosity rather than a sense of common ground. For heterosexual teachers, talking about one's family establishes basic humanness and a less-sexualized persona (such as mother, wife, aunt, or daughter), but for queer teachers, reference to family inevitably draws students' attention to the presumed contradiction between family and queer sexuality. This is often evidenced for me by students' questions about how I reconcile my queerness with my family: Do your parents still accept you? How, exactly, were you able to get pregnant? Are you worried that other kids will ridicule your child? And so forth. Rather than evoking normalcy and decency, talking about family places the sexuality of queer teachers even further under the spotlight.

Later in my career, when I began teaching as an "out" femme/dyke/queer professor, I started to reconsider the value of desexualizing myself in the classroom. Once I came out to students, it was impossible to control their (hetero)sexual gaze, but more importantly, I discovered that there was much to be gained by creating space for (queer) sexuality in the classroom, including my own. I could deliver a lecture about queer subculture and its erotic and campy elements, but students were far more engaged when I was willing to share a few examples from my own subcultural experiences (as a dancer in a queer burlesque troupe, as an attendee at dyke bathhouses, etc.). Continually asserting myself as queer *and* sexual (specifically, a femme attracted to butch women) *and* located within multiple families helped to circumvent heterosexual rescriptings of me as a lipstick lesbian attracted to other feminine women, an asexual and man-hating spinster, or a harmless, Rosie O'Donnell-esque soccer mom (though I can relate to elements of each of these lesbian archetypes!).

When I was pregnant and teaching, I noticed my desire to foreground the aspects of my sexual politics and queer desires that I imagined students would find most dissonant with the conventional script about pregnancy and motherhood. I shared with them that my female partner would be called "Dad," that we were hoping for a queer child, and that my queer burlesque troupe was talking about putting on a sexy pregnancy-themed revue featuring pregnant dancing lesbians. Students' shock occasionally made me wonder whether such disclosures would backfire, but the passionate and often insightful conversations that ensued—about the intersections of gender, heteronormativity, parenting, and public/private space—convinced me of their pedagogical value. In other words, while negotiating sexism in the classroom often means keeping our sexual lives private, queer pedagogy recognizes that the logics of privacy, appropriateness, and sexual decency are precisely those that undergird heteronormativity (Halberstam; Duggan).

Female Masculinity and Disruptions to the Maternal Frame

To be a queer woman in the classroom—especially a butch or otherwise gender nonconforming woman—stands to disrupt one of the primary gendered tropes of the teacher-student relationship, the one in which the female teacher functions like a mother to her students. Students often expect maternally coded responses from women teachers that they do not expect (or expect to a lesser degree) from men (Basow; Bennett). These include forgiveness and flexibility when they fail to fulfill their responsibilities, endless availability in office hours or after school, and sensitivity to their feelings and the complexities of their personal lives. Even as a conventionally feminine woman who is rarely read as queer until I pronounce myself to be so, I repeatedly find that heterosexual students expect less intense emotional labor from me once they know I am queer.

Yet for butch lesbian teachers, this effect is even more pronounced. Over the years, I have observed a number of butch women teachers in the classroom (as a Teaching Assistant, a colleague, or while watching my partner interact with her middle and high school students), and I have marveled at how quickly students learn to reconfigure their gendered expectations when confronted with a masculine female teacher. The gender of butch teachers is a source of interest and confusion for many students, but it is also the case that students ultimately figure out a workable system for relating to female masculinity. Faced with their teacher's butchness (and possibility sensing that she experiences some level of disidentification with femaleness), students rule out the maternal frame as the most suitable mode of interaction. They adapt to what typically takes its place—the social and cultural codes associated with male authority and caretaking. Butch teachers cue students to have more gender-fluid expectations by relating to them in cross-gendered, or male and often fatherly, ways.

In my personal (i.e., nonscientific) observations, this takes a couple of forms, one of which is establishing the kind of emotional distance typically associated with men and masculinity. My butch colleagues offer far less of the nurturing cues that I have long considered to be "part of my job" as a teacher, such as smiling frequently during my lectures, making self-effacing jokes to ensure that students are not intimidated by my authority, or offering non-academic guidance when students come to me with personal concerns (coming out issues, abusive relationships, eating disorders, sexual assault). Just as I have witnessed students extend respect to male teachers based more on their enthusiastic bravado and presumed competence than whether they are sympathetic or nurturing, so too have I watched students give up hope that butch dyke teachers will offer them the kind of "niceness" associated with conventional femininity. For instance, a butch friend and colleague of mine, a well-known scholar in the field of queer studies, is frequently described in student evaluations as brilliant, challenging, mean, aloof and difficult, yet never a "bitch," and never in sexualized terms (though the latter are common responses when these traits are paired with a feminine gender presentation). Though students may register homophobic responses to female masculinity, their sexism remains somewhat in check by an awareness that their basic conceptualization of female authority—for which mothers are arguably the original and quintessential model—apparently does not apply to butch dykes.

Another way that butch teachers produce cross-gendered responses from students is by communicating with them like peers. For instance, my partner commonly addresses her students—both male and female—as "dudes" (i.e., "hey, dude, where's your homework?"). As for me, I cannot imagine engaging my students in this way. Aside from not wanting to be perceived as a dude myself, my feminist and self-protective instincts caution me against this kind of equalizing playfulness (How will I maintain my authority if students start thinking of me as their friend?). But this kind of play-acting at being peers has long been associated with the gentle, fatherly form of male authority (in contrast with, say, the top-down, militaristic form). Fathers often refer to their sons as "buddy," evoking a kind of boundaried and egalitarian closeness with children quite distinct from the intensive and hierarchical relationship expected of mothers and their children. Traditionally, to be fatherly, like being a male teacher, is to be caring from a friendly distance. The father/friend model incorporates playfulness, coaching, and some degree of responsibility for pragmatic concerns (such as completion of a science project), but it circumvents the depth of emotional responsibility associated with mothering in part by suggesting a kind of equity between men and children.[1] By evoking friendship with students, butch teachers establish a similar relationship, in which attention is called more to their practical skills and less to their emotional sensitivity.

So what do I make of the apparent benefits of being butch in the classroom? For some time, as I reflected on the gendered dynamics of teaching, I felt resentful. While the privileges extended to men were evident (and have long been subject to feminist critique), weren't my butch comrades also conforming to, or benefitting from, a sexist gender binary in which masculinity is equated with emotional distance and automatic authority? Weren't they getting away with less work (i.e., less emotional labor)? And, shouldn't maternal forms of caring be expected of all of us, regardless of gender?

Though I still believe these questions take us in some productive directions, I want to highlight here the importance of thinking about "mothers" and "fathers" as performative categories that can be taken up by anyone who feels drawn to them, regardless of biological sex. As I reflect on gendered pedagogies, I discover that I am not personally interested in enacting the kinds of authority and relationality associated with masculinity; to do so would be in conflict with my most comfortable, and admittedly conventional, gender expression. If truth be told, I would also miss the emotional connection I have with students were I to abandon it for being too much work. However, I *am* deeply invested in making the broadest range of ways of relating to students (and children, more generally) available to female-bodied people, including what we might call "fatherly" approaches, just as "the maternal" must be extended to male-bodied people. This cross-gendering of the adult/child (or teacher/student) relationship distributes to female-bodied people the kinds of power associated with masculinity (should they desire it) and celebrates men divesting of masculinity and embracing the often less-rewarded labor of mothering. It also demonstrates to children the social constructedness of gender in very practical terms, introducing them to a broader range of relational options for both female- and male-bodied people. It sets the stage for them to later choose, for themselves, from the conventions associated with mothering, fathering, or both.

Dyke Dads and Fag Moms: Genderqueer Parenting

While the feminist movement has succeeded in disrupting the essential gendering of occupations (many people now acknowledge, for instance, that there are women who are doctors, and nurses who are men, and that there is nothing about women or men that makes them "naturally" suited to either), parenting roles remain deeply gendered and essentialist, such that female parents are always mothers, and male parents are always fathers. Even academic and popular writing on dyke parenthood presumes that women produce "two-mommy" families in which both women adopt the role and identity of mother, albeit with different styles and systems for negotiating the distinction between gestational and "other mothers" (Sullivan). Some feminist literature on motherhood extends the concept of maternalism to men, yet does so without recognizing the possibility of female fathers and male mothers (see Pagenhart and Murray Nossel's 2004 film *Paternal Instinct*, for exceptions). Yet why should "mother" and "father" refer to sex categories (woman with child, man with child) and not to a specific set of job duties and stylistic approaches available to all people regardless of sex or even gender (akin to the way we now understand work and occupations)?

To be clear, this way of thinking about mothers and fathers sits in contradiction with the argument that mothers and fathers are, or should be, "the same." Instead of flattening gender differences, queerness recodes traditional genders and celebrates their queer forms, such as transforming masculinity and femininity into butch and femme. Similarly, a queer approach to parenting recognizes differences that have long been associated with biological sex (some parents like to handle the sit-down emotional stuff, others prefer engaging kids in a series of physical activities; some want to parent fulltime, others find part-time parenting more enjoyable) and detaches them from male and female bodies. While our ultimate goal may be to imagine parenting models that transcend the mother/father binary, until we have achieved this total gender revolution, a queer approach recognizes that parenting, like all of our relationships, is gendered, and that we need not throw gender out of the picture in order to create just and fulfilling relationships with children. In fact, for many of us, myself included, gender is one of the great pleasures in life; this pleasure includes watching one's own gender evolve in the context of parenting, as well as witnessing the gendered surprises that children inevitably bring to our lives when we don't impose our own expectations upon them. In sum, we need to be clear about what, specifically, we imagine are the unique contributions that femininity and masculinity bring to parenting, and then make those parenting styles available to all people.

In my own life, I've found queer parenting very difficult to do in isolation. Not surprisingly, it takes a queer village to raise a child in genderqueer and counter-heteronormative ways. When my partner Kat and I first found out that we were expecting a baby, we had several conversations about how we would conceptualize ourselves as parents. Lesbian couples we know have chosen to be "mom" and "mommy," to use maternal terms taken from other languages, or to simply encourage their children to refer to them using their first names. None of these lesbian frameworks felt as though they provided us with the kind of specialness and recognition we wanted, as two equal but distinct parents (both of whom deserved our own holiday!). Kat also dis-identified with much of the gendered meaning assigned to motherhood, especially notions that equate motherhood with fertility, goddess energy, biological instincts, or the quintessential feminine (I am also very critical of these notions, though they are more incompatible with my poststructuralist tendencies than with my gender). And as we checked into the resources available for lesbian and gay parents in Los Angeles, we found that they too presumed a "two moms" or "two dads" arrangement and were generally very gender-normative in their conceptualization of both parents and children. Together we wondered about the possibilities of genderqueer parenting: what about dyke dads, fag moms, queer aunties and uncles?

With these questions in mind, my partner Kat and I founded the Los Angeles Genderqueer Parenting Group in 2009. Our aim was to build a community of genderqueer people who have close relationships with children—as parents, partners of parents, aunt/uncles, friends, etc., or people who are planning to someday have children. At our meetings, we talk about the difference between queer and lesbian/gay parenting (is there one? what is it?), how to relate to children in differently- and cross-gendered ways, how to parent or care for children without being totally integrated into private, consumer-based and homonormative domestic relations, and how to help create sustained space for children to explore gender, desire, and their own embodiment without imposing our own favorite gender systems on them (whatever they may be).

What has become clear to me is that queer adult/child relationships—whether parent/child or teacher/student—are not defined by the sexual identities of the people involved (such as same-sex couples having children), but by relating to children in ways that are informed by queer critique. This means that queer relationships with children can be the terrain of heterosexuals and queer alike. Queer adult/child relationships are those that reject normativity, "or conventional forms of association, belonging, and identification" (Halberstam 4). For instance, this can mean encouraging children to form attachments to many adults other than ourselves (as parents), especially adults who will care for them in cross-gendered ways. Not only does this build children's caring communities beyond the bounds of blood relations, but it also means that children are witness to a broader range of gender expressions.

[1] I am not suggesting that this performance of equity is "real"—in fact, to the contrary, father/child relationships are often deeply hierarchical—but rather that buddyness is a rhetorical device offered to men as one means of distinguishing fathering from mothering (just as nurturance is the rhetorical device offered to women, regardless of whether they actually feel nurturing).

Works Cited

Basow, Susan A., Julie E. Phelan, Laura Capotosto. "Gender Patterns in College Students' Choices of Their Best and Worst Professors." *Psychology of Women Quarterly* 30.1 (2006): 25-35. Print.

Behar, Ruth and Deborah Gordon. *Women Writing Culture.* Berkeley: University of California Press, 1996. Print.

Bennet, Sheila Kishler. "Student Perceptions of and Expectations for Male and Female Instructors: Evidence Relating to the Question of Gender Bias in Teaching Evaluation." *Journal of Educational Psychology* 74.2 (1982): 170-79. Print.

Duggan, Lisa. *The Twilight of Equality? Neoliberalism, Cultural Politics, and the Attack on Democracy.* New York: Beacon, 2004. Print.

Halberstam, Judith. *In a Queer Time and Place: Transgender Bodies, Subcultural Lives.* New York: New York University Press, 2005. Print.

Pagenhart, Polly. "Confessions of a Lesbian Dad." *Confessions of the Other Mothers: Nonbiological Lesbian Moms Tell All.* Ed. Harlyn Aizley. Boston: Beacon Press, 2006.

Paternal Instinct. Director/producer: Murray Nossel. 2004.

Sullivan, Maureen. *The Family of Woman: Lesbian Mothers, Their Children, and the Undoing of Gender.* Berkeley: University of California Press, 2004.

Ward, Jane. *Respectably Queer: Diversity Culture in LGBT Activist Organizations.* Nashville: Vanderbilt University Press, 2008. Print.

Pedagogy of the Obsessed

Infertility, IVF and How the Search for Maternity Affects Teaching, Learning and a Feminist Self

REBECCA L. UPTON

> ...The normative female body is, and should be, fertile.
>
> —Lisa Handwerker (359)

I AM PROFOUNDLY UNCOMFORTABLE WITH kinship charts and family trees. I experience a kind of love/hate relationship when it comes to teaching them to students. I love the study of kinship; indeed, I am a direct descendent of many mentors who trace their own intellectual lineage from some of the most kinship-versed anthropologists in the discipline. Kinship is the absolute backbone of much of socio-cultural anthropology and frames much of our methodology. Kinship gives us entrée, a way to ask a community in which we are immersed not just who is related to whom but who has power, where do gifts go, who has social weight? Why and how does that matter? And perhaps most importantly, who is *not* part of this community and what happens to them as outsiders? I hate the study of kinship because while I am a good teacher, a feminist and a scholar in both the U.S. and Africa, I am a woman without children.

In my undergraduate classrooms in the U.S. and in Botswana (I have taught and done research in southern Africa for the past fifteen years), I choose to use my own family tree to illustrate how to go about constructing a kinship taxonomy in typical American fashion. Recording and analyzing the various marriages and divorces, opposite and same-sex relationships, and biological and non-biological kin on one particular individual helps to demonstrate how we situate ourselves within our charts, why they make sense to "us," and how we might have to explain the graphic depiction to the "them" who don't fully understand the intimate bonds and the power of the lines drawn between symbols on the chart. Yet if I am being honest, I always experience a profound disquiet as I draw the chart and fill in my own symbols and lines. Do I put in pregnancies? Do I erase miscarriages? Do I even bother to list attempts to get pregnant and if so, how do I delineate various technologies and options tried? I am all for creativity in kinship charts, but just how do I go about illustrating my life on the board? It is never a comfortable moment, even if I have prepared well for the pedagogical point of the exercise.

It is an awkward moment but one that (literally) embodies what we mean when we talk about true teaching moments. The intellectual bravery that emerges on all sides of such a teacher/learner experience and the ability to tackle issues of fertility and other boundary-crossing concerns are always worth any discomfort I may experience on a personal level. I am not merely illustrating the efficacy and power of symbols to convey meaning about familial ties. Ideally, I am creating a moment in which I and my students collectively begin to find a language through which we can begin to challenge cultural beliefs about what is normative, deviant, feminist, awkward and Other (cf. Strathern).

Maternal Pedagogy and the Ideology of (In)fertility

In this essay, I explore some of the complicated terrain covered by the idea of maternal pedagogy and ponder what happens to our concept of ourselves as teachers, as learners, as women and as feminists when the pursuit of maternity becomes all-consuming. What happens to an idea of maternal pedagogy if maternity is not achieved? What happens to the boundaries between teachers and learners, "deviants" and normal persons? For those of us who are cross-cultural researchers, what can we learn that helps us situate some of these complicated questions and answers? And just what does it mean to be fertile, feminist or someone who aspires to practicing maternal pedagogy, though without children?

Maternal pedagogy appears to be a kind of simultaneously all-encompassing and yet incredibly specific term. It can be broadly understood as a pedagogical approach where nurturance, mothering and feminist ideologies are placed centrally in academic discourse. As an extension of that feminist approach, maternal pedagogy can be understood as a way to challenge and reshape the boundaries and strictures around what we have understood to be relations of power in a classroom and in contrast to more rigid, traditional and patriarchal forms of pedagogy. But I wonder: does being a practitioner of maternal pedagogies mean one has to have experienced childbirth/bearing/rearing? Certainly my undergraduate students were confused about the meaning of this book's title. When asked, students responded that maternal pedagogy must be "something about teaching about motherhood," must mean "putting your parenting skills into the classroom," probably means "telling us about how to be good women and mothers while we have a career and do it all." Of course at one point a student bluntly asked: "Why are you asking us this anyway? Maternal means children and you don't have any, do you?" … a point I return to and consider below.

(In)fertility in the Classroom

"Just be careful you don't end up talking about it all the time, or come across as obsessed or whatever, when you are teaching kinship, just make something up for yourself, it's easier than having to explain," said a colleague of mine about the blurry boundaries that arise between personal and professional lives for female faculty engaged in the pursuit of fertility. Another person, a member of a fertility support group, said "you are deviant, damned and totally disabled—marked as 'not the norm'—if you are potentially infertile" (see also Harwood and Terry and Urla). However, the topic (and state) of infertility can be an asset for a feminist teacher, a powerful lens for bringing into focus the fact that in patriarchal cultures, women (but not men) are almost always marked (and often valued) as reproducers. Thus it is no wonder that teaching about infertility disrupts and de-centers patriarchal discourses and pedagogies.

To help students understand Western, patriarchal, and mechanistic constructions of the body, I first ask them to read Emily Martin's now classic discussion on the woman in the body and her critique of the Cartesian view of menstruating as "failed reproduction." Then I assign a very different kind of exercise: I ask students to take a piece of paper and *draw* infertility. Typically, students draw barren fields, desiccated stick figures with X's across their bellies, farmland with dead animals or wilted crops. I ask whether these images are offensive. If people do not have children, is it appropriate to ask them if they are infertile? Is posing this question different from asking about other cultural and physical disabilities? These are important questions, but ones for which there are no easy answers.

Significantly, in every single class in which I have used this exercise (both in the U.S. and in Africa), there are at least a few students who present visual alternatives or solutions to infertility: these students draw pictures of adoptions, IVF (in-vitro fertilization) clinics, or women engaged in "othermothering" activities. Sometimes, students depict a woman and her family covered with smiles and hearts, symbols that these persons have "hope" for a family; in these instances, the female figure is always drawn first and is most prominent. Perhaps most importantly, there are always students who ask if anyone drew people as just plain happy, without children. Unlike those who drew pictures of barren fields, these students openly question the common association of infertility with deviance, disability, and tragedy.

Another way in which I ask students to critically examine the patriarchal conception of women as reproducers is to have them discuss real or imaginary case histories. As we discuss the female faculty member who was offered a vial of sperm for insemination (the vial was "extra," leftover from a friend's successful implant), the idea of a different kind of kinship tree arises. Students tend to like (and want to visually portray) the idea that the children would be related through faculty friends/parents more than they like the idea of two women simply choosing the same sperm donor. They like the idea that the artificially conceived kids would "at least" know each other and share a kind of recognized (i.e., biological) family. The consideration of surrogacy also challenges beliefs about the boundaries of the body and kinship in obvious and powerful ways. I share the case of a colleague who finally conceived a child via in-vitro fertilization—without (having sex with) her husband. She likes to say that she "got pregnant when her husband was out of town" (he was at a conference) but as students astutely observe, this is only a public and amusing story if you know that she was able to carry that pregnancy to term and know that the woman and man (still married) now have a child. Others observe that it's fortunate they "finally had a kid, otherwise she looks kind of obsessed about it," an equally astute but troubling observation.

Finally, I use a cross-cultural approach to the topic of infertility to demonstrate to my students that notions of infertility are socially constructed and intersect with numerous other elements of a given culture. For example, as Handwerker points out in her work on infertility in China, fertility itself is a flexible concept and subject to other kinds of relationships and social conditions. Whereas in the West, infertility might be defined as lack of children after two or three years of marriage and "trying," in China it is often defined as having no male children, a concept laden with patriarchal and marital assumptions that may or may not differ from those in the West. By contrast, in Botswana (a country where there are no assisted reproductive health facilities—nothing to aid conception or adoption, technological or social) one would not even consider marriage to a woman unless she had already had a child, giving rise to the oft quoted, albeit not entirely empowering expression "you know a cow is a good cow if it has a calf." In the U.S., of course, childbearing before marriage and certainly among youth is considered problematic; despite its growing popularity in teen media, the phenomenon is not a culturally sanctioned way to prove one's fertility status for future relationships (Upton 2011).

In short, interesting things arise when infertility enters the classroom. In the U.S., infertility can be an explicit topic on a course syllabus and can be used to challenge the concept that the normative female body is a "fertile" body. A professor also can present as problematic the fact that many students (and many faculty) assume that discussions of infertility will focus on far-removed and highly medicalized *female* problems. In Botswana, infertility is fairly foreign in the classroom, almost taboo; it is a topic one talks about outside the walls of academe—and not something one wants to discuss if one is worried about the valence of discourse with respect to witchcraft and malevolence. Tswana students will often tell me that an aunt or close female relative has bewitched them as a result of jealousy and that if it continues without reparation, they risk their future fertile lives. I suggest at times such an explanation of witchcraft to my physician and students in the U.S. in order to gauge their willingness to consider everything as data and truth.

(In)fertility in the Field—From Botswana to My Own Backyard

I explore issues related to fertility/infertility in very different ways through my ongoing anthropological research in both Botswana and the contemporary United States. In Botswana, where I have worked for over fifteen years, the social and physiological constructions and intersections of infertility have important ramifications for social status, personhood and health. Indeed, as I argue elsewhere, the experience of infertility can render one socially invisible (Upton 2001, 2002) despite some real and important medical outcomes of that invisibility. In Botswana, an extremely pro-natalist country ravaged by the HIV/AIDS epidemic, demographic and health care interests lie with those who have children, or with those who may have children in an era of such great disease risk. In "traditional" scholarly analyses of the problem of infertility in Botswana and other African countries, rarely do demographic perspectives on African people take social stigma into account; instead, assumptions of hyper-sexualized and risky behavior take center stage. In addition, as Marcia Inhorn and others point out, fertility *desires* among women (and men) themselves are rarely taken into consideration as accurate measures of public health and remain unseen in qualitative and quantitative research on reproductive health. My work has focused on and continues to emphasize the need to look at the cultural importance of fertility desires and infertility as related to personhood and social status precisely because of the direct influence of such overlooked issues in HIV/AIDS prevention research. I argue, for example, that knowledge about condoms is in fact quite high among the Tswana, but policy makers fail to recognize the significance of childbearing and thus remain frustrated by the low use of prophylaxis among young Tswana females—who are trying, prior to protecting themselves from HIV and STDs, to fulfill a culturally sanctioned desire to prove their fertility, bear children, and thereby achieve full personhood.

In the U.S., I work on perceptions of "failed" fertility, reproductive technologies, and the actual cultural imperative to have (even a certain number of) children in order to be considered a genuine "family," despite research and feminist work to the contrary. Specifically, I have spent about a decade researching and following couples who grapple with the cultural perception and obligation to have two children in dual-earning households. For the vast majority, despite the perceived cultural obligation to have two children in order to become a "family," it is the advent of that second child that most challenges the roles, responsibilities and identities of working women and men in contemporary society. In this research and over time in Botswana, an interesting thing has happened that places the idea of maternal pedagogy squarely at the center of my fertility research.

My identity as a bona fide and knowledgeable fieldworker and member of a community (both in Botswana and in the middle-class United States) has sometimes come into question when those with whom I work realize that as a result of my failed reproductive status, I don't know certain things that seem obvious to them. For example, when I ask people in Botswana about infertility, HIV, and traditional ways in which women can become pregnant, some tell me that by now, I "should know this already"; I am presumably asking ridiculous questions that I should know the answers to—both because I've lived in Botswana for so long and because it's assumed that I have children somewhere back in the U.S. The scenario is much the same when I work among American families. Most assume that I am much "like them" and therefore am asking ridiculous and obvious questions in the field when I pose questions such as "What led you to decide to move to part-time work after the birth of your second child?" In both Botswana and the U.S., many are shocked to discover that I am not culturally empowered in the ways that mothers (biological or otherwise) are and therefore need some help, need some answers, perhaps personally as well as professionally.

In Botswana I have managed to become a part of the community despite not having children of my own. I rely on the obligations to my research assistants' families and children to help solidify my commitment as an adult and person and remind people that I am trying to have children (this does lead to awkward moments, such as one memorable occasion when I woke to find a group of men who offered to help me after my main field assistant let it be known that I was actively trying to "fall pregnant"!). I currently research how and why assisted reproductive technologies are not available in the country, which ironically affords me some measure of credibility as well as gives me inroads with women and men who struggle with this under-researched topic. In the U.S., the people I work with also grant me both insider and outsider status. I am constantly in the role of educator as well as one in need of education and thus find myself in situations where people who are themselves grappling with infertility issues ask about reproductive technologies and options, as well as situations with those who are more than willing to let me know what their lives are like after having children and how they strive to balance their identities and obligations. In both places, I find that I am walking that fine yet classic anthropological line between participant and observer, pivoting in either place on the issue of fertility—both its potential stigma and its (successful) negotiation.

Some Conclusions

What am I doing in this volume? Far from being deviant, damned or totally disabled, I would argue that an exploration of infertility and the almost frenetic pursuit of fecundity can take center stage in a text on the real value of maternal pedagogies. Perhaps it is the absolute proof that we need, in academia and beyond, to situate fertility studies and maternity outcomes and challenges at the very center of any discussion on parenting and pedagogy, from petri-dishes to policy. Many, in various disciplines, have observed that mothering has often little to do with academic thinking on feminism. Mothering and motherhood are often invisible in those kinds of discussions and the pressures of perfection are pushed aside in the pursuit of feminist agendas that leave little room for the role of family, care-giver or woman (Swanson and Johnston). If motherhood and maternity is invisible, infertility is even more so.

It is ironic yet so often the case that infertility or just the lack of children is seen as an advantage in the pursuit of academic or career success. But cross-cultural research and lived experience demonstrate quite clearly how very fictitious such a view can be. Personhood, failed motherhood, and unattainable desires for motherhood are at stake when one begins to consider the path of infertility and just what one is going to "do" about it (cf. Landsman). How far are you going to go to "fix" the problem and what about guilt and fault? The steps you take are implicit indicators of just how serious you are about maternity, pedagogy, and feminism. Walking that fine line between being serious researcher, academic, teacher and potential parent needs to be carefully negotiated.

Feminist pedagogy and its extension, maternal pedagogy, are not unilinear, univocal or static approaches. They make sense to me as matters of process and practice. Kinship charts are a work in progress, not a fixed snapshot of who and what "family" means in any given culture in the same ways that at various points in time, I have indeed "had" children, achieved maternity, however briefly and unrecognized by a broader society. Comparisons of cultural and individual assumptions from the field to the classroom help illuminate non-maternal, non-nurturing and non-feminist approaches and challenge those normative and essentialized theories that reify a reproductive norm. Feminist pedagogy and by extension, maternal pedagogy, must have room within it to accommodate those who are not essentially mothers or even considered normative by reproductive standards. It is not a single discourse, but multiple voices; my contribution adds to that discussion by offering up some thoughts on the pursuit of maternity, the looming fear of infertility, and the challenges of keeping one's feminist head above the essentialist water.

Infertility is key in the development of maternal pedagogy because it suggests in a very real way that women cannot "have it all." If feminist pedagogy is to continue to be efficacious in challenging patriarchal norms in academia and beyond, then recognition of the relative invisibility of infertility must be examined further. As I suggest, however, that recognition is fraught with tension. If you are desperate to fill in that kinship chart, if you erase the attempts but leave the palimpsests to indicate that there might just be some sort of problem with your ability to fulfill cultural expectations to "do it all," you leave yourself subject to scrutiny and query, although ideally and quite possibly, you also initiate an honest discussion of women's bodies and socially sanctioned roles with a new generation of feminists. As I embark upon another venture down the path toward fertility, the fears are great and who knows when, if, or how I will conceive. Now my obsession is not with fertility per se, nor with the navigation of kinship charts, but with the idea that we can talk about these issues with feminist and maternal voices in the ever-expanding cross-cultural classroom.

Works Cited

Handwerker, Lisa. "The Hen That Can't Lay an Egg (*Bu Xia Dan de Mu Ji*): Conceptions of Female Infertility in Modern China." *Deviant Bodies*. Eds. Jennifer Terry and Jacqueline Urla. Bloomington: Indiana University Press, 1995. 358-387. Print.

Harwood, Karey A. *The Infertility Treadmill: Feminist Ethics, Personal Choice and the Use of Reproductive Technologies*. Chapel Hill: University of North Carolina Press, 2007. Print.

Inhorn, Marcia C. "Missing Motherhood: Infertility, Technology and Poverty in Egyptian Women's Lives." *Ideologies and Technologies of Motherhood*. Eds. Helena Ragone and France Winddance Twine. New York: Routledge, 2000. 139- 167. Print.

Landsman, Gail. "'Real Motherhood': Class, and Children with Disabilities." *Ideologies and Technologies of Motherhood*. Eds. Helena Ragone and France Winddance Twine. New York: Routledge, 2000. 169-187. Print.

Martin, Emily. *The Woman in the Body*. (rev. edition) Boston: Beacon Press, 2001. Print.

Ragone, Helena and France Winddance Twine, eds. *Ideologies and Technologies of Motherhood*. New York: Routledge, 2000. Print.

Strathern, Marilyn. "An Awkward Relationship: The Case of Feminism and Anthropology." *Signs* 12.2 (1987): 276-92. Print.

Swanson, Debra H. And Dierdre D. Johnston. "Mothering in the Ivy-Tower: Interviews with Academic Mothers." *Journal of the Association for Research on Mothering* 5.2 (Fall/Winter 2003): 1-10. Print.

Terry, Jennifer and Jacqueline Urla, eds. *Deviant Bodies: Critical Perspectives on Difference in Science and Popular Culture.* Bloomington: Indiana University Press, 1995. Print.

Upton, Rebecca L. "Infertility Makes You Invisible: Gender, Health and the Negotiation of Fertility in Northern Botswana." *Journal of Southern African Studies* 27.2 (June 2001): 349-362. Print.

Upton, Rebecca L. "Perceptions and Attitudes Towards Male Infertility in Northern Botswana: Some Implications for Family Planning and AIDS Prevention Policies." *African Journal of Reproductive Health* 6.3 (2002): 103-111. Print.

Upton, Rebecca L. "Using Infertility, Useful Fertility: Cultural Imperatives on the Value of Children in the U.S." *The End of Children.* Ed. Graham Allen and Nathanael Lauster. Vancouver: University of British Columbia Press, 2011. 60-78. Print.

Reclaiming Maternal Pedagogies in a British Columbia Aboriginal Head Start Program

MARGARET MACDONALD

> We all carry worlds in our heads, and those worlds are decidedly different. We educators set out to teach, but how can we reach the worlds of others when we don't even know they exist? Indeed, many of us don't even realize that our own worlds exist only in our heads and in the cultural institutions we have built to support them. It is as if we are in the middle of a great computer-generated virtual reality game, but the "realities" displayed in various participants' minds are entirely different terrains. When one player moves right and up a hill, the other player perceives him as moving left and into a river.
>
> —Lisa Delpit (*Other People's Children* xxiv)

LISA DELPIT ADVISES THAT THE debate over appropriate curriculum for minority groups and marginalized families should not be restricted to instructional methods or content but should also include discussions about relationships and power. She encourages us to ask questions that yield a greater understanding about the involvement and engagement of students and families. These more fundamental considerations call into question many "taken for granted" practices that have been the hallmark of student-teacher interactions shaped by centuries of cultural assumptions about the role of the teacher as curriculum expert, mother as "surrogate teacher," and the student perceivably as empty vessel, blank slate, absorbent sponge, or malleable ball of clay—one who is in need respectively of filling, scribing, sopping or shaping under the watchful eye and wisdom of the teacher within the classroom context.

The Normative Parent and Child

In many of today's early childhood classrooms across North America, routines and learning activities tend to reproduce messages that emphasize individualism and support discrete skills and responses typical for the child's age or development. Children's social construction of knowledge within a family system and the connections between the child and his or her family are often overlooked or receive only modest attention in our teaching methods, curriculum, classroom organization, and evaluation. Commonly, classrooms separate the child from his or her teachers within the family and community, and separate the family and community, including their knowledge, from the classroom. Such practices have created an image of the "universal normative child," one who is independent, rational, and functions within the constructs of the classroom and school system and the values these dominant institutions represent.

Thomas Popkewitz refers to this modernist construction of the cosmopolitan child as "an inscription device of governing" where the anthropological "other" is reconstructed as a cosmopolitan, self-regulated, active, lifelong learner operating in a family system where "the parent [often the mother] is pedagogized as a surrogate teacher whose child rearing practices follow the didactic principles of teaching children" (37). This contemporary narrative of the cosmopolitan child and modernist maternal pedagogue favors the behaviors of a child who is self-directed and self-regulating and who demonstrates appropriate independence with respect to self-help skills (e.g., managing his/her own belongings with minimal guidance, following directions, "working" independently, and conforming to routines and imposed structures). Similarly, in classroom communities we conceptualize the ideal parent, typically the mother, as someone who supports the teacher by taking part in at-home activities that reinforce the school curriculum: helping with homework, talking and reading with her child(ren), attending school functions, and guiding her child(ren)'s behavior in socially sanctioned ways. Because of these embedded goals we both consciously and unconsciously privilege children's listening and independent reasoning skills and regard the mother's ability to assist the child in complying with didactic instructional methods as hallmarks of the child and parent's competence. Even in "idealized" models of parent participation, the roles are prescriptive; parents are usually invited to help teachers with classroom tasks such as numeracy and literacy exercises or read aloud sessions, but deeper consultation and collaboration around curriculum development and routines does not take place (see Borba; Scott; Nichols, Nixon and Rowsell; and Strickland, Morrow, and Neuman).

In Canada, linguistically and culturally this normative universal "cosmopolitan" child and parent are ones who are fluent and literate in one or both official Canadian languages, can reason mathematically and scientifically, and can employ the methods and rational logic of contemporary thinkers. To conform to our typical standards and expectations of the school community, the child must work independently for the majority of the time and collaboratively during sanctioned social moments. Typically this means that the child is able to understand and conform to social nuances and rules around listening and speaking, group processes, play entry, temporary ownership of collective "school" or "classroom" property, and respect for private and personal property and for the feelings and boundaries of others.

Reclaiming and Revitalizing Stó:lō Language and Culture: From Residential Schools to the BC Aboriginal Head Start Program

We come by many of our dispositions toward teaching and learning as they are modeled to us and embedded in our early experiences with and observations of others. Typically this process begins with familial role models such as our mothers, grandmothers, siblings and cousins, who help us embrace the traditions and ethical values that our family and culture revere. These include such fundamentals as our language(s), occupational skills, roles within our family and community systems, ways of nurturing and guiding the young, and wisdom that we hold dear and pass on through our generations. Initially, the cultural traditions and beliefs of the Stó:lō people of the west coast of British Columbia were passed on through family-based systems of intergenerational kinship ties that linked families to the land. But during colonization, these lines of cultural knowledge were disrupted and replaced by Eurocentric languages and worldviews. This especially was the case with the separation of aboriginal children from their families during the era of residential schools, when church-run, government-funded and sanctioned schools were used as a way to colonize Stó:lō youth and integrate them and other native children into mainstream Canadian society (see <http://archives.cbc.ca/society/education/topics/692-4003>).

This practice began in traditional Stó:lō territory in 1863 (in what is now referred to as the Fraser Valley of British Columbia) when St. Mary's boarding school established a residential school for aboriginal boys. Five years later, in 1868, separate dormitories were created and the first girls were admitted. For over a century (St. Mary's closed in 1973), this school was a site of cultural disruption affecting multiple generations. Stó:lō children were exposed to Xwelitem (white persons') views and institutional organization, including a highly gendered curriculum. Subjects such as cooking, sewing, and cleaning were taught to the girls, while farming, woodworking, and industrial and millwork were taught to the boys. As Keith Carlson notes,

> Boys and girls slept in separate dormitories, ate in different dining rooms and, until as recently as the 1950s, learned academic subjects in different classrooms. In many areas they were not allowed to speak to each other—even if they were related—and they were certainly not allowed to speak their Aboriginal languages. (68)

Residential schools like St. Mary's were part of the colonial construction of a new world "citizen." They imposed on Stó:lō youth a foreign language and Eurocentric values that interrupted parental modeling and the transmission of the Halq'eméylem language and Stó:lō traditions over multiple generations.

Not surprisingly, when articulating their aspirations for their own children, today's Stó:lō mothers describe their own feelings of alienation from the public school system and a strong desire for their children to fare better than themselves, saying such things as "I don't want him to feel like I did" or "I want her to feel good about herself" (personal communications, July 2007).[1] The desire of these mothers (and fathers) to improve the educational system led to the founding of the Aboriginal Head Start Association of BC in 2001. Through culturally relevant teachings and learning structures, the Head Start programs honor and help preserve the language and traditions of the indigenous community. Not only do the programs introduce pre-schoolers to songs and stories in Halq'eméylem, but they also give mothers, grandmothers, and other Stó:lō Elders the opportunity to participate in twice weekly, play-based learning activities in the classroom.

The Halq'eméylem Language and Stó:lō Identity

In the Stó:lō tradition, people and communities are tied to rhythm and patterns of the land, in what is referred to as the Seasonal Rounds. Words describing the seasons, and the ceremonies and occupations associated with those seasons, connect the people to the land and their traditional livelihoods. For example, the Halq'eméylem word *Temqw'iles* or Spring ("when everything comes up") signals a time when families celebrate the first spring salmon caught, hold the First Salmon Ceremony to give thanks to the Creator, and share fish among members of the community. Such events represent a collaborative sharing of culture and traditions based on Stó:lō connections to place.

In a similarly collective way, the benefit of multiple perspectives and opinions, particularly the knowledge of the Elders, is central to Stó:lō ways of constructing knowledge. Stó:lō teachers construct their understandings with Elders. Children typically learn by being involved in community activities and by observing the work of others. In the Stó:lō tradition, children are also taught to reflect on and synthesize the lessons of stories told to them at an age when they are deemed ready to receive them. Many words in Halq'eméylem demonstrate the importance of familial connections to persons within the community and extended family, both past and present. For example, the word *Xwélmexw* refers to human beings who speak the same language, thus illustrating the importance of ties between linguistic or cultural communities. Words that convey kinship relationships across marriages also exist. In Halq'eméylem, the word *qeló:qtel* refers to kinship relationships that acknowledge the blood ties between fourth cousins, that is, children who are connected through marriage to common great great great grandparents (Carlson). The language also has words that connect the present generation to both the past and the future, with referents to generations who have passed away and those yet to be born. This connection of the current generation to eternity is very different from referents in English and many other languages, showing a fundamental difference in thought and world views around time, place, space and stewardship. In an interview, Head Start Teacher Selisewet Bibiana Norris describes the importance of these Halq'eméylem words and relationships as follows:

> You know identity is very important to me—I teach my children about their identity especially our teaching that people need to

> know who you are, even when it goes as far as just giving an introduction. I'm Bibiana Norris, my Indian name is Seliselwet, I come from Matsqui, my mother was Tseloyóthelwet, Shirley Julian, and give the whole history of who you are. If you could go back, I'd say four generations that would be good, but there are not many of us that can go that far because to me that is our identity. If we know who we are and where we come from that is our identity, I feel I'm richer if I know that. (Bibiana Norris, August 2007)

BC Aboriginal Head Start Programs

Following some of the traditions of the Stó:lō community described above, BC Aboriginal Head Start programs have set out to give native children from birth to school age both a head start in preparation for elementary school, and pride in their indigenous heritage, language, and cultures (Dunning). Describing the Chilliwack-based Head Start Family Program, Early Childhood Development Manager Mary Stewart explains:

> Funding was obtained for the program in 1998, in response to the Indian Residential School era, where the majority of the Stó:lō/First Nation students were not exposed to "parental observance" nor experienced a nurturing upbringing; for they were raised by religious figures. In response to this, Stó:lō Nation had mandated that their Aboriginal Head Start Program would be family-oriented and have full participation from the parent/caregiver and include the extended family.
>
> One of the goals of the Stó:lō Nation Aboriginal Head Start Program is to rebuild strong close-knit Aboriginal families and Aboriginal communities—the way it was in pre-contact. We believe that exposure of the Halq'eméylem language and Stó:lō/Aboriginal cultural enrichment is pertinent in developing the positive self-esteem and self-identity as an Aboriginal amongst the Head Start participants. [To this end] Each family receives a copy of the audiocassette Halq'eméylem language library, consisting of six tapes.
>
> The age-appropriate information contains culturally relevant and culturally sensitive materials on the month's themes and songs,

> traditional and contemporary [developed by Mary Stewart]. This ensures that the Halq'eméylem language is reinforced within the home. This will also be beneficial to the children when they enter the Aboriginal all-day kindergarten class within the Chilliwack School District.
>
> One of the teachers has informed me that the Stó:lō Nation Head Start preschool children arrive to kindergarten with a wealth of the Halq'eméylem language.[2] (Mary Stewart, Personal Communication, April 2009)

Several aspects of the Head Start classroom program and routines reinforce and support Stó:lō traditions and practices that are holistic, community-based and transmitted across generations. A respect for Elders is modeled by having these community members consulted on language, protocol and traditions, as well as by having them present in the classroom and serving them first during mealtime. The wisdom of the Elders is also honored by basing classroom themes on a Seasonal Activity Chart designed by Stó:lō Elders in the 1970s. This chart highlights times in the calendar year that relate to traditional fishing and harvesting practices and serves as a guideline for classroom-based themes such as participation in the community salmon ceremonies (Mary Stewart, Personal Communication, May 2009).

In addition to introducing these culturally appropriate themes and community practices, the teachers and Stó:lō adults in the Head Start program urge other adults to actively participate in the transmission of knowledge to the community's children. Stó:lō songs and activities are taught to the children's family members—especially to mothers and grandmothers, who then help classroom teachers pass this knowledge on to their children. As a result, children explore materials and comfortably engage in classroom routines within a supportive, intergenerational, community context.

Other ways of transmitting indigenous values and traditions include introducing children and families to Halq'eméylem through the teaching of prayers and songs. For example, during the pre-meal prayer, the teacher shares information about the cultural origins, meaning, and value of the song, and all members of community listen and participate collectively. In addition, the built or classroom environment includes posters, pictures, and images that are unique to the First Nations community, with the words often written in Halq'eméylem.

Classroom Learning Environments as a Worldview

In early childhood education, so much of our current practice has been built on past practice or traditions and theoretical paradigms that are historically rooted in restrictive interpretations of child development theory, and values that often reflect narrowly defined outputs rather than culturally appropriate curriculum practices (Cannella; Cannella and Viruru). It has been argued that our modern, Eurocentric traditions have locked us into particular ways of doing things that are counterproductive to an educational image of young children as capable, competent and able to enter into prolonged investigations, develop elaborate theories, discuss concepts, forge relationships, and make deep meaningful cognitive and socio-emotional connections (Dahlberg and Moss; Dahlberg, Moss, and Pence; Egan; MacDonald).

As Margie Mayfield notes, Eurocentric cultures have a long tradition of valuing individual work over collaboration and of closely observing children to identify individual learning needs. Because of the requirements of teacher credentialing and licensure, as well as a conscious desire to prepare the children to be comfortable and successful in the classrooms that await them in the formal school system (kindergarten or grade 1), some aspects of the Aboriginal Head Start Program classroom environment are influenced by Eurocentric traditions and values, particularly some of the play-based routines and instructional activities using individual question and response patterns. However, because of the frequent classroom presence of Elders and the teaching of native traditions and language, the Stó:lō emphasis on community-based and collaborative learning is never absent from books, arts and crafts projects, and circle time songs and routines. Moreover, urging mothers, grandmothers, and other family members to share in the teaching of the community's youth ensures that both in and outside the classroom, young Stó:lō have numerous adults communicating the importance of Indigenous knowledges and ways of knowing.

Final Thoughts

Sadly, in our Eurocentric culture of teaching and learning, parents often have been sidelined and had no or little input into pedagogical or curriculum decisions. Many teachers and school administrators view parental, and especially maternal, knowledge as inferior or secondary, considering parents limited in their abilities to educate their children. Wrongly, some also assume that parents are disinterested in collaboration; rather than imagining parents or community elders as partners, they are seen as "outsiders" and sometimes as hurried, uncaring, and disengaged. To be sure, some parents may in fact have these attributes or come from cultures that revere the teacher as "expert," thus making them hesitant to get involved in curriculum decisions (Hujala et al.). But more often, these attitudes have been shaped by a view of teachers as the only individuals fit to uphold educational standards (Gordon and Nocon 2008).

In Early Childhood Education we believe that learning is socially constructed and have developed strategies to support socially mediated learning (Bodrova and Leong). But ironically, we generally view and assess a child's performance not as part of a collective effort, but as an individual response. In First Nations communities, we are only beginning to understand the ways that opportunities for shared, communal teaching and learning can be cultivated through carefully selected curricular materials and play-based activities that can be used both in and outside the traditional classroom (Curtis and Carter, Archibald).

As noted at the beginning of this essay, school children can feel alienated when parents and teachers both consciously and unconsciously hold different world-views, and when neither party has a way of connecting to or fully understanding the others' cultural values and beliefs. For members of the Stó:lō community on the west coast of British Columbia and many other aboriginal women and men in Canada, reclaiming indigenous pedagogies and knowledge through community-based educational institutions like the Aboriginal Head Start program is proving to be an effective way of preparing aboriginal pre-schoolers to enter a Eurocentric school system not only with confidence, but with great pride in their heritage.

[1]In a separate project, in-depth interviews were conducted with eight new mothers attending a Baby Time program at the Stó:lō Health Centre.
[2]To date, because of sensitivities around empirical data collection on an individual level, no formal evaluation has been conducted on the performance of these children in early elementary.

Works Cited

Archibald, Johanne. *Indigenous Storywork: Educating the Heart, Mind, Body, and Spirit.* Vancouver: University of British Columbia Press, 2008. Print.

Bodrova, Elenor and Deborah Leong. *Tools of the Mind: The Vygotskian Approach to Early Childhood Education.* 2nd ed. Upper Saddle River, NJ: Pearson Education/Allyn and Bacon, 2007. Print.

Borba, Michele. "Caring Closes the Language-Learning Gap." *Phi Delta Kappan* 90.9 (2009): 681-685. Print.

Cannella, Gail Sloan. *Deconstructing Early Childhood Education: Social Justice and Revolution.* New York: Peter Lang, 2002. Print.

Cannella, Gail Sloan and Rahdika Viruru. *Childhood and Postcolonization: Power, Education, and Contemporary Practice.* New York: Routledge-Falmer, 2004. Print.

Carlson, Keith Thor. *A Stó:lō Coast Salish Historical Atlas.* Vancouver: Douglas and McIntyre, 2001. Print.

Curtis, Debra and Margie Carter. *Designs for Living and Learning: Transforming Early Childhood Environments.* St Paul, MN: Redleaf Press, 2003. Print.

Dahlberg, Gunilla and Peter Moss. *Ethics and Politics in Early Childhood Education.* London: RoutledgeFalmer, 2005. Print.

Dahlberg, Gunilla, Peter Moss, and Alan Pence. *Beyond Quality in Early Childhood Education and Care: Postmodern Perspectives.* London: Falmer Press, 1999. Print.

Delpit, Lisa. *Other People's Children: Cultural Conflict in the Classroom.* 2nd ed. New York: New Press, 2006. Print.

Dunning, Paula. "Aboriginal Head Start." *Education Canada* 39.4 (2000): 38. Print.

Egan, Keran, *Getting it Wrong from the Beginning: Our Progressivist Inheritance from Herbert Spencer, John Dewey, and Jean Piaget.* New Haven: Yale University Press, 2002. Print.

Gordon, Virginia and Hornorine Nocon. "Reproducing Segregation: Parent Involvement, Diversity, and School Governance." *Journal of Latinos and Education* 7.4 (2008): 320-339. Print.

Hujala, Eeva, Leena Turja, Maria Gaspar, Marika Beisson, and Majnula Waniganayake Manjula. "Perspectives of Early Childhood Teachers on Parent-Teacher Partnerships in Five European Countries." *European Early*

Childhood Education Research Journal 17.1 (2009): 57-76. Print.

MacDonald, Margaret. "Developmental Theory and Post Modern Thinking in Early Childhood Education." *Canadian Children* 32.2 (2007): 7-10. Print.

Mayfield, Margie. *Early Childhood Education and Care in Canada: Contexts, Dimensions, and Issues*. Toronto: Prentice Hall, 2001. Print.

Nichols, Sue, Helen Nixon, and Jennifer Rowsell. "The 'Good' Parent in Relation to Early Childhood Literacy: Symbolic Terrain and Lived Practice." *Literacy* 43.2 (2009): 65-74. Print.

Popkewitz, Thomas S. "Governing the Child and Pedagogicalization of the Parent: A Historical Excursus into the Present." *Governing Children, Families and Education: Restructuring the Welfare State*. Ed. Marianne N. Block, Kerstin Holmlund, Ingeborg Moqvist, and Thomas S. Popkewitz. New York: Palgrave MacMillian, 2003. 35-62. Print.

Scott, Peggy. "Successfully Bringing Parents into the Classroom." *Education Digest* 73.2 (2007): 47-49. Print

Soto, Lourdes Diaz, ed. *The Politics of Early Childhood Education*. New York: Peter Lang, 2005. Print.

Strickland, Dorothy, Lesley M. Morrow, and Susan Neuman. "The Role of Literacy in Early Childhood Education." *The Reading Teacher* 58.1 (2004): 86-100. Print.

2. Being a Recipient of Maternal Pedagogies

The Child/Student's Point of View

Re-searching Mommy

Narrating My Inquiry of Maternal Pedagogies

JENNIFER WATT

Gestation: Telling a Maternal Pedagogy

I WAS WORKING ON THE coursework component of my Master's of Education when I met Wayne—my then-instructor, my now-doctoral supervisor. In my life BC (Before Children), I taught secondary school English Language Arts in England. When my daughter was born we moved back to Canada. The time, space, and self that existed before I became a mother often felt distant, even though many of my courses prompted me to reflect on teaching, learning, curriculum, and pedagogy. I began my Master's degree when my daughter was just a little over a year old. I was looking for something to balance my life as a stay-at-home mother, often expressing to others that graduate school was "something for my brain," somehow dismissing the intense cognitive processing that was part of my mothering. I had not yet discovered or acknowledged maternal thinking (Ruddick). That comes much later in my story. At the time, school was my place for academic "head" work and home was my place for nurturing "heart" work.

I sensed there was something different and profound about Wayne's teaching from the first moments that he began our graduate class. I am saddened that I cannot capture on paper the gentle and genuine presence Wayne created through his posture, voice, and words that reassured me that what we were about to learn, read, and discover had not yet been fully determined. "The course will develop only as we get to know each other," he said, "First, we need to get a sense of who we are as people and what we need from this learning space."

It was during this first class that Wayne explained that the assignment for the course would be to conduct an inquiry into language and/or literacy development. This inquiry was to be more than a make-work project and become more than a final mark: the inquiry should be based in the context of our practice and become personally meaningful. Wayne did not suggest protocol or methodology. He simply invited us to pay close attention to something we wanted to know more about and to allow ourselves to be surprised through the process.

The open nature of the assignment unsettled some of my classmates. There were a lot of questions: What do you mean? What does that look like? How many pages? The practical concerns of the assignment did not worry me—I like some creative wiggle room. However, my head was spinning with the idea of where I would base my inquiry. I was out of practice, was I not? I did not have a school or a classroom, students or colleagues. And then as quickly as the anxiety had overwhelmed me, it washed away. "Could I," I asked incredulously, "Could I study my daughter? She is 17 months old. If I carefully wrote a journal about her emergent language and literacy for six weeks, would that count?" I felt foolish asking; perhaps mommy journaling had no place in the academy, even if I did connect it with scholarly literature. Wayne was enthusiastically encouraging and for the first time I felt that my identities as new researcher and new mom, which I had guardedly kept separate, could be integrated and interrogated.

The result of the inquiry was a story of my daughter and how she made sense of language, literacy, and life at eighteen months. It also became a story of discovering myself as mommy through the reading and writing of our experiences. It is only now that I recognize how those stories have become the beginning of a new inquiry into transformative approaches to teaching and learning. I believe now that my instructor used a maternal pedagogy as he taught our class. Although he did not call it that himself and might be surprised by the label today, his approach to teaching fits my still developing understanding of the term. The remainder of this paper explores how I am coming to understand and articulate the idea of a maternal pedagogy, by juxtaposing the literature and theories of mothering research with my lived narratives as a teacher, Ph.D. student, and mother of small children. I also bring my questions to this semiotic space (Gee): What is maternal and how does it connect to teaching? Is the meaning of maternal culturally universal? Will the term "maternal pedagogy" exclude men or women who are not mothers because they may not be able to identify with or invest in the concepts the term embodies?[1] How do we promote the living, naming, and valuing of empowering maternal pedagogies by new and experienced teachers? Stories and questions are helping me "give birth" to my understandings (Belenky et al. 217) of a maternal pedagogy and helping to preserve, nurture, and shape its acceptability in my current and future learning, teaching, and mothering.

Labour: Situating the Narratives of Research, Theory, and Self

Confession time: when I proposed this essay, I named my instructor-advisor's teaching as a maternal pedagogy based entirely on intuition. Until I saw the call for papers on the topic of maternal pedagogies, I had never heard the term. I certainly did not have a set definition to which I compared Wayne's practice. Maternal pedagogy just felt right, and this intuitive fit of my experience to the proposed linguistic expression inspired me to embark on the more laborious process of discovering what exactly I meant when I used the term.

Pedagogy is commonly defined as the art, science, profession, or craft of teaching. It is a term often combined with a descriptor to further explain the focus or philosophy of the teaching choices, approaches, and strategies employed: feminist, ecological, critical, or radical to name a few. I believe I need to unpack the descriptor "maternal" before I can use it to describe what I understand as an empowering maternal pedagogy.

The study of motherhood, mothering, and the maternal is a vibrant and growing scholarly conversation. Fiona Green suggests this academic dialogue began largely in response to Adrienne Rich's *Of Woman Born:* "Adrienne Rich is the first person to have acknowledged that motherhood is a complex site of women's oppression and a potential location for women's creativity and joy" (125). As Andrea O'Reilly observes, Rich differentiates the terms motherhood, "the patriarchal institution of motherhood that is male-defined and controlled and is deeply oppressive to women" and mothering, "women's experiences of mothering that are female-defined and centered and potentially empowering to women" (*From Motherhood to Mothering* 2). Thus maternal, depending upon the context in which it is being used, can refer to what is characteristic of or related to either motherhood or mothering. If maternal refers to the patriarchal institution of motherhood, it can often become romanticized or patronizing. However, if maternal refers to mothering, especially feminist mothering as defined by Fiona Green, Andrea O'Reilly, and Sara Ruddick, it can become inspiring or empowering—this is the sense of the maternal that I embrace in a definition of a maternal pedagogy.

I believe in this discussion of maternal pedagogies there needs to be a parallel drawn between the concepts of motherhood and mothering and the concepts of education systems and teaching. Just as motherhood can be seen as a patriarchal institution that controls and oppresses, education as a systemic concept is a patriarchal institution, similarly male-defined, and very often controlling and oppressive. Education systems define who can learn what, when, and how. Teaching, on the other hand, is more often practitioner-defined and potentially empowering. Motherhood limits and influences mothering, just as education systems limit and influence teaching.

In *Maternal Thinking*, Ruddick conceptualizes mothering as a practice in which mothers engage in the protection, nurturance, and training of their children. O'Reilly explains that engaging in the mothering practice "gives rise to a specific discipline of thought, a cluster of attitudes, beliefs and values which Ruddick calls maternal thinking" (3). O'Reilly also directly compares maternal thinking to pedagogy:

> Good teaching requires conspicuous thought and not just about content delivery. It necessitates reflection on practising in intentional ways that are effective for learning to take place, beyond or outside of the expectations of others. This and other similarities indicate comparisons can be made, *between maternal thinking and highly reflective pedagogy,* providing greater understanding of both practices. (*Maternal Thinking* 8)

Maternal thinking and excellent teaching require reflective and intentional practice aimed to "meet the demands of vulnerable 'children' for safety and well-being" (O'Reilly and Ruddick 17). Whether the "children," or rather learners, in question are adults in the classroom of a post-secondary teacher or toddlers in the care of their mother, a scrutinizing consciousness is engaged to meet the needs and expand the opportunities of those being nurtured. I recognize the patterns of thinking, decision-making, and reflecting from my teaching experiences as I now engage in mothering my two small children. I also recognized the consciousness developed in my mothering when I recently returned to teaching teacher-candidates.

Denise Ferris explores the connection of maternal thinking to her practice as a university teacher of fine arts, although I believe a great deal of her argument can be applied to any level or subject of teaching. She writes, "It occurred to me there were correlations between the considerations I made in my teaching practice and certain deliberations of my mothering life" (121). She narrates how colleagues would sometimes refer to her "nurturing" teaching style almost more as a liability than a strength. However, she poignantly defends her pedagogical choices: "A kind of thought, modelled on the maternal form, does matter.... In a university we teach with a potent opportunity to guide the evolving maturity of emergent individuals who will imminently have an impact socially and culturally" (121).

Ferris bases her teaching on the three essential activities that Ruddick names as comprising maternal thought: protection, nurturance, and training. I feel tension when using the term "training" because of its Latin root, which means "to drag along," so I prefer the term "educating." However, true to Ruddick's and Ferris' work, I will use the term training for continuity of argument. Ferris states, "Protection may be understood as using hierarchical power wisely ... and providing the security of support" (123). Teaching requires setting boundaries for the personal, physical, and emotional safety of all involved in the community of learning. "Suitable nurturance promotes confidence and self-esteem," Ferris explains (123). She then refers to her context of teaching art, "where decision-making relies on the confidence to initiate and innovate for speculative outcomes" (123). When students have had their confidence and sense of self nurtured, they are more able to identify as accountable, responsible, and empowered agents. Within the nurturing environment, they become willing to take the risks needed to learn new ways of doing and being. Finally, Ferris describes training as a promotion of "understanding of methodology and ability, in other words the comprehension and insight to repeat outcomes by fostering critical thinking that relishes ongoing questions and problems" (123). Whether the training is in art, English literature, educational research, or simply in how to live as caring individuals, Ferris argues that teaching is a process of communicating with students and inviting them to engage within a community of learners. I believe Ferris's description of the maternal thinking within her art teaching is an example of a maternal pedagogy in practice.

I return, for a moment, to the opening narrative of my experience in Wayne's class. Embedded within the story, I can easily identify the aspects of maternal thinking that Ferris describes in her teaching practice. Wayne provided protection for us as students through his encouragement of personal and emotional safety. He responded to the worries of those who felt the need for more structure and clarity in the inquiry assignment by building in a proposal process in which our ideas could mature through the dialogue with him as an instructor and with the class as a community of inquiry. We checked in regularly, both formally and informally, throughout our inquiries and were given space and time to ask questions, seek advice, vent frustrations, suggest resources, and/or gain perspectives. We were nurtured in our emerging identities as re-searchers of our practices. Written and spoken feedback was generously offered about how we were conducting our inquiries and we were given ample examples of other researchers who used inquiries to guide their work. Wayne encouraged us to use the inquiry as an opportunity to practice nurturing the individuals we were studying. As Ferris articulates, "Trust is built from recognition that a vigilant teacher conducts these sessions in positive ways and knows about an individual's progress and process, a consequence of what Ruddick names 'careful attention'" (125-126). From this, I recognize how Wayne used the assignment, and his pedagogical approach, as an opportunity to educate (rather than train) us as teacher-researchers—stressing the importance of carefully attending to the individuals we were teaching and viewing every moment in the classroom as an opportunity to learn about our practice.

Delivery: Problematizing and Practicalizing the Pedagogy

As I begin to grasp a sense of what maternal pedagogies are or are not and how they could be lived and defined, I feel the need to look a little closer. I have the responsibility to adopt a critical lens to examine beyond the warm and fuzzy exterior of a "really good idea" to reveal the more uncomfortable assumptions that exist within. It can be hard to render visible what easily remains hidden beneath personal, cultural, and social biases, but ignoring hegemony does not make it less individually or collectively damaging. I felt intuitively drawn towards the term maternal pedagogies because I believe mothering and maternal thinking need to be more valued in our society and I believe a great deal of excellent teaching is a living example of mothering on a community level. However, I believe there are many aspects of naming a way of teaching as a "maternal pedagogy" that could be insensitive or damaging if not carefully and critically acknowledged.

I need to claim this pedagogy as empowering and inclusive, rather than to assume that this is how it will be interpreted and applied within educational systems.

When I taught, I described myself as very "mothering" of my students. I called the students in my classes "my kids," and I felt a responsibility that could sometimes turn into anxiety for their well-being. I tried to get to know my students' lives and interests out of school—I had a good sense of the dramatic stages of the ever-changing romantic relationships unveiling themselves in our midst, I attended carefully to how "my kids" were getting along in other classes with other teachers, and spent many lunch hours, breaks, and after-school hours listening to stories of troubles at home or dreams for the future. In many of the ways that Green describes the "good" or "ideal mother," I felt as a teacher I should always have "a connection with [my] children, never … an ill feeling towards them," believing I was "completely responsible for caring for and nurturing" all the students in my classes—and my colleagues (127). I worked hard to get past rough edges, rolling eyes, and bad reputations, trying, alongside my teacher colleagues, to compassionately imagine the stories that these students carried with them. Like the "ideal mother" Green critically scrutinizes, I believed that I should "never get angry" because I found teaching "to be the most meaningful part" of my life. ("Feminist Mothers" 127) On days when "I lost it" and shouted at a kid or a whole class, I was plagued with feelings of lack of confidence and competence, remembering how I had vowed during my teacher training to be a "good enough" teacher that I would never need to resort to yelling.

I learned early in my career that this ideal notion of the perfect teacher that I had set for myself, in accordance with the expectations of the patriarchal educational system, was impossible. It was impossible as long as there were dreaded Thursday last periods of the day (or any other last period of the day), when groups of hot, sweaty, just-finished Physical Education 15-year-olds erupted in my classroom, angry they had to be in English class, frustrated they had to learn romantic poetry for national exams, and uninterested in how much time or energy I had poured into lesson planning. It was impossible to remain ideal when gang or race conflicts came to brawls in my classroom. I could not be perfect when I needed to teach *Macbeth* to new immigrants with little to no knowledge of English who had witnessed the murder of their parents in their home countries or experienced other atrocities, while at the same time offering support and individualized instruction to twenty-seven other students with high literacy needs. I, alone, could not provide all the care that all of the students and staff that I worked with needed. There were students I did not connect with, no matter how hard I tried, and there were many times I harboured ill-feelings towards students. And I got angry—red, flaring, ragingly angry. I lost my temper and raised my voice, shouted and occasionally cursed. When I experienced these less than ideal, but incredibly normal (and usually justified) feelings, I inevitably felt guilty. Despite not always being able to be the "good teacher" or the "ideal teacher," I believe I was still effective, caring, and vibrant.

I also believe my desire to teach in a way that fit the "good mother" or "ideal teacher" model greatly influenced my reasons for stopping classroom teaching when I became a mother. "I don't think I have enough patience, care, time, and energy to be able to devote everything I feel I need to my students and to my children. I can't see how I would be able to do both well because I couldn't give my whole self to either," I explained to colleagues, friends, and family when I chose to stay at home with my small children rather than return to classroom teaching. I could not imagine how I could fulfill the expectations of selflessness in two arenas. Although I have no evidence other than my own story to back this claim, I believe that the patriarchal expectations of the self-sacrificing mother and teacher may play a part in the attrition rates of both male and female teachers in the public school system and may account for the reluctance of some female academics to combine mothering with a career as a professor.

I can now recognize that I defined my teaching and my mothering by the "intensive" motherhood standards that O'Reilly identifies as an "ideology of care whose standards are impossible for any woman to meet, guaranteeing that her efforts are anxiously and relentlessly directed in specifically predictable ways" (Trimble 179). Within this discourse of "intensive mothering," I confront one of the concerns about the term maternal pedagogy that I experienced when I read Ferris: "It is the intensity in teaching and my comprehension of the importance of that intensity, which allows me to speculate on the similar qualities of … teaching and the maternal" (122). Do we really want to encourage a maternal pedagogy that endorses the impossible standards of intensive practice? Do we want to encourage "putting others first in pedagogy" (Ferris 128) above a more empowering definition of a maternal pedagogy where the needs and complete life of the teacher are as equally acknowledged and valued as the students? I think the word "maternal" can be a slippery slope that easily leads to discourse of self-sacrificial, martyr-style teaching in which the "ideal" leads to burn-out or attrition. However, I believe we can find firm footing by claiming maternal as an empowering recognition of the teacher as an important part of the pedagogical equation.

O'Reilly provides a compelling definition of empowered mothering that I believe could be used, in part, to define a practical, empowering, and inviting maternal pedagogy. It is possible to read the following quotation in two ways, as is depicted in the following table. The first column provides O'Reilly's original definition of empowered mothering. In the second column, I suggest replaceable maternal pedagogical terms that are depicted in italics:

Empowered Mothering	**Maternal Pedagogy**
Empowered mothering begins with the recognition that mothers and children benefit when the mother lives her life and practices mothering from a position of agency, authority, authenticity, and autonomy. This perspective, in emphasizing maternal authority and ascribing agency to mothers and value to motherwork, defines motherhood as a site wherein mothers can affect social change through the socialization of children at large through political-social activism (*Feminist Mothering* 6-7).	Empowered *[maternal pedagogy]* begins with the recognition that both *[teachers]* and *[students]* benefit when the *[teacher]* lives her life and practices *[teaching]* from a position of agency, authority, authenticity, and autonomy. This perspective, in emphasizing *[teacher]* authority and ascribing agency to *[teaching]*, defines *[teaching]* as a site wherein *[teachers]* can affect social change through the socialization of *[students]* at large through political-social activism (*Feminist Mothering* 6-7; brackets and italics not in the original).

In this definition of a maternal pedagogy, we read the teacher as an active, empowered agent who is valued and effects real change. The definition addresses how both teachers and students benefit from an empowered teacher who is able to engage in pedagogical decisions that foster relationships that re-distribute power. Like the above passage, the following quotation from Green can be read first as her description of the ways in which relationships can be fostered through feminist mothering and then again as a possible way of explaining a maternal pedagogy:

Relationships in Feminist Mothering	**Relationships in Maternal Pedagogy**
Rather than exercise power over children, they strived for relationships based on respect, responsibility, and accountability. They encouraged their children to think critically about their own and their mother's ideas. They also acknowledge the experiences and knowledge of their children and encouraged them to talk about their own understandings and experiences with them in respectful dialogue (167).	Rather than exercise power over *[students]*, they strived for relationships based on respect, responsibility, and accountability. They encouraged their *[students]* to think critically about their own and their *[teacher's]* ideas. They also acknowledge the experiences and knowledge of their *[students]* and encouraged them to talk about their own understandings and experiences with them in a respectful dialogue. (167; italics and brackets not in the original)

Within both the definition of the role of the empowered teacher and the description of the relationships this would enable with students, I find there is the potential for an inclusive invitation for people of all genders and cultures, whether they choose to be parents or not, to adopt a maternal pedagogy.

However, I now question whether I find these definitions so inviting because of my position as a white, middle-class, heterosexual, currently able-bodied woman from a linguistic majority who is the biological mother of two children. From my privileged position, I am okay with this version of a maternal pedagogy. In fact, I find it exciting. Both the definitions of empowering feminist mothering and empowering maternal pedagogies help me to imagine how to combine my mothering with teaching—not just surviving, but thriving in each mutually enhancing role. Yet, I recognize that the idea of maternal is not universal and, therefore, it is not necessarily inclusive or inviting. At first, I found this very disturbing—enough to almost abandon the phrase. Why bother coming up with another term that might potentially further divide teachers and/or feminists who are trying their best to effect change and promote equality through their work in classrooms? Do we really need another big word to unpack and interrogate? However, it is the process of naming that gives value to the maternal and provokes searching into what the term might mean. It is the claiming of the term by individuals from varied backgrounds that brings pedagogical perspectives of privileged and oppressed groups into dialogue. This is a needed and worthy process and it is within a collection such as this that this dialogue of differentiation begins to happen. Just as my mothering is unique, so is my living of a maternal pedagogy, but both are enriched by honest and open sharing of diverse perspectives.

I circle back to the narrative that opens this paper. In the midst of conducting the case-study inquiry of my daughter, I reflected on why the assignment had become so transformational in my learning and to my identity:

> I was surprised what an extremely emotional experience it has been to record these everyday moments that I may have easily overlooked and most likely forgotten had I not been giving myself a reason to record my daughter's achievements. Here she is: learning, growing, developing, changing, making meaning, and expressing her will—and I have captured some of it (some of her) on paper. So my first surprise? The case study has figuratively and literally become my baby.... Here is my life. It is right here. Exposed. How deeply grateful I am that I was honest and let myself be vulnerable and open to this experience and let it surprise me. (Progress Report of Else's Case Study: March 9, 2006)

It is four years later and I still feel the same gratitude for the process, because it is ongoing and still surprising me. In order to make sense of what I was experiencing as I researched my daughter's experiences, I contextualized my inquiry within the academic literature and theories of language and literacy and the methodologies of parent-research. Dorothy Cohen, Virginia Stern and Nancy Balaban suggest, "Taking this sort of recording 'time out' during a busy day can be viewed as putting 'time in' since it provides teachers and caregivers a deep view into the lives of their children" (177-178). At the time of the original inquiry, I found in this quotation a justification to allow my role as mother and researcher to integrate and inform one another. Now, I find the quotation even richer. Not only has the time out that I now routinely devote to recording my mothering work provided me a deep view into the lives of my ever-changing daughter and son, but it also provides a deep view into my own life. It was through first recording my daughter that I became aware of my intensive mothering style and the intensive guilt that accompanied it. Reading and writing my mothering readied me to begin inquiries of a wider socio-cultural, political, and historical scope, affording me the opportunity to discover a more empowering feminist mothering praxis. At this early stage in my Ph.D. program, taking time out to connect mothering to teaching once again allows me a deep view into my ever-changing conceptualizations of myself as a teacher, mother, and researcher. The inquiry does not end: it simply begins again with new questions, birthing new possibilities for empowered mothering, maternal pedagogy, and feminist research.

[1]After writing this essay, I realized my rhetorical choice to include subtitles referring to the biological process of birthing is in itself a potentially exclusive structure. Within what I had originally considered "clever" subtitles comparing pregnancy and birthing to the process of coming to know a new pedagogical stance, there exists an unintended, yet problematic privileging of mothers who can identify with the experience of giving birth, then raising the children they have delivered.

Works Cited (Afterbirth)

Belenky, Mary Field, Blythe McIvar Clinchy, Nancy Rule Goldberger, and Jill Mattuck Tarule, eds. *Women's Ways of Knowing: The Development of Self, Voice, and Mind.* 10th anniversary ed. New York: Basic Books, 1997. Print.

Cohen, Dorothy H., Virginia Stern, and Nancy Balaban, eds. *Observing and Recording the Behaviour of Young Children.* 4th ed. New York: Teachers College Press, 1997. Print.

Ferris, Denise. "The Mother in Mr. Chipps: Educating Artists and Maternal Thinking." *Maternal Thinking: Philosophy, Politics, Practice.* Ed. Andrea O'Reilly. Toronto: Demeter Press, 2009. 120-130. Print.

Gee, James Paul. "Semiotic Social Spaces and Affinity Spaces: From *The Age of Mythology* to Today's Schools." *Beyond Communities of Practice: Language, Power, and Social Context.* Ed. David Barton and Karin Tusting New York: Cambridge University Press, 2005. 214-232. Print.

Green, Fiona Joy. "Feminist Mothers: Successfully Negotiating the Tension between Motherhood as 'Institution' and 'Experience'." *From Motherhood to Mothering: The Legacy of Adrienne Rich's* Of Woman Born. Ed. Andrea O'Reilly. Albany: State University of New York Press, 2004. 125-136. Print.

O'Reilly, Andrea. "Introduction." *Feminist Mothering.* Ed. Andrea O'Reilly. Albany: State University of New York Press, 2008. 1-22. Print.

O'Reilly, Andrea. "Introduction." *Motherhood to Mothering: The Legacy of Adrienne Rich's* Of Woman Born. Ed. Andrea O'Reilly. Albany: State University of New York Press, 2004. 1-23. Print.

O'Reilly, Andrea. "Introduction." *Maternal Thinking: Philosophy, Politics, Practice.* Ed. Andrea O'Reilly. Toronto: Demeter Press, 2009. 1-13. Print.

O'Reilly, Andrea and Sara Ruddick. "A Conversation about Maternal Thinking." *Maternal Thinking: Philosophy, Politics, Practice.* Ed. Andrea O'Reilly. Toronto: Demeter Press, 2009. 14-38. Print.

Ruddick, Sara. *Maternal Thinking: Toward a Politics of Peace.* Boston: Beacon Press, 1989. Print.

Trimble, Sarah. "(Un)usual Suspects: Mothers, Masculinities, Monstrosities." *Feminist Mothering.* Ed. Andrea O'Reilly. Albany: State University of New York Press, 2008. 177 - 190. Print.

African Maternal Pedagogies

Sociological and Educational Implications

ADWOA NTOZAKE ONUORA

Ma'at: "The Catalyst for My Remembering"

THE BATH WATER IS HOT. I resist being lulled to sleep by the aroma of lavender-scented incense mixing with quiet notes of peppermint oil. With each exhale fog droplets ascend, coating the bathroom mirror. I lie on my back, water covers all but my protruding stomach. Blissful, I bask in the last few moments of "me time."

I imagine what it will be like when Ma'at arrives. No more silence perhaps? I think that I will soon have to surrender what was once my time to this person I carry in my womb. I embrace the deafening silence, waiting for the lesson that it brings, realizing that there will be fewer of these moments of silence in the years to come.

My body grows weary. I close my eyes and am carried away by ripples of thoughts. I remember.

* * *

Afro-indigenous maternal pedagogy has been a topic of limited interest to scholars of the past. To date, there is a crucial gap in comparative analyses of the cultural knowledges of mothers of African descent, honing in on how these women have blurred—and continue to blur—the boundaries between teacher and learner. This chapter attempts to fill this critical gap. In examining African maternal pedagogies, it locates the African mother as a vehicle for the transmission of African indigenous knowledge and more importantly, the survival of African indigenous cultures. Guided by the philosophy of African-centred feminism(s) and Afro-indigenous theory, it asks and, wherever possible, proposes answers to the following questions: What are some indigenous educational practices women of African descent engage in while mothering? How, why and under what circumstances have these practices of knowledge production and dissemination changed? Are the pedagogical tools employed by women of African descent transferable or even relevant to African-centred educational settings or to African Diasporic contexts such the Caribbean and Canada? In sum, what are the "epistemic consequences" (Grosfoguel 211) of validating African maternal pedagogies?

Using the methodology of autoethnography, I draw on my embodied experience and individual memory as sources of knowledge in an attempt to answer the above questions.[1] The reader thus enters my layered streams of consciousness as I go back and forth between my introspective ethnography (written in literary prose) and my central thesis, written in conventional social science prose. My intention here is to be able to use my personal anecdotes to encourage new understandings and generate new conversations about the ways in which mothers and othermothers of African descent both draw upon and are central to the dissemination of Afro-indigenous knowledges.

The Journey of Transformation

My academic journey into the study of Afro-indigenous maternal pedagogies coincided with my own personal journey when I, a daughter, was becoming a mother. From the moment I discovered I was carrying a child in my womb, I found numerous questions impinging upon my consciousness: Would I be able to live up to the images of the African mother as strong superwoman and all-knowing sage, images frequently presented to me in movies, books and other popular cultural mediums that sought to (re)present women of African descent? Was it even necessary for me to do so, or was it more important to expose my vulnerabilities to my child so she would learn that all humans have them? As a 25-year-old Jamaican-born woman who had been living in Canada for the past twelve years, would I be able to tap deep into the roots of my ancestral/blood memory to unearth all the knowledge that had been passed on to me, then effectively transmit these knowledges to my child? Would this female African child "discover [her] mission, fulfill or betray it?" (Fanon 206). To what extent was her success contingent upon my mothering? These self-reflexive moments plunged me far back into my childhood, where I began to relive the distant yet vivid memories of growing up in Kingston, Jamaica. What follows here is the story of my growing understanding of, appreciation for, and commitment to engaging in Afro-indigenous maternal pedagogies.

* * *

"Mommy Said": Memories of a Pedagogy Beyond Gestation

A loud knock on the bathroom door startles me. "Yes," I grunt.

"Oh, just checking to see if someone is in there," my suitemate Safyia responds. "Will you be out soon?" she asks.

An awkward pause follows. I begin to think about the trials and tribulations of living in a shared campus space with strangers. At this point I am frustrated—totally pissed as a matter of fact! I'm not really sure why she has come knocking on this door when there are two other bathrooms right down the hall. "Just keep cool, respond nicely and you will diffuse the situation more easily," I think to myself.

In that moment I try to place myself in the shoes of my four suitemates. I imagine how difficult it must be for them to have to live with a cranky, hormonal, pregnant suitemate. This would not be their optimal choice of spaces to live in, if indeed they had been given a choice. In this case, they were not given a choice. But come to think of it, neither was I; the little one just showed up quite unexpectedly three weeks into the semester. I would not have knowingly chosen to share a space with four women (well, five if you count Ma'at, who makes her presence known through my frequent bathroom visits and constant heaving). The bottom line is we're stuck with each other for the remainder of the school year, and everyone (including me) will just have to find creative ways to deal with the pregnant woman in suite 4-24.

"I'll be out in a few more minutes," I say. She scurries down the hallway and slams one of the other bathrooms' doors. Relieved that she has now decided to take the option that was available to her all along, I go back to my daydreaming.

* * *

I was the second child of my mother and the first child of my father, both of whom were thrust into the role of parents at a very early age. My parents were not 'married' (at least not in the way that Eurocentric cultures define marriage) and in fact ended their relationship shortly after my birth. I lived with my father, later visiting my birth mother during holiday breaks from school. Though I was raised in my father's household, I spent the majority of my time before entering school with his partner, who assumed the role of my mother. It did not in the least matter to this woman, whom I affectionately called 'Mommy,' that she had not given birth to me. She acknowledged and accepted—indeed welcomed and cherished—her responsibility for nurturing the seed that was my being. This woman, in staying true to our Afro-Jamaican sense of communalism, threw herself into the role of my mother. She cared for me, sang to and played with me, and meted out spankings; she taught me lessons in much the same way that my aunts and grandmothers (who partially mothered me) instructed my cousins and other children in the village.

One of my most vivid memories of Mommy is seeing her in the kitchen talking to her female friends about a disagreement that had occurred between her and my father the night before. I remember her in tears and being very shaken by the conversation; I could not understand why mommy and the other women would endure these (I suppose what seemed to them cathartic) sessions when the solution to the problem, at least to me, was clear. Even at such a young age my thoughts were developed perhaps beyond my age, as I remember asking her, "Why stay Mommy, why?"

Now anyone who has grown up in Jamaica (or the Caribbean for that matter) knows that this is not the type of questioning a child should engage in. In many Jamaican households, there is an unspoken rule that children are to be seen and not heard, especially when adults are discussing, to use the common Jamaican vernacular, 'big people tings.' Although I anticipated a thorough thrashing for my insolence, I instead received a gentle reply from Mommy: "Di hag ask him mumma ow yu mouth so lang an di mumma seh, yu a grow yu wi know." The English translation of this saying reads: "The hog asked his mother why her mouth was so long, to which the mother replied: you are growing; you will soon understand."

* * *

As I remember that day—Mommy's words and Mommy's friends—I realize how blessed I was to have been surrounded by this sisterhood of women and to have been exposed to their warmth, their knowledges, and their love of one another and each other's children. I realize how fortunate I am to have learned many of life's lessons through proverbs, metaphors, and stories that stirred my imagination and spoke to my emotions as well as my intellect. The reverberating echo of Mommy's voice lingers still; like white noise it accompanies almost all my thoughts. With that epiphany, I awake to realize that my bath water has now turned cold. How long did I drift off this time around? I wonder to myself. Shivering, I reach for a towel, wrap my body, and exit the bathtub.

* * *

Towards an African-centred Feminist Epistemology on Maternal Pedagogy

Indigenous knowledge and African-centered feminism are the major discursive frameworks guiding the questions asked and assumptions presented in this chapter. Importantly, both discursive frameworks function as strategic bases from which colonized peoples can begin the intellectual struggle for self-representation and epistemological centeredness (Daniel 63). This is particularly true for the indigenous framework whose goal is that of countering the dominating, universalizing and imposing tendencies of Eurocentric patriarchal discourses (Dei 6). In this regard, and as Beverly-Jean Daniel points out, indigenous knowledge functions discursively to provide worldwide indigenous peoples space to reclaim and validate the values, practices and beliefs that inform their existence and that have shaped the survival mechanisms developed in response to dominant Eurocentrism's epistemological debasement (63).

It is important to note, however, that while the indigenous discursive framework presents tremendous possibilities in functioning as an anti-colonial tool for disrupting dominant Eurocentrisms' positional "superiority" in relation to indigenous knowledges, one has to be mindful of the ways in which indigenous knowledge systems can also reproduce sites of disempowerment for women (Dei 8). This is of particular importance since in producing counter narratives we cannot approach a study of indigenous knowledge systems uncritically. Hence, in this chapter, African feminism functions to render visible the ways in which African women's contributions have been undervalued and invalidated within patriarchal institutions such as the school, home, workplaces and especially within academia. In this regard, African feminism complements the indigenous theoretical framework to the extent that it allows one to focus in on women of African descent as significant sites of knowledge production and dissemination.

African feminism functions specifically to challenge the Eurocentric agenda of Western (read: white) brands of feminism. It also serves as a counter narrative to dominant cultural representations about African womanhood. As part of the white imagination, these representations often (re) inscribe the African woman as always and already an inept, subordinate, dysfunctional "[M]Other" who is rendered simultaneously visible and invisible because of her supposed fecundity. In the above encounter with my suitemate, one is able to unpack the racist logic that results in women of African descent being positioned within this realm as hypersexualized "Other," "as bodies out of place" (Ahmed 55).

Though I cannot say with absolute certainty that Safyia (and my other suitemates) had internalized Eurocentric, racist discourses about young single mothers, especially unwed young mothers of African descent, it is quite possible that they had projected on to me the all-too-common stereotype of the promiscuous, irresponsible, overly fecund African/Black woman. If this was indeed the case, I would have represented a real and perceived threat to white middle-class standards of normalcy, including the "ideal" nuclear family. Their very gestures towards me, though not necessarily communicated in words or always expressed overtly, were but outward manifestations of the discomfort they felt in having this stranger that was my pregnant Black body invade and contaminate their space (Ahmed 39).[2]

Being frequently read as a young teenage mother (even though at the time of my pregnancy I was a 25-year-old and in a partnership) is sadly an everyday reality which mothers of African descent face. As an Afro-Jamaican woman, I know that value judgments about my youthfulness, and my perceived inability to "properly" mother without always and already being a long-term social burden to the state, remain the dominant perception. This is so despite my ancestral history of coming from a long line of African women who were from a different pedagogical reality and who mothered effectively, using proverbs and stories to teach lessons and to stimulate both African and non-African children's imaginations and thinking. It is for this reason African feminism serves as a counter narrative though which women of African descent can challenge these Eurocentric tropes and instead, usher in stories that, to borrow from Njoki Wane, "evoke the power, not paralysis of African women, account[ing] for their triumphs without underestimating the gravity of their circumstances" (31). As women of African descent, we need spaces where we can focus on issues that are relevant to us as women, and which are informed by our gender but that also take into consideration our racial, sexual, and class identifications (Daniel 56). In recounting some of my autobiographical experiences, I attempt to open up space where African women (mothers and community/other mothers in particular) can feel comfortable telling their own stories in their own voices and feel empowered to name the issues that are important to them in the applied arena of mothering or community/other mothering.

At this juncture, I would be remiss if I did not mention that mothering is something that not only women in our communities do. Such an assumption is at best faulty, and at worst, reifies a false dichotomy, further fixing the role of mother to the biological act of giving birth. The fact is, some African men can and do mother as much as African women do. Case in point: with my daughter Ma'at, her uncles, who are part of my village, perform the role of othermother (in my absence or presence) in the same way her aunts or other women in the village do. By default, this renders them equally capable of imparting cultural knowledges unto her. Having said this, I must also say that I am cognizant of the problems that inhere in trying to pinpoint the pedagogical (albeit male or female) experiences that can be rendered salient in the discussion on maternal pedagogy. Notwithstanding the difficulty of distinguishing between the pedagogical teachings and strategies that emanate from males and those that come from females in our village, what is clear is that because of the gendered nature of mother work, Ma'at spends most of her time learning from women. The disparity between the time spent with her uncles when compared to the time she spends with her aunts/community mothers is not due to the fact that she is biologically a female child, but rather stems from the fact that most households in the African community (due to combination of historical, cultural and systemic reasons too complex to detail here) are headed by women. Moreover, in many instances, even in what is considered a 'normal' heterosexual, monogamous household family arrangement, women generally take on the lion's share of the duties of childrearing.[3] Therefore, it is the frequency and intensity of female interaction with children in the village, and not biology, which positions women as foundational elements in the African child's spiritual, social, emotional and educational development. African centered feminism is therefore used here as a discursive lens through which to foreground the role mothers and community mothers play in this regard. African feminism calls for the centering of African women as vital producers, collaborators and contributors in the creation of Afro-indigenous cultural knowings. This is of tremendous importance given that my political and academic project is to (1) make sense of the educational imperatives of mothers of African descent who are birth mothers and community/other mothers and (2) to reinstall African women as creators of African feminist theory and key contributors perpetually engaged in theory building around Afro-indigenous knowledges.

Reflections in Praise of the Epistemic Saliency of Mothers of African Descent

June 11th, 2010. With little over a week left to the submission deadline, I labour, quite begrudgingly, on the first draft of a chapter I admittedly had been given more than enough time by the editors to complete. Ma'at is now two, and her bouncing on my lap makes the process of completion all the more difficult. What can I say? I am supposed to be an academic! Isn't procrastination part of our socialization as doctoral students? Dare I betray my roots by completing the chapter way before the eleventh hour? Word to the wise: choosing to stay true to one's roots can have serious consequences for sleep deprivation.

As I sit at my desk writing this chapter, Ma'at climbing from floor to lap, I continue to reflect on words spoken to me as a child. Back then, my mother's repeated sayings seemed like mere gibberish in times when I desperately sought a straightforward answer to a question I posed. Would it not have been much simpler for her to explain what was meant? Could she not have spared me the internal battle I experienced trying to make sense of it all? I now realize much later that in repeating the adage, she was imparting a lesson. This lesson was two-fold. At one level, she was teaching me to become familiar with and value the proverbs and speech patterns and parlance of Afro-Jamaican culture. At another, equally important level, she was urging me to view metaphor, proverbs, and narrative as effective vehicles for the transmission of knowledge—as ways of communicating that make people take the time to ponder the meaning, implications and applications of a saying or a story. Finally, in the case of the particular proverb I quoted, Mommy was teaching me something at the core of Afro-indigenous ontology—the notion that many lessons must be learned through experience and as one matures.

Writing this chapter, I am forced to reflect on how it is that my experiences growing up in Jamaica helped shape my identity as an Afro-Jamaican woman, daughter and mother. As a mother, I now embody the richness of experiential knowledge. I, as well as Ma'at's community/other mothers, am her abundant storehouse of knowledge. I therefore see it as my duty to impart lessons through the same proverbs and 'folk' sayings told to me by Mommy and the other women who took part in my upbringing. I read Anancy stories and sing Jamaican digging tunes with my daughter Ma'at, so much so that at two years and barely speaking intelligible language, she confidently sings the tunes I grew up singing, and to my astonishment, performs them much in the way I did as a child. Just as I emulated my mother and community/other mothers, I now watch in amazement as Ma'at mimics me. Today, having grown and matured like Mommy said I would, I am able to appreciate the pedagogical moments which she provided me, realizing that perhaps were it not for my community/other mother(s), the women I spent much of my time with as a child, I would not have grown up with an awareness of and appreciation for the richness and efficacy of the cultural knowings that I now so proudly pass on to Ma'at.

Reflecting on my childhood experience, I am able to see the challenges before me and other daughters poised with the task of raising our African children in social contexts that are not conducive to imparting such cultural knowledges. For our generation, and those to follow, are tasked with negotiating the tensions that arise as we straddle the precarious boundary of a culture of individualism which conflicts with our Afro-indigenous communal ethos. This seems an impossible feat, particularly when one considers the additional structural impediments of racism, classism and sexism that African women encounter in spaces like Canada and that make it all the more difficult to mother in the same way our foremothers did. The challenge becomes even more apparent given the fact that the Canadian landscape has demoralized African women (particularly those of working class backgrounds) so much so that putting food on the table or working multiple jobs to eke out a still substandard living militates against recreating pedagogical moments such as the one presented in my personal narrative. This is compounded by the general lack of appreciation (in some cases) within the dominant culture for the significance of Afro-indigenous cultural knowledges.

My personal narrative begins to clue us into the *why* of this chapter.

More specifically, it provides a starting point for understanding that the fundamental way we as a people have learned in the historical and contemporary context is through intergenerational cultural transmission. My personal anecdotes, recalled as memories, are instructive as they not only illustrates how this knowledge is transmitted through life experience, but also reinforce the fact that women of African descent have played a central role in laying the foundation for the continuation of these cultural knowings within the diverse communities where our people reside.

How, then, can African mothers and community/other mothers living in Canada recover, maintain and transmit important cultural knowledges, given the threats of neo-liberal globalization on Afro-indigenous spaces and cultures? What of this experience of being a daughter and now a mother can I share with educators so that they will begin to see the pedagogical richness of the experience of being an African mother or community/other mother? How can we begin to develop a theoretical framework for understanding and validating the maternal pedagogies of mothers and community/other mothers of African descent living in spaces like Canada? Given our contemporary situation that seems so dire and hopeless, how do we begin to unearth possible answers to these questions so as to find a way forward for the African community?

Challenging though these questions may be, the task of disrupting the "patriarchal colonizing practices of educational institutions" (Dei 4) demands that we create counter hegemonic, anti-colonial epistemologies that move us further towards a radical critique that ushers in social transformation (Grosfoguel 215). We need to create spaces within educational research for further examination of the possibilities and challenges that inhere in maternal pedagogies. This chapter by virtue of its positioning of motherhood as a site of learning, presents an answer to this call of creating a radical departure in our understanding of knowledge, learning and teaching. By placing mothers of African descent at the centre of discussion on motherhood and education, we can begin to develop new strategies for praxis on educational transformation that will not only benefit Afro-indigenous women, but will also validate the cultural knowledges of all racialized women.

[1]Bochner and Ellis define autoethnography as an autobiographical genre of writing and research that displays multiple layers of consciousness,

connecting the personal to the socio-cultural. Autoethnographers look inward, exposing the vulnerable self. Usually written in the first person voice, autoethnographies can appear in a variety of forms ranging from short stories, poetry, fiction, novels, photographic essays, personal essays, journals, to fragmented and layered writing as well as social science prose (see Ellis and Bochner 739).

[2]Although my suitemates might have had difficulty understanding or uncertainty about how to receive this "unusual" case of having a perceived single pregnant woman as their suitemate, in Jamaica, it is quite common and acceptable for a man and woman to live in separate households or raise children together without legally being husband and wife. Furthermore, the Eurocentric nuclear family is not the norm amongst working class Jamaicans. Rather, in many cases, a group of female and male "othermothers" (a village, a neighborhood, a circle of friends and relatives) take collective responsibility for teaching, guiding, and protecting a community's children, many of whom (for a combination of reasons too complex to detail here) are growing up in female-headed households. In Jamaica, there is no social stigma associated with being a 25 year-old mother. Relative to my younger cousins living in Jamaica, in my family I was often seen as the odd child who had decided to delay pregnancy in pursuit of degrees. In fact, by the time I was pregnant with Ma'at, some of my cousins in Jamaica had already had one or more children in their early twenties.

[3]I place the word normal here in quotes to problematize the notion of a standard (read: heterosexual, monogamous) family arrangement, and that this normalcy always translates into the optimal family condition which simultaneous yields the best results for a child's social, spiritual, emotional and educational development. My personal politics dictates that I recognize, respect and honor the diversity of family arrangements that exists within the human experience.

Works Cited

Ahmed, Sara. *Strange Encounters: Embodied Others in Post-Coloniality*. London: Routledge, 2000. Print.

Daniel, Beverly-Jean. "Researching African Canadian Women: Indigenous Knowledge and the Politics of Representation." *Critical Issues in Anti-Racist Research Methodologies*. Ed. George J. Sefa Dei and Gurpreet Singh Johal. New York: Peter Lang, 2005. 53-78. Print.

Dei, George J. Sefa et al. "Introduction." *Indigenous Knowledges in Global Contexts: Multiple Readings of Our Worlds.* Ed. George J. Sefa Dei, Budd L. Hall, and Dorothy Goldin Rosenberg. Toronto: OISE/University of Toronto P, 2000. 3-20. Print.

Ellis, Carol, and Arthur Bochner. "Autoethnography, Personal Narrative, Reflexivity: Researcher as Subject." *Handbook of Qualitative Research.* 2nd ed. Ed. Norman K. Denzin and Yvonna S. Lincoln. Thousand Oaks, CA: Sage Publications, 2000. 733-768. Print.

Fanon, Frantz. *The Wretched of the Earth.* New York: Grove Press, 1968. Print.

Grosfoguel, Ramón. "The Epistemic Colonial Turn: Beyond Political-economy Paradigms." *Cultural Studies* 21.2-3 (2007): 211-223. Print.

Wane, Njoki. "Black-Canadian Feminist Thought: Drawing on the Experiences of my Sisters." *Back to the Drawing Board.* Ed. Njoki Wane, Katerina Deliovsky and Erica Lawson. Toronto: Sumach Press, 2002. 29-53. Print.

"If I Had a Normal Job, I Couldn't Do This"

Exploring the Economics of Disability Advocacy Motherhood and Inclusive Education

SAMANTHA WALSH AND ELISABETH HARRISON

Elisabeth

WHEN I ASKED MY MOTHER—Valerie—how she was able to successfully advocate on behalf of me and my sisters in seeking disability accommodations for us in the educational system, she said, "If I had a normal job, I couldn't do this." Many mothers of children with disabilities spend enormous amounts of time and energy trying to ensure that their children's educational needs are met. But are boundless time and energy available to all mothers? What else enables mothers to succeed in this area? The purpose of this paper is to interrogate the role of gender, class, and race privilege in advocate mothers' navigation of the school system. We reflect on how gender, class and race inform and animate mothers' advocacy, and how mothers' presentation of both social and cultural capital—as theorized by Pierre Bourdieu—influences their work as advocates. Our work is grounded in our experiences as disabled children of advocate mothers, and in our more recent roles as disability scholars theorising about the structural factors that have allowed us to occupy such a role. The paper is also, of course, further animated by the ongoing dialogue between the two of us and our mothers.

Samantha

In thinking about the advocacy work of mothers, I am called to reflect on both my own experience as a child whose mother acted as a primary advocate in the education system, and my current work as a graduate student and member of a disability advocacy organization. I identify as a white woman who comes from a middle class background in the city of Waterloo. My family moved from Toronto when I was six years old both because my father got a new job there, and because my mom—Karen—felt that moving to a city with less special education infrastructure would ensure that I and my twin sister—who is also disabled—would be able to attend our new community's public school. In Toronto, we had been denied access to our local school due to being "high needs" children. We had attended kindergarten in a mainstream class, but the school was not located in our neighbourhood and the arrangement had been on a probational basis, for that year only.

To ensure that we were treated equitably by the Waterloo school system, my mom quit her job as a law clerk and bookkeeper and became a full-time advocate. She employed her experience as a businesswoman to chair education committees and set up meetings. She also got help from a network of professionals; for example, she would have friends who were lawyers call the school if my sister or I were being denied services. My mother also became very involved in the community, leading Girl Guides groups and chairing church functions not only to establish and maintain support networks, but also to ensure that my sister and I would be "allowed" to participate in youth organizations.

While I benefited from my mom's involvement and am grateful for it, I wish to now unpack the explicit and implicit manifestations of gender, class, race and privilege that enabled her to be successful in her advocacy work. As Pierre Bourdieu defines it, "cultural capital" refers to practices, interactions and material goods that improve or create one's social status (47-51). "Social capital" refers to the value inherent in being recognized as a member of a group, or having robust connections to a network of others (51-3). Bourdieu writes, "The volume of the social capital possessed by a given agent depends on the size of the network of connections he can effectively mobilize and on the volume of the capital (economic, cultural and symbolic) possessed in his own right by each of those to whom he is connected" (51).

My mom's own access to education and her former work as a legal secretary (which gave her both knowledge of the law and access to a support network of powerful and privileged people) made it fairly comfortable for her to challenge inequities in the educational system. Additionally, having a good command of the English language, access to financial resources, free time, and a number of power suits, my mom had both the social and cultural capital to successfully negotiate the school system.

However, as she advocated for me and my sister within an often hostile environment, my mother employed arguments which sought to either erase or marginalise disability. For example, my mom often argued that I was smart—it was just my legs that didn't work. Other than that, she proclaimed, I was "just like everyone else." As Rod Michalko notes, such assertions accommodate and perpetuate rather than seek to eliminate mainstream society's discomfort with disability and disabled people (148-50). With equal frequency, my mom would claim that I was not really *that* disabled. Michalko's writing asks us to ponder what happens when a person implicitly claims that their own (or in this case, their child's) value is dependent upon *not* belonging to a particular marginalized and oppressed group (20-1). By asserting repeatedly that I was "smart" and/or "not really that disabled," what was my mom implying about students understood as "not smart" or "really disabled"? What happens when disability is quantified as something that is manageable only in small doses? In short, my mom's advocacy, while effective, relied on her performance and endorsement of valued social norms as well as my normalization. The premise became not that disability and disabled people deserve to be acknowledged, valued and respected, but rather that I deserved to be valued and respected because my disability was only a minimal part of my identity.

My mom's performance of privilege sought to erase or cover the existence of disability. The result was that the school and its community made allowances for my sister and me not in an attempt to celebrate and explore disability, but rather because disability was only an incidental aspect of the identities of an otherwise privileged mother and daughter triad. In other words, the disability was excused in the face of a profound illustration of privilege.

Moreover, my mom did not seek alliances with other disability groups unless their members shared her class privilege and advocacy strategies, and I myself sought to avoid others with disabilities unless they were also performing some kind of normalizing of their disability. Moreover, I sought to be normative in my performance of social roles; I managed my weight and appearance, was careful in my choice of friends, worked hard to be academically successful, and took on a number of valued roles both in school and within extra-curricular activities.

Most of these roles allowed me to negotiate access to school and community activities that typically exclude physically disabled students. I was on the board of the local youth council so the buses for trips were made accessible—not for the sake of universal access or because I was concerned with ensuring that other students using wheelchairs could participate, but only because I was interested in attending. I went skiing with my seventh grade class, not because, as a student in the class I would obviously attend, but because I was already taking adapted skiing lessons. My mother arranged for the instructor to come with the class and bring my ski. Reacting to this, everyone commented that I was "a very brave girl" for learning how to ski, and said that my mom's idea of organising my participation in the trip was a great idea. No one mentioned that had I not come from a family that could afford adapted skiing lessons, or if I didn't have a mother with the negotiation skills to facilitate instructors and equipment for the trip, none of this would have happened. Nor was there a discussion that other disabled students were left out of this particular excursion.

It was only because my mother and I had adequate economic, social and cultural capital that I was able to participate in many of the aspects of school life that ordinarily exclude disabled students. Rather than highlighting the inequities in the school system or the taken for granted positioning of disability as a deficit, my mother and I worked to ensure that I would be understood as separate from disability (or, at worst, as overcoming disability). Erasing my disability allowed for my movement through the school system without making any changes to the system itself, and it perpetuated the individualistic narrative that the onus is on disabled people and their family members to fill the gaps that society does not.

Elisabeth

My mother is white, Canadian born, and English is her first language. She has a Bachelor's degree in Communications and is married to my father, who is also white and English speaking. My father was a university professor before he and my mother started their small business, an advertising agency, in the late 1980s. My mother has three children, all of whom have disabilities that have necessitated accommodations in the educational system—my older sister has a learning disability, and my younger sister and I have psychiatric disabilities.

My mum's career as an advocate began when my older sister entered the school system in 1987 in Brockville, a small town near Ottawa in eastern Ontario. It soon became clear that she wasn't meeting some of the learning milestones on time. My mother's initial reaction was that my sister might just need extra help, so she began working with her at home in the evenings. When that didn't seem to help, mum thought that my sister might have a learning disability. She began scheduling meetings with classroom teachers, "special education" teachers, and school administrators, demanding that my sister receive an educational assessment by an educational psychologist from the school board. Because of my mother's persistence, my sister was finally diagnosed with a learning disability when she was in Grade Two. After that, my mother was in constant contact with the school, helping to plan and participating in my sister's Individual Education Plan and negotiating access to special education resources while ensuring that my sister's needs were also met in the "regular" classroom.

I wasn't identified as disabled until much later, during high school, when I was diagnosed with schizophrenia at the age of 16, during the summer after I had completed Grade 10. As a result of my periods of hospitalisation and the effects of the medications I was made to take, I was unable to attend class regularly, carry a full course load or meet deadlines. Again, my mother went to many, many meetings with teachers and administrative staff, and I was eventually granted accommodations for all of these needs. When I asked her about this, my mother said, "My attitude was that, you know, I would basically make sure that they did what was necessary so that you could finish high school—come hell or high water."

My mother also told me that she explained my diagnosis of schizophrenia to school staff as being a "medical condition" in order to make them understand that it was a legitimate, real, thing. She pointed out that my illness was being treated with pharmacological interventions, and told staff that I was "sick, but still the same person underneath." She mentioned that she appealed to teachers' memories of my having been a good student prior to my diagnosis in order to convince them that I deserved the accommodations I needed. "I told them, you were still really smart, but you had a medical problem, and the medication you were taking had a lot of side effects, so you just needed some extra help until you got better." While this strategy was effective, it also negated any possibility of recognising "mental illness" as socially constructed (Porter 9; Kutchins and Kirk 23), or as a space of positive or even neutral difference (White and Denborough), as many mad or antipsychiatry activists and theorists argue it is. My mother claimed that my diagnosis was real, but it wasn't an important aspect of my identity or my experience. Instead, it was simply a medical problem that was being treated and would hopefully "disappear" in that it could be improved enough to restore me to my previous level of functioning.

Indeed, although my ability to function well in my daily life was significantly impaired by the effects of the medication I was taking, my mother encouraged me to act, as much as possible, as though I was still my "normal" self and nothing was really wrong. The fatigue I experienced was so severe that whenever possible, I slept for 20 hour periods. Despite this, my mother insisted that I keep my weekend job at a restaurant, saying that I would feel better if I "kept active" and continued my usual routine. Maintaining control of my body was also an enormous challenge for me. My muscles were so weakened that I was often unable to stand or walk, or even to hold my mouth closed, with the result that I frequently drooled. I often felt too tired to shower, style my hair, or put on makeup. Mum worked also to ensure that I maintained as close to a normal appearance as possible. She carefully monitored my personal hygiene and how I dressed in order to maintain my image as an ordinary teenage girl. She also kept a close watch over my diet and activity levels so that I would not gain the weight that is often a result of treatment with "antipsychotic" medication (Martin et al.).

My mother believed that it was important for me to "keep up appearances" so that I would be seen—and valued—as myself, and not be associated with the negative image of the mentally ill individual. Otto F. Wahl points out that the knowledge that the majority of people have about mental illness comes from mass media representations (3), most of which depict mentally ill people as "recognizably different from others in both manner and appearance, [standing] out as deviant and bizarre" (36). Further, many studies have shown that most mass media depictions of people with mental illness characterise us as frightening and dangerously violent (Anderson; Blood and Holland; Cassey; Cross; Cutcliffe and Hannigan; Dietrich et al.; Nairn; Olstead; Wahl), and even sometimes as sub-human (Glasgow Media Group; Selling Murder; Wahl 36-55). My mother was aware of these stereotypes, and this knowledge informed her efforts to enhance the normalcy of my appearance and behaviour, but it did not lead her to challenge the basis or accuracy of the stereotypes.

Several years after my sisters and I had completed high school, my mother resumed her advocacy work when my younger sister, who was attending university, required accommodations as a result of her psychiatric disability. My sister had asked my mother to intervene on her behalf, and, noting that administrators were initially resistant to this because my sister was an adult, mum said, "I just ignored that and did it anyway." When administrators at the university seemed unwilling to take my sister's needs seriously, mum was confident that the people in charge would listen to her, so she maintained regular contact with the staff of the Dean of Students. She also used her expertise in the field of advertising to put pressure on them, telling them that their position on a disability-related concern they weren't addressing might not look very good to members of the public, and she could issue a press release on the matter. This was, apparently, an effective strategy, and my sister's needs were ultimately accommodated.

My older sister's disability needs had required the largest commitment of time from my mother, which is what she meant when she said that if she had a "normal job"—as opposed to owning a small business, which made her schedule very flexible—she couldn't have been as successful in her advocacy. But mum used the same skills in negotiating access to education for all her children. She reported that she used her social identity as a businesswoman and a university graduate whose husband had been a university professor, to "develop a certain camaraderie—the idea that 'I'm one of you'" with teachers and school officials. Just as she encouraged me to maintain my culturally acceptable appearance in order that I be perceived as legitimate, my mother also used her own physical appearance to underscore the legitimacy of her claims. She relates,

> The medium is the message. Part of it is the way you look, the way you act, it's the whole package. I was dressed a certain way. It's totally ridiculous on one hand, but the message is "I'm a professional, I'm well turned-out"; these are visual cues that "I cannot be fooled around with." I'm not going to lie down, and they're not even going to attempt to talk down to me or feel like they can get away with dismissing my concerns—because that's not going to happen.

She really was "one of them" in the sense that she is white—the population of Brockville is overwhelmingly so, as were many of the members of the administration of the university that my sister attended. My mother was also university-educated and very articulate, like the people with whom she was dealing. She was able to schedule many meetings and make innumerable phone calls during business hours on behalf of my sisters and me because she and my father ran their own business, which gave them a very flexible schedule. Additionally, she was married to the father of her children, which also gave her social capital in the context of dealing with the administrators of Catholic schools. And as a woman, she was fulfilling the culturally valorised role of the "good mother" (Stoppard) in seeking to ensure that her children's needs were met—"come hell or high water."

My mother never reached out to other parents of disabled children, and never sought to effect broader changes in the educational system or in the ways that people understand learning disabilities or mental illness. She regarded my and my sisters' disabilities as individual "problems" or "issues" with individual solutions, rather than as being related to unjust social relations or oppressive stereotypes circulating in our culture. She seems to understand other children's disabilities in the same way, telling me that when it comes to disabled children's education, "Well, if parents don't get involved, the kid will pay the price."

Samantha

Why should the disabled children of mothers who lack social and cultural capital "pay the price"? While our mothers might believe that parents who don't get involved with their disabled children's education are simply failing in their duty to their children, we contend that this opinion is a manifestation of the ideology of individualism that permeates our culture, and that our mothers' success in making our schools accommodate our needs was highly dependent on their access to social and cultural resources that many parents cannot access. We know that as it "stands," the education system is a primary means of legitimising the oppressive norms of society (Nicholson 73-9). We can understand how this process occurs when we think about our mothers' stories, and when we ask ourselves: What happens to disabled children whose parents don't speak English? To non-white families whose disabled children attend schools with racist, white-majority hierarchies? To children whose parents are themselves disabled? To disabled children with single parents? What about those children whose parents are not highly educated? Or children whose parents can't afford to take time off work to make phone calls, attend meetings, and participate extensively in Individual Education Plans?

There are many disabled children in these circumstances, and the "price" of failing to accommodate their needs is very expensive indeed. We propose that an alternative to individual activism can be found in coalition-building. This would create a means to bridge activist movements, as well as an opportunity to incorporate and link individuals with communities seeking social change. Further, it would reveal systemic histories of oppression, establish a critical mass of support, and create links between marginalized groups. It is far easier to exhaust and silence a single individual than a group. Moreover, when disability issues are linked with other social justice issues through the creation of coalitions between equity-seeking groups, people in power might be better able to understand that a large faction of the community is invested in equity. This may help create a climate in which the rights of disabled students—along with students who are disadvantaged as a result of other forms of oppression—cannot be ignored. This type of collaborative work may also afford opportunities to foster connections between parent advocates of disabled children and the broader disability activism community, which could assist in improving some of the problematic aspects of parent advocacy work, such as the tendency toward individualism and the over-valorisation of normalcy.

The cost of advocacy work for mothers must also be recognized. While I am grateful for all of the work my mother did on my behalf, and for the many sacrifices she made, I continue to feel perplexed by the fact that it was necessary for her to give up her career and many of her interests, completely change her life, and to deploy a huge amount of resources in order to provide me with the type of meaningful school experience that a non-disabled student might take for granted.

From a research perspective, we need to examine the price that is paid by mothers who modify their own identities to ensure their children are not marginalized. What happens when they quit jobs they enjoy or become involved in organizations in which they are not truly interested? For instance, my mom has none of the skills or interests that Girl Guides promotes, but she volunteered as a leader anyway so that my sister and I could be included. What happens to mothers who have put aside their careers and interests once their children no longer require a full-time advocate? And of course research is required to further explore how schools might become more inclusive, especially given their tendency to reify the social positioning of individuals.

It is imperative, in all of these areas of action and inquiry, that we think beyond the level of the individual and address systemic inequities. It is only when marginalisation is understood as a manifestation of social organisation and not as a hallmark of individual deficit that lasting and effective social change can be created. This will support both disabled children and their parents in achieving equity and moving away from the margins.

Works Cited

Anderson, Martin. "'One Flew Over the Psychiatric Unit': Mental Illness and the Media." *Journal of Psychiatric and Mental Health Nursing* 10 (2003): 297-306. Print.

Blood, Warwick and Kate Holland. "Risky News, Madness and Public Crisis: A Case Study of the Reporting and Portrayal of Mental Health and Illness in the Australian Press." *Journalism* 5.3 (2004): 323-42. Print.

Bourdieu, Pierre. "The Forms of Capital." *Education: Culture, Economy and Society*. Ed. A. H. Halsey, Hugh Lauder, Phillip Brown and Amy Stuarts Wells. Oxford: Oxford University Press, 1997. 46-58. Print.

Cassey, Jo. "Mental Illness." *Understanding Representation*. Ed. Wendy Helsby. London: British Film Institute Publishing, 2005. Print.

Cross, Simon. "Visualizing Madness: Mental Illness and Public Representation." *Television and New Media* 5.3 (2004): 197-216. Print.

Cutcliffe, J. R. and B. Hannigan. "Mass Media, 'Monsters' and Mental Health Clients: The Need for Increased Lobbying." *Journal of Psychiatric and Mental Health Nursing* 8 (2001): 315–21. Print.

Dietrich, Sandra et al. "Influence of Newspaper Reporting on Adolescents' Attitudes Toward People with Mental Illness." *Social Psychiatry and Psychiatric Epidemiology* 41 (2006): 318-22. Print.

Glasgow Media Group. *The Media and Mental Distress*. Ed. Greg Philo. London: Longman, 1996. Print.

Kutchins, Herb and Stuart A. Kirk. *Making Us Crazy: DSM – The Psychiatric Bible and the Creation of Mental Disorders*. New York: The Free Press, 1997. Print.

Martin, Andrés et al. "Weight and Leptin Changes Among Risperidone-Treated Youths With Autism: 6-Month Prospective Data." *American Journal of Psychiatry* 161.6 (2004): 1125-1127. Print.

Michalko, Rod. *The Difference that Disability Makes*. Philadelphia: Temple University Press, 2002. Print.

Nairn, Raymond G. "Media Portrayals of Mental Illness, or is it Madness? A Review." *Australian Psychologist* 42.2 (2007): 138-46. Print.

Nicholson, Linda J. "Women and Schooling." *The Education Feminism Reader.* Ed. Lynda Stone. London: Routledge, 1994. 73-83. Print.

Olstead, Riley. "Contesting the Text: Canadian Media Depictions of the Conflation of Mental Illness and Criminality." *Sociology of Health and Illness* 24.5 (2002): 621-43. Print.

Overboe, James. "'Difference in Itself': Validating Disabled People's Lived Experience." *Body and Society* 5.4 (1999): 17-29. Print.

Porter, Roy. *A Social History of Madness: Stories of the Insane.* London: Weidenfeld and Nicolson, 1987. Print.

Selling Murder: The Killing Films of the Third Reich. Prod. Steward Lansley. Dir. Joanna Mack. Domino Films, 1991. Videocassette.

Stoppard, Janet M. *Understanding Depression: Feminist Social Constructionist Approaches.* London, Routledge, 2000. Print.

Wahl, Otto F. *Media Madness: Public Images of Mental Illness.* New Brunswick, NJ: Rutgers University Press, 1995. Print.

White, Cheryl and David Denborough. "Companions on a Journey: The Work of the Dulwich Centre Community Mental Health Project." *Introducing Narrative Therapy: A Collection of Practice-Based Writings.* Ed. Cheryl White and David Denborough. Adelaide: Dulwich Centre Publications, 1998. 1-15. Print.

3. Learning With and From One's Children

Some Mothers' Experiences

The Baffled Mother

Maternal Puzzlement in Narrative, in Pedagogy, in Academia

MARTHA SATZ

> All families are surprise families. Parents and children meet as strangers and grow up together, surprising one another with interests and talents that are not exactly what had been expected. And they continue to love each other anyway.
> —Lynne Reiser (commenting on her children's book, *Surprise Family*)

MARIANNE HIRSCH WRITES IN *The Mother/Daughter Plot*: "The story of female development, both in fiction and theory, needs to be written in the voice of mothers as well as in that of daughters. Only in combining both voices, in finding a double voice that would yield multiple female consciousnesses, can we begin to envision ways to 'live afresh'" (161). In the first decade of the twenty-first century and in the last years of the twentieth century, a number of authors fulfilled Hirsch's request. Surprisingly, three prolific and accomplished female authors penned novels with remarkably similar plots, offering anguished maternal chronicles of experiences with young adult daughters who disappoint, oppose, and baffle their protagonist mothers. In Mary Gordon's *Pearl* (2005), Carol Shields' *Unless* (2002), and Anne Roiphe's *Lovingkindness* (1987), three fiercely feminist mothers confront and work to understand what they take to be the bizarre decisions of their daughters, who in their strength validate their mothers' views of women but in their actions confound them.

I must confess that in my present stage of life, I am attracted to these books, greedily reading them to discover something about myself, how to lead my life, and how to think about it, as I once read *Little Women* or later *Middlemarch*. Indeed, at this time, they have become, to use Lee Edwards' phrase, the "books of my life."

Decades ago, I became entranced with Sara Ruddick's work that analyzed and detailed in a philosophical way a phenomenon I was experiencing and grappling with—maternal thought, a notion, she thought and I believed, that could be applied to the greater world of people and institutions. She maintains in *Maternal Thinking* that maternal practice and thought culminate in the virtue of "attentive love," which contains both a cognitive capacity and the virtue of love—in the case of maternal love, seeing the world from the perspective of the child, without the mediation and intervention of maternal desires. Ruddick, incorporating and interpolating the thought of Iris Murdoch, writes, "The difficulty is to keep the attention fixed on the real situation or as I would say on the real children. Attention to real children, children seen by the patient eye of love ... teaches us how real things [real children] can be looked at and loved without being seized and used, without being appropriated in the greedy organism of the self" (122-3).

In the blush of my daughter's early years, Ruddick's principle guided my child rearing, and I thought I could come quite close to attaining that ideal. However, only recently have I come to understand my inadequacies and failures in this regard and to appreciate the full demands of attentive love and its consequences. I share my initial faulty comprehension, I believe, with both the narrators and authors of the novels I discuss. For indeed, the novels paradoxically both present a challenge to Ruddick's work and instantiate it, conjointly furnishing a partial guidebook for feminist mothers of young adult daughters, demonstrating that attentive love becomes more difficult as one's child becomes older and reflects back, perhaps, on the gaps in the attentive love one had offered her as a child. For if one has nurtured one's daughter to be independent, then inevitably, and wrenchingly for the mother, the daughter will have values and ways of living different from one's own. It is the test, then, of feminism and maternal thought to appreciate and respect those differences. The novels discussed wrestle with this issue and have much to teach their readers in areas both domestic and academic.

Twenty-three years ago I adopted as an infant a bi-racial (African American and white) daughter. I was enchanted with her and the experiences that she brought me. I relished my maternal merging with her as well as the separation from her that the introduction of racial difference and adoption brought. As an example, I believed and wrote about the fact that I thought I had experienced the closest facsimile of racism a white person could because of my maternal identification with her. Yet I experienced that phenomenon as a white person because of my inevitable separation from her and valued the experience for its rarity. Such experience also better enabled me to incorporate into my maternal practice strategies to help her contend with a racist society, an area of maternal thinking that some critics of Ruddick claim she neglects (see, for example, Bailey; Di Quinzio). I also thought that the fact my daughter was adopted and racially different from me privileged our relationship because these obvious markers of distinction might guard against my over-identification with her. For all children differ from their parents, all daughters from their mothers, yet it is easy to forget this fact when genetic bonds bind mother and daughter together, sometimes creating in mothers the anticipation that their daughters will replicate their best selves. To my chagrin, I discovered that the facts of trans-racial adoption did not render me immune from such an expectation. However, I was unprepared for quite how different from me my daughter would be, how she would drop out of high school in the tenth grade, how she would defy me and all my values, how she disdained the middle-class life that I expected her to lead, how she fought with me at every turn. So, I was brought up short when a colleague commented that it was surprising the extent to which my daughter resembled me. I inquired, "Whatever could he mean?" He replied, "She is so strong. She is so unconventional. She always defies expectations."

Aaah, I had been deceived by appearances and traditional signs. She did resemble me. And I had relied too much upon external markers of difference to safeguard me from identification. In the last years, our relationship has improved as she has begun to cobble together a life that suits her. I support as I can, and we have renegotiated our connection. I have learned a good deal about the intensity and limits of maternal love, thought, and practice. In a parallel fashion, I believe, the narratives I have mentioned authored by mature women with maternal experience contend with the perplexities, difficulties, and sheer bafflement of mothers with adult daughters who make choices incomprehensible to their mothers. The authors and narrating protagonists declare themselves to be mothers that seek to enlarge and extend their understanding of maternal love and maternal thought, as they struggle to understand and keep faith with the daughters that both resemble and differ from them. Yet, perhaps additionally these novels and the mothers' narrative, psychological, and philosophical methodology within them suggest a paradigm for academic maternal feminists dealing with their students and their younger colleagues, realizing that neither maternity nor feminism automatically confers identification, understanding, nor a satisfactory relationship with their "daughters."

In *Lovingkindness,* the protagonist's rebellious, counter-culture daughter phones her thoroughly secular mother from an ultra-orthodox kibbutz in Israel, explaining that she looks forward to an arranged marriage and seeks her mother's approval. In *Unless,* the oldest of three daughters disappears from her conventional, happy home and college life and reappears homeless, sitting on a street corner every day holding a sign that says "Goodness." Similarly, in *Pearl,* the mother receives a Christmas-day phone call, informing her that her daughter is near death in Ireland, chained to the doors of the American Embassy on a hunger strike.

The text of each of these novels emphasizes, indeed foregrounds, the professional achievements and feminist commitments of their narrating protagonists. And perhaps most notably, the narrators mentally linger over the self-conscious child-rearing they have lavished upon their daughters, having broken with their own personal history and the conventions of their culture, confident that in their daughters they would create women embodying their re/vision of the female. However, the actions and decisions of their adult daughters bring these mothers up short, creating unprecedented crises in their lives, forcing them to reexamine all their former assumptions. Most critically, even as their worldviews churn and spin, they must choose how to respond to their daughters' pressing needs. Their struggles, their decisions, and the outcomes of their choices constitute reflections by these feminist authors on feminism, motherhood, morality, as well as intellectual and political humility that may suggest for their maternal readers, no longer basking in the first bloom of a new wave of feminism or new motherhood, ways of interacting with the world, other women, and their daughters.

The narrators' feminism permeates these novels. All have personally and financially rewarding careers: Annie, the protagonist of *Lovingkindness,* teaches and has authored a scholarly book on New England spinsters; Reta, the narrating mother of *Unless,* enjoys a career as a successful writer of fiction and as a translator; and Maria, the mother in *Pearl,* expresses her political activism by founding and administering several daycare centers in disadvantaged neighborhoods. Moreover, each of these women expresses avid feminist views: Annie argues endlessly with the leader of the kibbutz about the roles the community has allocated to women, who will never be allowed to lead or speak publicly; Reta expresses her despair over her daughter in rambling letters to book editors and television show producers, critiquing them for their neglect and exclusion of women; and Maria—even in an emergency—insists that she not be addressed as "Mrs." Yet in spite of their feminism, these women find, sometimes to their surprise, that maternity lies at the emotional and psychic center of their lives. Annie admits that at times, because of their motherless state, she felt sorry for the New England spinsters about whom she wrote, and Reta understands the essential place of her daughters in her life as she reflects back on a radio interview:

> The radio host in Baltimore asked me—he must have been desperate—what was the worst thing that had ever happened to me.... I couldn't think of the worst thing. I told him that whatever it was, it hadn't happened yet. I knew, though, at that moment ... that it would be socketed into the lives of my children. (112-113)

And in the most effusive narrative, Maria meditates on the intensity of maternal love, recalling when her daughter was first presented to her:

> Hello, my own, Maria said to Pearl. She had been saying that to her with every sentence since that moment, believing ... that no one will ever know her so well and she will never be known so well. I am the beloved and the beloved is mine. The ellipse of the most ecstatic sex is ragged, partial, next to this. (89)

Entranced by this maternal love, these women pour their most fervent feminism into raising their daughters. As *Pearl* opens on Christmas day and Maria feels hurt that her daughter has not called on such a significant occasion, she quickly revises her view, reminding herself, "But that was what she wanted, wasn't it? A daughter who did not feel obligated, who felt free to pursue her life, her interests, her pleasures, her adventures" (4). In *Lovingkindness,* Annie also has clearly formulated feminist goals for her child. Recalling a conversation about parental ambitions she and her friend Louise had had a decade earlier in a shoe store, Annie recounts:

> While the children tore through the aisles, climbing over the seats we talked of our plans for their adulthood—education of course, but dedication to a cause also, beauty and comfort but concern for others and love of music and books, and Louise wanted her son to have a working acquaintance with the Orient and a love of travel and a capacity for sexual pleasure and decent affection, and then we confessed to each other that we wanted our children to cast a small shadow over the planet, maybe build houses or design new methods of production or improve our health-care delivery system. We wanted them to change the order of things, to fight it and improve it. By the time the shoe salesman arrived to wait on us we had tagged the future and felt confident we knew its contents. We wanted children who would take up our work and carry it further. It seemed a simple, modest ambition. (104-5)

Consistent with such self-conscious mothering, each of the narrating mothers grapples with how she will respond to her daughter's actions. Annie vacillates about whether to support her daughter's choice to, in Annie's view, "[live] forever under a shawl, arms covered, eyes down, pious and pregnant" (104) or to kidnap her daughter as the parents of her daughter's intended bridegroom attempt to do with their son, his mother whispering to her "reclaimed" son, "We know what is good for you and all we are doing is taking care of you. Trust me" (238). On her part, Reta agonizingly adopts the position of watchful waiting with her daughter who sits on a street corner, observing her from afar, hoping "she will grow out of it," and allowing her other daughters to sit supportively with their sister on Saturdays. In contrast, Maria rushes across the ocean, wondering, "Isn't my love enough to keep my child alive? What did I do wrong, what did I do wrong?"(39), vowing to preserve her daughter's life, only to be blocked by a maternal psychiatrist in charge of her daughter's case. She spends the intervening time trying to make the incomprehensible comprehensible, trying to figure out why her daughter wants to die.

In the end, Annie succumbs to her daughter's choice and betrays her new friends, the prospective groom's parents, allowing the kibbutz to recover their son and clearing the way for her daughter to marry him. In *Unless,* Reta's daughter has a fortuitous bout with pneumonia, leading to the discovery of at least a partial explanation of the young woman's mysterious behavior: she had experienced the trauma of failing to save a Muslim woman who had immolated herself before her eyes. This discovery allows the daughter to be restored to the family with some familial comprehension of her behavior. And Pearl, after being tested, reunites with her daughter on terms different from before.

What have these narrating feminists mothers learned, and, in turn, what can they teach their older, somewhat world and child-rearing-weary maternal readers? As ambivalently as they feel, two of the maternal protagonists, Annie and Reta, regretfully honor their daughters' decisions, understanding that to negate their daughters' choices would be to violate their love for their daughters. In contrast, Maria, the protagonist of Pearl, alone remains undeterred, sometimes histrionically achieving her goals, willing to invade all her daughter's boundaries to save her daughter's life. Nevertheless, eventually her daughter's motherly psychiatrist thwarts her path, and thus she, too, learns respect for her daughter's autonomy. The novels offer no easy moral or parenting prescriptions, for in each case, the outcomes are ambivalent.

Annie, in *Lovingkindness,* resigns herself to an ambiguous future. She yields her daughter to what she takes to be a patriarchal world but clings to a fantasy for her potential granddaughter:

> When my granddaughter is eighteen and restless with all she has been taught, I will invite her to visit me. Once she is here I will slowly introduce her to science and math and deductive reasoning and Chekhov and Dostoyevsky, Locke and Susan B. Anthony and when she is ready I will suggest to her that she become a doctor and stay here and go to college.... She can change her name to Jane for Jane Austen or to Charlotte for Charlotte Bronte to Simone for Simone de Beauvoir to Amelia for Amelia Earhart. (264)

Evidently, she cannot fully abnegate a maternal role that influences and shapes. And Shields' work, which seems to offer a pat comedic ending—with some effort, a temporarily transgressive daughter is restored to her family—signals at every turn that readers should not accept its manifest content. The novel flashes its metafictional nature, employing a passage from George Eliot's *Middlemarch* as an epigraph to alert its reader that as a novel, it will concern itself with the weighty, interpersonal nature of morality. Also the particular quoted passage makes apparent that even within those closest to us, say our daughters, a whole world lies hidden.

Furthermore, Shields explicitly casts doubt on the tidy ending of *Unless* in which an identifiable trauma explains Reta's daughter's behavior. For within *Unless,* not only does Reta discuss the conventions of fiction where narrative strands are neatly tied up at the end, but Reta comments "The problem is, I'm not sure I believe in the thunderclap of trauma. A stubborn screen of common sense keeps getting in my way and cancelling the filigree of fine-spun theory" (269). In addition, Reta owns up to the fact that she has been projecting her own discouragement onto her daughter: "it is also probable that I was weighing her down with my own fears, my own growing perplexity concerning the world and its arrangements, that I had found myself in the middle of my life, in the middle of the continent, on the side of the disfavored, and it may be that I am partly right and partly wrong" (310).

In the end, these narrating feminist mothers and the maternal feminist authors who have produced them have learned the limitations of both feminist theory and their own maternal love—or perhaps most essentially of their own finitude, that their love no matter how intense, and their vision, no matter how idealistic and grandiose, cannot mold their daughters into who they want them to be. They may have also learned that it may not be desirable to do so. Yet there is consolation as well: neither their love for their daughters nor the strength of their dedication has been in vain. Their daughters have basked in their mothers' love and absorbed their strength in order to passionately pursue paths, albeit ones that are not in accord with their mothers' original design, or even feminist principles as they conceive them.

The narratives discussed testify to the difficulty, perhaps the impossibility of the ideal of attentive love when one's children are young. The maternal self intervenes, unwittingly projecting an idealistic future on one's children cast in one's own image. It may take the weight of the daughters' adulthoods, their stubborn female selves, imitative of one's own, to reveal one's earlier maternal self-deception. Yet, as the mothers discussed have done, one may still renegotiate the loving maternal contract—by ceding them their autonomy, endeavoring to see things from their perspective while attempting to persuade them of one's own, and never for one moment allowing one's love to lapse.

In their separate works, Patricia Hill Collins and Maria Lugones offer methodologies for entering the world of the other, in their emphasis, a method for a member of the dominant culture to understand the world view of minority subjects. Perhaps it is not far-fetched to believe that mothers and daughters and also by extension, teachers and students, and older and younger colleagues, participate in a power differential as well, so that Collins' and Lugones' theories and methodologies are appropriate, although clearly the differential involved is much less significant than the one these theorists invoke. Collins phrases it, "Such a project requires among other things learning to listen attentively to marginalized people [and] ... critical self-examination" (137), while Lugones advocates traveling to each other's "worlds," to understand each other's realities—but, significantly, in a playful manner, an attitude that involves "openness to surprise, openness to being a fool, openness to self-construction or reconstruction" (288). I was reminded of Lugones' prescription as I jousted with my daughter over some household chores. When she said, "I'm very busy. I have to send out these resumes," I responded, "Well, I'm very busy too." She rejoined, "But you already have your career. You have tenure. I'm just starting out." With her penetrating reply, she forced me to look at myself. Indeed, her anxiety differed from my own, and I placed my own anxieties in perspective.

What happens narratively in the novels I have discussed is that mothers confront their daughters in an incomprehensible guise. As a result, the mothers interrogate themselves and the world and attempt to understand and persuade their daughters. When their attempts at persuasion fail and their efforts to comprehend fall short, they adopt some modesty, psychically remain with their daughter, realizing that the bonds between them will continue, whatever the differences. It is a model that I try to embrace in my own maternity, with my students who see the world very differently from the way I do, and with my younger colleagues who at times, for example, do not see the importance of Women's Studies as a category in the curriculum, who blithely it would seem, jettison history and hard-won battles. This extends, I believe, to women of other cultures who, for instance, might support the necessity of clitoridectomies. I cannot and should not impose my will on them, even though their views may be incomprehensible to me. It is their work; it is their lives.

Pearl, the novel with the most irrepressible, unrepentant, and invasive mother, ends in a heartening way, with mother and daughter laughing together, as the treating psychiatrist observes the unexpected scene of their reconciliation. "Of all the responses she would have predicted, laughter was not among them. Words of anger, gestures of recrimination, anxious sobbing, clinging followed by a push to separate: all these and many others had occurred to her. But laughter? No, she had not thought of that" (345). It is laughter initiated by the daughter who realizes and appreciates her mother's strength, inconsistency, and absurdity. Pearl reflects on her mother's devotedness:

> She had said to her mother: go and do this thing for me, and her mother had done it. She hadn't hesitated; Pearl had known she would not hesitate. Her mother is her mother. My mother is my mother and I am I. This seems quite amusing; she could repeat it to herself just for the pleasure of the words. My mother is my mother and I am I. (344)

The daughter recognizes both her mother's connection to and separation from herself. In many ways, all three novels echo this narrative laughter, wryly and sardonically gesturing toward the ludicrous intensity and disappointments of motherhood, but also to its bonding force as well. With warmth, perseverance, and humor, we learn from our experiences of motherhood and reach toward other women with perhaps not as much optimism as in earlier years, but with realism, humility, and humor.

My daughter has just completed a course of study at EMT school. She will save lives. I see her strength and admire her. I credit myself for her achievement only to the extent that I remained, watchfully waiting like the mother in Shields' work and yielding finally to her incomprehensible choices like the mother in Roiphe's novel. And we do often laugh together. I am grateful to the authors of the books discussed for their companionship and tentative guidance in this difficult time in my life. For the present, they stand as the "books of my life," for their teachings about mothering all those who substantively differ from me.

Works Cited

Bailey, Alison. "Mothers, Birthgivers, and Peacemakers: The Need for an Inclusive Account." *Philosophical Perspectives on Power and Domination: Theories and Practices.* Ed. Laura Duhan Kaplan and Laurence F. Bove. Atlanta: Rodopi Press. 1994. Print.

Collins, Patricia Hill. *Black Feminist Thought.* New York: Routledge, 2000. Print.

DiQuinzio, Patrice. "Exclusion and Essentialism in Feminist Theory: The Problem of Mothering." *Hypatia* 8:3(1993): 1-20. Print.

Edwards, Lee R. "Women, Energy, and Middlemarch." *Massachusetts Review* 13 (1972): 223-238. Print.

Gordon, Mary. *Pearl.* New York: Pantheon Books, 2005. Print.

Hirsch, Marianne. *The Mother/Daughter Plot.* Bloomington: Indiana University Press, 1989. Print.

Lugones, Maria. "Playfulness, 'World'-Traveling, and Loving Perception." *Women, Knowledge, and Reality: Explorations in Feminist Philosophy.* Ed. Ann Gary and Marilyn Pearsall. Boston: Unwin Hyman, 1989. 275-292. Print.

Reiser, Lynne. *The Surprise Family.* New York: Green Willow, 1994. Print.

Roiphe, Anne. *Lovingkindness.* New York: Warner Books, 1987. Print.

Ruddick, Sara. *Maternal Thinking: Toward a Politics of Peace.* Boston: Beacon Press, 1989, rprt. 1995. Print.

Satz, Martha. "Trans-Racial Mothering: Double-Edged Privilege." *Journal of Social Distress and the Homeless: Adoption across Race, Culture, and Class* Special Issue 17 (2008): 8-36. Print.

Shields, Carol. *Unless.* London: Fourth Estate, 2002. Print.

Maternal Pedagogies as a Function of Mothers' Ways of Knowing

TABITHA R. HOLMES AND LYNNE A. BOND

AS MANY SCHOLARS HAVE NOTED, the role of mother and teacher are similar in many ways. Both are socializing agents expected to define and reinforce behavioral, moral, and cultural values. Both are charged with teaching content and process, skills and ideologies. And both—either implicitly or explicitly—endorse certain pedagogical beliefs and practices that inform how adults and children interact and share knowledge. Although there is an extensive history of research in the psychological literature describing and distinguishing among mothers' styles of teaching their children (e.g., Baumrind), there is surprisingly limited work examining the factors that underlie and lead to these different pedagogies. Beyond the notion that mothers are influenced by models in their own lives (e.g., their own mothers, fathers, and significant others), an important question remains: why do specific women adopt particular maternal pedagogies? To address this question, our essay explores one important foundation of mothers' pedagogical styles—their epistemological perspectives or "ways of knowing"—in other words, the women's assumptions about the nature of knowledge and themselves as knowers. We argue that women's epistemologies shape their conceptions about how children learn and develop, and these ideas, in turn, significantly influence maternal pedagogies. We will describe these varied "teacher-student" relationships by drawing upon our research with diverse populations of mothers and their young children; then examining similar "teacher-student" relationships between diverse kinds of mothers and their adolescents.

A Framework for Understanding Variability in Maternal Pedagogies

Working from a constructivist perspective, we have found the Ways of

Knowing scheme helpful, although not necessarily complete, for thinking about the ways in which women make meaning of knowledge and knowing (Belenky, Clinchy, Goldberger and Tarule). This scheme relies on a semi-structured interview that asks the respondent to comment upon the nature of knowledge and truth, and upon the self as a knower and thinker. Interview responses are coded in relation to five primary epistemological perspectives that Lynne A. Bond, Mary F. Belenky, and Jacqueline S. Weinstock summarize as follows:

> 1) silenced knowing, where people think of themselves as generally mindless, voiceless, and unable to learn from others or figure things out for themselves; 2) received knowing, where people equate learning with passively receiving and storing information, with dualistic notions of truth and knowledge that are to be passed from expert to novice; 3) subjective knowing, where knowledge and truth are conceived as highly personal, private, and essentially incommunicable, and as such cannot be shared, evaluated, or developed with others; 4) procedural knowing, where people envision that knowledge and truth can be developed, identified, evaluated and communicated using systematic procedures; and 5) constructed knowing, where people conceive that knowledge and truth are constructions of humankind and, as such are dynamic, contextual, and evolving. (170)

In *A Tradition That Has No Name,* Belenky, Bond and Weinstock, argue that, although undoubtedly culture-bound, these epistemological perspectives likely emerge in a developmental order within majority cultures in Western technological societies (see also Bond, Belenky and Weinstock; Goldberger, Tarule, Clinchy, and Belenky). One exception to this Western trajectory involves Silenced knowing, a perspective that is not part of a typical developmental process; rather, it is believed to emerge from experiences of extreme marginalization and oppression.

It makes sense that women's assumptions and understanding of the nature of knowledge and its acquisition will powerfully affect their goals and strategies for supporting learning in others, including their maternal pedagogies. For example, a mother who has a dualistic notion of truth and understands knowledge acquisition as a process of passively receiving and storing information passed from expert to novice (i.e., a

Received knower) is likely to use highly didactic pedagogical strategies, to feel responsible for "filling" her child with the truth, to feel inadequate when her expertise is challenged (or insufficient), and to demand that her child be relatively passive and observant rather than actively engaged and experimenting in knowledge construction. In contrast, mothers who understand knowledge to be fluid, dynamic, and constructed by human engagement and interaction (i.e., Constructed knowers) are more likely to use pedagogical strategies that draw their children into active interaction and experimentation with constructs and ideas, and to create dialogue in which mother and child are partners in analyzing, testing, and generating understanding and knowledge.

Table 1 summarizes these hypothesized relationships between women's epistemological perspectives, their sense of themselves and their children as knowers and meaning-makers, and their maternal pedagogies. We have been struck by the consistency with which these relationships have been documented in our behavioral research with mothers and their young children (e.g., Belenky, Bond, and Weinstock; Bond, Belenky, Weinstock and Cook; Hutchins, Bond, Silliman, and Bryant). Repeatedly we have found that mothers' pedagogical approaches with their preschoolers reflect their ways of knowing and their understanding of the nature of truth and knowledge. This is true for mothers coming from diverse and varied backgrounds—isolated, extremely impoverished, Euro-American rural mothers of infants and preschoolers; middle- and upper-class Euro-American mothers of preschoolers residing in small and mid-size towns; and mixed income African American mothers and their preschoolers living in major urban settings.

Across samples, mothers with dualistic notions of knowledge as absolute and external to the individual (Received knowers) are more likely to provide answers and declarative statements to their child rather than pose questions, to manage "non-task" behavior (e.g., so her child would sit still, pay attention, etc.) rather than draw attention to the learning problem itself, and to call for replication of the mother's own perspectives rather than encourage innovation or experimentation. Mothers who envision knowledge and truth as highly personal, subjective, idiosyncratic, and therefore essentially incommunicable (Subjective knowers) are more likely to employ a laissez-faire approach to teaching rather than sharing perspectives in didactic or collaborative manners. Moreover, mothers who conceive of knowledge as emerging from systematic analysis, evaluation, and engagement (Procedural knowers) or from a dynamic and fluid col-

Table 1
Epistemological Perspectives of Self and Relation with Child[1]

Epistemology	Mother's View of Her Mind and Voice	Mother's View of Child's Mind and Voice	Mother's View of Child Rearing
Silenced Knower	Feels stupid, mindless and voiceless; feels she can't teach others; words are weapons	Child as mindless and voiceless; child can't learn; child's feelings are dangerous, not understood	Use raw power to influence child; neither listen nor explain; much yelling; no dialogue; enforce absolute rules
Received Knower	Goal is to receive, store, and transmit without modifying information; learns through memorization and recitation	Child learns by listening to elders; should be seen but not heard; child needs to be molded and filled with information	Inform child through lectures; teach right from wrong using rules, rewards and punishments; emphasis on training and modeling
Subjective Knower	Discover inner voice; truth comes from inner voice and experience, not authorities; values individuality	Child has own inner voice; each child is unique; delight in child's spontaneity	Let child think and speak for her/himself; laissez-fair; nonjudgmental
Procedural Knower	Goal is to articulate and examine thoughts and feelings uses procedures to evaluate and guide thinking	Child has thoughts and feelings to be developed; child can learn procedures for finding good answers	Ask for and provide reasoning and explanations; share processes behind each other's thinking
Constructed Knower	Can collaborate in construction of knowledge through dialogue with self and others; create new synthesis: not merely uncover information	Child has ability and reasonability to think through and make choices; can and should listen to heart and mind of self and others; inventor; artist and scientist	Draw out child's thoughts and feelings; ask questions and provide feedback; share, discuss, evaluate each other's perspectives; challenge, think, revise, and plan together.

laborative construction (Constructed knowers) are most likely to pose questions, draw their children into active engagement in the learning activity, and participate in a reciprocal and responsive give-and-take with their child in problem-solving.

A Study of Pedagogical Approaches to Parenting Adolescents

Building on our work with mothers of young children, we designed a study to explore how mothers' ways of knowing are related to their pedagogical approaches to parenting adolescents. We were interested in extending past research to families with teenagers for several reasons. First, adolescents are known for their propensity to challenge authority figures and those in positions of power. Our working model (in Table 1) suggests that the way in which mothers deal with these challenges will vary as a function of their epistemological beliefs. In addition, as adolescents become more sophisticated in how they think about the world, mothers must negotiate how to make sense of and respond to their teenagers' increasingly complex ways of knowing. This transition has interesting implications for our understanding of how mothers' perspectives on knowledge and knowing influence parenting beliefs and practices of children at different developmental stages.

The Study

As part of a larger project, mothers with adolescents volunteered to take part in a study about mother-adolescent relationships. These mothers completed extensive face-to-face interviews that included the Ways of Knowing Interview and a series of questions about their parenting beliefs, parenting practices, and patterns of mother-adolescent conflict. Mothers also responded to a series of vignettes that dealt with how mothers believe children learn from real-life situations. All interviews were transcribed verbatim and coded by a minimum of two independent researchers. Interviews were analyzed using inductive methodologies based on Grounded Theory (Glaser and Strauss) to identify conceptual ideas, themes, and interpretations that emerged from the mothers' stories, anecdotes, and meaning-making. Emergent themes were then examined as a function of three epistemological perspectives: Received, Transitional (i.e., women who are "transitioning" from received to procedural knowers with some qualities of subjective knowers), and Procedural.

Participant Demographics

The interviews were conducted with 62 mothers of adolescents currently living in the Northeastern United States. These mothers reported diverse backgrounds, personal characteristics, and living situations. Mothers ranged in age from 32 to 65 years with an average age of 44 years. Approximately half self-identified as White or Caucasian, 29 percent as Black or African American, and 13 percent as Hispanic or Latino. Slightly over half of the mothers were married, while 20 percent were divorced. There was variability in the amount of formal education that mothers reported, although the majority did not have a Bachelor's degree. The majority of mothers were employed; however, a variety of family incomes were reported such that 21 percent of the women reported an income below $20,000 and 20 percent reported incomes over $60,000 with the remaining falling between these two categories. Mothers had between one and nine children; half had one or two children and 25 percent had four or more. In many instances, mothers had some children who no longer lived at home; however, many others described living with and supporting adult children, extended family members, and non-related individuals.

Analysis of Pedagogical Processes

To explore maternal pedagogies, we focused on three main questions: 1) How do mothers think about challenges to their own authority during mother-adolescent disagreements? 2) How do mothers believe that adolescents learn new things? 3) Do mothers believe that adolescents can create and/or collaborate in knowledge generation such that they teach adults new things? We predicted that mothers' responses would vary as a function of their ways of knowing.

The Role of Maternal Authority

To understand a woman's pedagogical practices, it is important to understand how she views her role as teacher. Many traditional notions of teaching emphasize a component of authority; however, the degree and nature of this authority and its association with power can vary dramatically from person to person. Therefore, we focused a portion of our inquiry on ways in which mothers make meaning of their disagreements with their adolescents, exchanges that typically involve challenges to authority figures and systems of knowledge. Mothers were asked to describe a "typical" argument by detailing what a disagreement between themselves and their adolescent would look like if viewed by an outside observer. They were also asked to describe their role in the disagreement. Responses were then examined in relation to the mothers' epistemological perspectives.

Mothers described two contrasting styles of dealing with disagreements with their teens: Process-oriented versus Power-centered. In a Process-oriented approach to conflict mothers were focused on the processes or mechanics involved in disagreements with their adolescents. Accordingly, this strategy emphasized activities such as asking questions, listening, thinking things through, understanding different perspectives, and presenting a compelling argument. Thus, mothers who described this approach to conflict portrayed disagreements with their adolescents as an active, dynamic "dance" that involves interaction between the adolescent and mother. This is illustrated in the following interview excerpt:

> And my right isn't always the only right. There can be two rights to an answer. It might not be the one I like, but there can be two rights to an answer.... What's the rationale for your answer? Give me a reason, give me a valid reason. I can be swayed, you know?... I want him to think for himself. So, any answer can be the right answer if you have the good reason for it, you know?

For this mother, knowledge is not equated with a definitive authority; rather, knowledge is the product of reason and analysis, tools that are accessible to adolescents. In comparison to Process-oriented mothers, Power-centered mothers tended to take a unidirectional, parent-centered approach to conflict characterized by non-negotiable positions. As one mother said, "I'm still what I say that day. That's it; I will not change. When I say 'don't', I mean 'don't' and when I say 'go' or to 'come,' I mean 'Come.'" For these mothers, conflict is dealt with by squelching discussions and debates. In fact, they often view adolescents who attempt to present their side of an argument as disrespectful. As one mother said, "If you're butting me, you're not listening to me. Shouldn't be, but if you hear what I have to say, it's a 'Yes' or a 'No.' It's not, 'Well if' and not, 'Oh, but.' It's a, 'Yes Mom' or 'No Mom'."

As the above examples illustrate, mothers have striking differences in how they think about their authority and react to conflict with their teenagers. Importantly, these differences appear to be related to mothers' epistemological perspectives. In our analysis, 100 percent of the Procedural mothers (those mothers who believe knowledge can be articulated, evaluated, and improved through analysis) endorsed a Process-oriented approach to dealing with conflict and disagreements. In comparison, 60 percent of Transitional mothers and ten percent of Received mothers referred to the processes of a disagreement. Another pattern was evident in the Power-centered responses. Fifty percent of the mothers with a Received perspective described Power-centered behaviors, in comparison to only ten percent of mothers with a Procedural perspective. These findings support the notion that maternal pedagogies, as defined by mothers' styles of dealing with mother-adolescent conflict, are related to how mothers think more generally about the nature of knowledge.

Modes of Learning

Equally important to understanding how mothers view themselves as authority figures is how they view adolescents as learners and thinkers. Accordingly, we were interested in the degree to which mothers endorsed adolescent learning as a passive activity or as one characterized by active cognitive and interpersonal processes. To explore these pedagogical differences, mothers were read a series of six short vignettes that detailed a situation in which an adolescent approaches his or her parent for advice or information (e.g., a friend has shoplifted). Mothers were then asked what they thought would be the best way for a parent to respond to each situation.

Elaborating upon the work of Lynne Bond, Mary Belenky, Jacqueline Weinstock and Toni Cook, mothers' open-ended responses were coded into one of three categories: Direct authoritative, Didactic, or Interactive. These categories vary along a continuum with regard to how much they require adolescents to think and process information actively and ultimately independently. In a Direct Authoritative response, for example, mothers describe providing the adolescent with all information and a directive on what to do in a given situation; this approach is unilateral and does not require the teen to actively engage in problem-solving. In a Didactic response, mothers supply teens with a directive; however, they accompany their advice with a rationale that encourages teens to think about and understand the mother's perspective. In an Interactive response, the most cognitively demanding of the three, mothers and adolescents work together to actively co-construct a solution through discussion, dialogue, and the sharing of ideas. As an example, one scenario required mothers to describe how they would respond if their teen approached them and confessed to cheating on an exam. Examples of three mothers' responses, as they were coded, included: 1) "I have a fit. Maybe have her talk to the teacher and tell her that she cheated and will take the test over" (coded Direct Authoritative). 2) "I told her not to do it again because you know maybe she passed by cheating, but then later on in life she's not going to accomplish nothing by cheating because then she's not going to learn. Why, just to pass a grade? So I told her it's not a good idea and this is why" (coded Didactic). 3) "I would probably ask her what she needs to do to make it feel better. Talk to her about it.... They need to practice figuring out how to deal with stuff" (coded Interactive).

We examined which strategy each mother endorsed the most frequently across the six scenarios. In instances in which two strategies were endorsed equally, the higher code (reflecting the most cognitive demand) was used in our statistical analyses. These scores for each mother were then analyzed in relation to the mothers' epistemologies. Analyses confirmed that mothers' parenting strategies differed significantly as a function of their epistemological perspectives. As expected, Procedural and Transitional mothers endorsed parenting strategies that were more cognitively demanding; they described pedagogies that required adolescents to actively engage in knowledge construction and collaboration. Conversely, mothers with Received perspectives described more Direct Authoritative and Didactic strategies in which advice was dispensed and enforced. These findings clearly indicate a relationship between mothers' ways of knowing and their pedagogical beliefs. Some mothers believe that teens learn through thinking through solutions to problems and engaging in conversation. Others believe learning is the product of being told what to do and how to do it (either with or without an accompanying rationale). Thus, pedagogical approaches differ in how much the learner is called upon to participate in the co-construction of knowledge, a difference that has clear epistemological roots.

Adolescents as Teachers, Mothers as Learners

Building on the question of how mothers believe that adolescents learn is the question of how mothers think about their own learning, as influenced by parenting adolescents. This question sheds light on the degree to which mothers view learning and knowledge acquisition as a bi-directional, evolving process or one that is unidirectional and fixed. At a basic level, a general pattern that we identified was that mothers with Procedural and Transitional ways of knowing were more likely than mothers with Received perspectives to describe learning by listening to what their teens have to say and by trying to understand their adolescents' point of view. As one mother said:

> How could you be thinking that way? But really trying to understand what is it because, you know, you know when you think you are right about something? Someone else thinks they were that right too. So what is making them think that way?... Everyone comes from a different angle. There is never the same angle. We are all built that way, we're built differently. So you have to understand where they are coming from.

As this quotation illustrates, some mothers acknowledged the existence of multiple realities and the importance of understanding that there can be different interpretations of the same experience. The implicit meaning of such a pedagogical approach is that young people have knowledge that can be shared, communicated, and co-constructed with adults.

To explicitly explore mothers' pedagogical views on their own personal learning we asked mothers to describe what, if anything, they learned from their teenagers. Nearly all mothers described learning something from their adolescents. Mothers differed, however, in whether they described content-based learning, that is, acquiring new information from their teens (e.g., how to use technology) or process-based learning, that is, new ways of interacting in or thinking about the world (e.g., how to be more patient). Mothers who focused on content-based knowledge emphasized learning information that centered upon on their teens' interests and youth culture such as computer skills, popular culture, and music. On the other hand, mothers who focused on "process-based" learning described changes in self-awareness, communication skills, and interpersonal strategies. From an epistemological perspective, these two types of learning are quite different. In the content-based learning, knowledge originates in the world of young people as they teach their mothers how to tweet and twitter. In this way, adolescents are the experts teaching those with less experience in a particular arena. Conversely, mothers who described learning from their teenagers how to be more accepting and open to difference, for example, had to unlearn or relearn something in which they already had experience and knowledge. Thus, these mothers described a pedagogical view that de-emphasizes power and reinforces the idea that knowledge evolves over time. As might be expected, these mothers tended to have procedural ways of knowing.

Final Thoughts

From images in the media to comparisons between play date participants, most people recognize that mothers differ in how they parent. Some appear relatively dogmatic and unyielding, confident that "mothers know best." Others appear more flexible in their approach, using questions and dialogue to draw out their children's ideas and thoughts as a way to co-construct knowledge. Our contribution to understanding these different strategies and styles of mothering has been to explore the epistemological contribution to maternal pedagogies—how women's overarching assumptions about the basic nature of knowledge and knowing play a role in how mothers think about their children's minds and parenting. To demonstrate this relationship, we analyzed mothers' reports of the ways in which they parent their adolescents and respond when confronted with parenting challenges. Our findings build on and support past findings with mothers of small children, illustrating a consistent relationship between epistemological perspectives and parenting beliefs and strategies.

Although our research addresses the "why" behind maternal pedagogies, one question we have not addressed involves why women endorse particular ways of knowing. As Belenky, Clinchy, Goldberger and Tarule describe in their landmark book *Women's Ways of Knowing,* approaches to knowledge develop from a variety of experiences and sources, across formal and informal classrooms, communities, and relationships. Moreover, epistemologies are not static and permanent; rather, they change and develop over time. This can occur naturally, as women experience new challenges, contexts, and collaborations or through more formally organized programs, as demonstrated in the Listening Partner's Program (Bond, Belenky, and Weinstock), a project designed to support rural, impoverished women to recognize the power of their own minds as a source of knowledge. Thus, regardless of route, women develop ideas about knowing as they interact with friends and supervisors, read newspapers and books, and participate in their neighborhoods and families. Accordingly, although we have presented parenting as being informed by mothers' epistemological perspectives, we suspect that ways of knowing are also influenced by being a parent. As one mother in our study said, "Kids keep you on your toes. You think you know something and then 'Wham!' they show you that you don't."

[1]Adapted, with the authors' permission, from Bond, Belenky, Weinstock, and Cook.

Works Cited

Baumrind, Diana. "Current Patterns of Parental Authority." *Developmental Psychology Monographs* 4 (1971): 1-102. Print.

Belenky, Mary F., Lynne A. Bond and Jacqueline S. Weinstock. *A Tradition That Has No Name: Nurturing the Development of People, Families and Communities.* New York: Basic Books, 1997. Print.

Belenky, Mary F., Blythe M. Clinchy, Nancy R. Goldberger, and Jill M. Tarule. *Women's Ways of Knowing: The Development of Self, Voice and Mind.* 2nd ed. New York: Basic Books, 1997. Print

Bond, Lynne A., Mary F. Belenky, and Jacqueline S. Weinstock. "The Listening Partners Program: An Initiative Toward Feminist Community Psychology in Action." *American Journal of Community Psychology* 28.5 (2000): 697-730. Print.

Bond, Lynne A., Mary F. Belenky, Jacqueline S. Weinstock, and Toni Cook. "Imagining and Engaging One's Children: Lessons from Poor, Rural New England Mothers." *Parents' Cultural Belief Systems: Their Origins and Consequences.* Ed. Sara Harkness and Charles Super. New York: Guilford Press, 1996. 467-495. Print.

Glaser, Barney G. and Anselm L. Strauss. *The Discovery of Grounded Theory: Strategies for Qualitative Theory.* Chicago: Adeline, 1967. Print.

Goldberger, Nancy R., Jill M. Tarule, Blythe M. Clinchy, and Mary F. Belenky, eds. *Knowledge, Difference, and Power.* New York: Basic Books, 1996. Print.

Hutchins, Tiffany, Lynne A. Bond, Elaine R. Silliman, and Judith B. Bryant. "Maternal Epistemologcial Perspectives and Variations in Mental State Talk." *Journal of Speech, Language, and Hearing Research* 52 (2009): 61-80. Print.

Crossing Bridges

Maternal Pedagogies for the AD(H)D Child

KAREN I. CASE AND VICTORIA PROULX-SCHIRDUAN

I want to live in the rain forest with tigers when I grow up. (Martin, seven years old)

I thought you wanted to be an engineer. (Martin's Mother)

I can build bridges in the rain forest. (Martin, seven years old)

MARY OLIVER'S POEM "THE SUMMER DAY" queries, "What is it you plan to do with your one wild and precious life?" This question holds particular resonance for many mothers of children with Attention Deficit Disorder and Attention Deficit Hyperactivity Disorder (AD(H)D). Like most mothers, these women regard their children as precious, often treasuring rather than lamenting the high energy levels commonly associated with AD(H)D. However, the "wildness" typical of children diagnosed with what many label "disorders of volition" (Garro and Yarris 559) is not well understood or appreciated by the culture at large, including the teachers these children encounter when they begin school. In addition, individuals outside and even inside the family may regard children with AD(H)D as "bad" (ill-mannered, poorly behaved, out of control), with the result that many teachers assume these students to be "below average" in intelligence.

In this essay, we focus on how mothers of children with AD(H)D developed and employed maternal pedagogies to positively build on their children's capacities. They used maternal pedagogies to educate teachers and administrators how to recognize, value and accommodate the curriculum to meet their children's needs. Throughout a decade-long collaborative research relationship we collected interviews and case histories, as well as narratives based on our advocacy on AD(H)D list-serves.[1] We found that mothers' recognition and awe regarding their children's intelligences were quite evident. This represented a positive dimension to what has traditionally been thought of as a childhood disorder that negatively impacts the family (Deater-Deckard 65). To provide examples of how mothers viewed and used maternal pedagogies to positively build on their children's behaviors, in publications we have used, whenever possible, the voices of mothers who have children with AD(H)D.

These women were predominately white and middle class; some were single and others married. Whether they had obtained high school or college degrees, almost all were employed outside the home in either a full- or part-time capacity. Their stories suggest that to fully employ maternal pedagogies they crossed three bridges. Crossing over the first bridge, mothers recognized and accepted their child's differences and became cognizant of the need to eliminate their own feelings of guilt, inadequacy and self-blame. This in turn allowed them to traverse a second bridge in which they created child-centric maternal pedagogies developed during everyday mother/child interactions. A third bridge provided them with avenues by which they could use maternal pedagogies as a form of tactical and negotiative advocacy in partnership with teachers.

Mothering a child outside the norm, specifically mothering a child with AD(H)D, has been described as frenzied, conflict-laden, and emotionally and physically draining (Cronin 84). Research has shown that when mothering "other-than-normal" children, mothers progresses through four stages: (1) becoming a mother of a disabled child, (2) negotiating a new meaning of mothering, (3) facing a new life as a mother and family, and (4) embarking on a process of acceptance or denial (Nelson 520). Oftentimes, the mother of an AD(H)D child confronts maternal and pedagogical challenges during the toddler years, during which manifestations of AD(H)D characteristics (inattention, impulsivity and/or hyperactivity) tend to emerge. Challenged by the demands of raising a child with AD(H)D, mothers realize that life as they knew or imagined it will no longer be possible. Mothers may feel stigmatized as "bad mothers" and internalize feelings of guilt and self-blame. Expected to be in control of their children's behavior in private and public settings, women's maternal anxieties are doubled when aligned with "professional and lay discourses of maternal blame" (Malacrida 139). Thus it is not unusual that the mothers fear being viewed as 'bad' parents

(Cronin 86). Remarking on the relief his mother felt regarding his diagnosis of AD(H)D, an adult male explained: "My mom was so happy to find out I had AD(H)D. Oh, thank God," she said, "All these years I just thought I was a bad mother" (Proulx-Schirduan, Shearer, and Case 114).

The coming to terms with public scrutiny leads some mothers to cynicism and sarcasm. One exclaimed: "How very inconvenient for others to be temporarily irritated when my child acts out in public. Poor things!" Another mother remarked adamantly, "I won't listen to any insinuation that I'm a bad mother because I'm not. Or that he's a bad kid. He's a great kid with a huge challenge." Mothers of children with AD(H)D counter feelings of guilt with an empathetic understanding of their child. Addie stated, "We naturally carry guilt when our kids fail or lack certain 'graces' and we hurt when they hurt and we make it our job to be the voice of reason and source of comfort." Janice asked, "What is it that I am supposed to learn from this experience? What am I supposed to do with it?" answering her own question with, "The only thing I've figured out is that I have to let go of my emotional baggage, the guilt, the anger and become a 'voice' on behalf of my child and continually choose to deliberately pick up that chain and drag that mountain another inch, every single day."

Moving away from guilt and the need for external validation, these mothers crossed the first bridge and gradually began to shape the maternal pedagogies that had the greatest potential to move mountains for their children. Hardly a new phenomenon, as early as 1914, Florence Hull Winterburn in *The Mother in Education* wrote that it is "not the learned mother who is most competent to instruct her children but the mother who understands them" (149). Mothers' descriptions of their children with AD(H)D varied. Conformity, however, existed regarding their understanding of their child's aptitudes and abilities. An unexplored theme in much of the literature on AD(H)D is the maternal awe and gratitude mothers' experience when they contemplate the energy, drive and intellectual gifts of these learners. As one mother commented, "When I see my son, I see a boy who has a love for life and the energy to express it." Along with an understanding that their child is in some ways different from other children, mothers also recognized their children's early capacity for learning. Their descriptions ranged from she was a "ball of energy since she was born" to "I was in awe of his limitless energy and insatiable curiosity as a toddler." Acknowledging her son's precocity, one mother stated, "Martin was always the wild independent one, fixing his own microwave eggs at two, trying to walk to the store to buy candy alone at three. He was pretty much convinced he could do whatever he wanted because he believes he's just that smart." Describing her middle school age son, Shanna maintained he's a "kind kid, loves animals, painfully honest about himself, funny, and genuine" adding "I don't know how he gets through the day though, incredible math and science skills but can't remember his house key."

Maternal pedagogies arose from the "getting through the day" strategies mothers derived from the daily interactions they had with their children. From these they developed an understanding of their children's cognition from a child-centric standpoint. One mother came to understand that for her daughter, "ideas were like lots of fish swimming around, and sometimes a fisherman just comes and plucks one out and other times, it seems like one of them jumps out on its own." Shanna stated that "My son is quick to cry and you would be too if your mind was buzzing all the time. I'm amazed he can function at all." Quite simply, as Linda maintained regarding her son, "he just seems to have too many things floating in his head at once. He thinks constantly."

"Thinking constantly" is perhaps one of the most apt descriptions of children with AD(H)D. Mothers walked an emotional tightrope when employing maternal pedagogies to positively build on their children's everyday behaviors. Vested in an appreciation of children's unique talents and intelligences, maternal pedagogies can be thought of as using instructional tools readily and serendipitously in the child's day to day life. For example, after losing sight of her daughter briefly in a mall, Tara came upon her daughter examining the security devices attached to store clothing. Instead of punishing her daughter for leaving her side and causing anxiety, Tara checked her first instinct, instead going down on her knees to spend "time on the floor of the store investigating the devices and discussing how they [the devices] work."

Mothers have often employed the surrounding environment to create positive learning experiences for children. Researchers have claimed that animals (Proulx-Schirduan, Shearer, Brantan and Case 33) and green spaces (Louv 103) may be meditative and instructional for children with AD(H)D. For example, one mother employed an adopted German Shepherd mix to act in the dual role of alarm clock and calming presence. The use of the canine allowed the mother to absent herself from the battle of waking her son for school. "Luna wakes him up for me. She comes into the room, licks his face and climbs up on the bed. She's calming for my son." One mother revealed that her daughter would say, "let's look at the sunset or look at the moon and we'd be there for a long time just looking." Callie remembered using readily available instructional tools with her son.

> When he was a toddler, I would give him a stick in the yard and he would be entertained for hours! As he got a little older, he would find a stick and build pretend campfires. He loved to pick flowers and plant seeds and watch them grow like pumpkins. In fifth grade, he started building stone walls all over the yard. As a preteen, he would and still does take care of the yard. He does all the landscaping and is very meticulous, making paths in the orchard.

Mothers also used play objects in their child's world to make the link from home to school. Beth Ann described connecting her son's ability with Legos to his school work. She explained, "Legos encompass so many educational areas: planning, spatial, problem solving. He practices his hand writing by copying the Lego instructions and making signs and stuff for his creations."

The recognition of the "what and the how" of their child's thinking represents an important step connecting maternal pedagogy to what Mulley (1997) calls a "kitchen table activism" (311). While contrasting everyday learning outside of school with traditional classroom pedagogy, mothers became aware that their children with AD(H)D could be academically and socially marginalized in the classroom. Thus mothers crossed over the third and final bridge, moving from the private moments of mother-child interaction to the more public displays of maternal pedagogy as a form of advocacy and activism.

This did not occur without frustrations and sustained effort on the part of the mothers. "I was ready to jump off a bridge," Nancy remembered regarding her first attempts to work with the school, explaining that her free time had been completely devoted to getting her son all of the necessary services and curriculum modifications available. After hearing from one of his teachers that her son made the school day "less than enjoyable" for him as an educator, Diana recalled that she was "at her wits end" and had "cried for three days." "But then there came a feeling of resolve and Diana learned "not to give up," and vowed "to fight every day, go to his locker get his work and have him finish it." She continued by stating that the teachers and the principal are "probably sick of me. But he is intelligent and I refuse to let him fall into the cracks."

Mothers viewed teachers' denigration of their child's talents as the result of a lack of empathy and often countered feelings of frustration by making themselves available to the teacher. They acknowledged a "Catch 22" inherent in their participation. One mother protested, "I feel like teachers complain if parents aren't involved. They complain when we're too involved. I'm dammed if I do, dammed if I don't." Some mothers' advice was at best treated with indifference, and at worse with disdain. Jennifer recounted that

> Every year I meet with his new teacher within the first week sometime. I explain the situation, weaknesses, strengths, what works, what doesn't. Every year this falls on deaf ears. I can just see the look on teachers' faces as I explain this. They smile and nod, give compliments about what a nice boy he is. Behind their eyes I see what they are thinking: "I know, I know, I've been teaching for 25 years, I know how to deal with these students."

Debbie claimed that she generally tells a teacher "what incentives work for her son"; however, if a teacher "refuses to implement any of the techniques I'm showing her and prefers to blame my child for everything, it's useless." Marta explained that "The first day I was met by the teacher, I was wide eyed, a deer caught in headlights. I'm not sure what she said to incite me, but I ended up telling her that if she couldn't do her job, then point me to who can." For mothers, teacher selection became important. Tonya stated that in the "right" environment, her child had "thrived" and spoke of a young long-term substitute teacher who had taken the place of an older "regular" teacher. "I praised the young teacher's ability, and the substitute teacher's reply was, 'If a child in grade school is failing anything, it isn't their fault, it's mine. I'm the one not doing something right.'" Tonya queried, "If a new teacher can do this, it should be a snap for a seasoned teacher to help my son! Right?"

Mothers concluded that their own knowledge of their children was fairly comprehensive, spanning years, while teacher knowledge was finite and concentrated (Proulx-Schirduan, Shearer, Brantan and Case 120). They also learned that just as they needed to "double think," often ignoring their first impulse when interacting with their children, they also needed to restrain initial reactions when responding to teachers and principals. They devised tactical and negotiating strategies to work with school officials. Tactical strategies comprised a "how to" form of advocacy. Moving beyond learning the logistics of special education placement procedures, mothers strategically employed their knowledge of school policies, politics, and dynamics, collecting documentation and discovering when and when not to communicate with teachers and administrators. Nancy explained that when the principal called her on the phone, she refused to answer. "I wanted to force the principal to put all communication in writing." Mothers reported that they "worked the system" by "making noise" and employed negotiating or communication strategies. Descriptions of negotiating strategies ranged from "bug the crap out of them [educators]" to "communicating with the teachers is part of your job as a parent." Maggie recalled that in her experience, "having the school 'on your side' is a heck of a lot easier than fighting them." Some mothers of children with AD(H)D gradually became well-versed in negotiation strategies, which entailed the seeking and providing information regarding their children's progress. Shared information resulted in joint learning. For example, Tina noted that though other parents had suggested that she have her son removed from one teacher's class, she had balked. Instead, she told the teacher to let her know "if any situation arises." Tina, exclaimed, "Well, she let me know alright! I have over 300 e-mails! I counted them! I answered each and every e-mail." At the end of the school year, Tina acknowledged their partnership by stating "I told her we both learned from this."

Maternal pedagogies do not create unidirectional learning, but are rather rooted in reciprocity. As some mothers interact with children with AD(H)D they learn unique instructional strategies designed to change potentially negative situations into positive joint learnings. In this essay, we have suggested that mothers cross three bridges related to the development of maternal pedagogies. Initially, mothers crossed an emotional bridge from feelings of guilt and anger to an acceptance of a diagnosis of AD(H)D, thus gaining an understanding of their child's unique cognition. This understanding subsequently led to the crossing of a second bridge, whereby mothers employed and refined maternal pedagogies during day-to-day interactions with their child and at times linked these to the more structured academic world. When mothers used maternal pedagogies in the form of advocacy, they crossed a third bridge in which they employed tactical and negotiating strategies to advocate and share proven pedagogies with those responsible for their child's academic success. The crossing of all three bridges provided mothers with the hope that like Martin in the rain forest, their children could become the engineers of their own lives.

[1]From 2000 to 2010, the authors have researched AD(H)D and multiple intelligence theory, conducting a national study on AD(H)D and M1 in Schools Using Multiple Intelligence Theory (SUMIT) and in non-M1 sites. They found that students with AD(H)D display strengths with naturalist and spatial intelligences.

Works Cited

Cronin, Anne F. "Mothering a Child with Hidden Impairments." *The American Journal of Occupational Therapy* 58.1 (January/February 2004): 83-92. Print.

Deater-Deckard, Kirby. *Parenting Stress.* New Haven, CT: Yale University Press, 2004. Print.

Garro, Linda and Kristen E. Yarris. "A Massive Long Way: Interconnecting Histories, a 'Special Child,' AD(H)D, and Everyday Family Life." *Culture, Medicine, and Psychiatry: An International Journal of Cross-cultural Health Research* 33.4 (2009): 559-607. Print.

Louv, Richard. *Last Child in the Woods: Saving Our Children From Nature Deficit Disorder.* Chapel Hill, North Carolina: Algonquin Books, 2005. Print.

Malacrida, Claudia. *Cold Comfort: Mothers, Professionals, and Attention Deficit Disorder.* Toronto: University of Toronto Press, 2003. Print.

Mulley, Linda. "Lesbian Motherhood and Other Small Acts of Resistance." *The Politics of Motherhood: Activist Voices from Left to Right.* Ed. Alexis Jetter, Annelise Orleck, and Diana Taylor. Hanover, NH: University Press of New England, 1997. 311-321. Print.

Nelson, Antonia."A Metasynthesis: Mothering Other than Normal Children." *Qualitative Health Research* 12.4 (2002): 515-530. Print.

Oliver, Mary. "The Summer Day." *The Truro Bear and Other Adventures: Poems and Essays.* Boston: Beacon Press, 2008.

Proulx-Schirduan, Victoria, C. Shearer, C. Branton and Karen Case. *Mindful Education for ADHD Students: Differentiating Curriculum and Instruction Using Multiple Intelligences.* New York: Teachers College Press, 2009. Print.

Winterburn, Florence Hull. *The Mother in Education.* New York: McBride, Nast and Co., 1914. Print.

4. Pedagogical Othermothering

The African-American Teacher as Othermother

1863 to the Present

MARGARET AUGUSTE

> Monday, October 23, 1854: I will spare no effort to prepare myself well for the responsible duties of a teacher and to live for the good I can do my oppressed and suffering fellow creatures. (Forten 26)

CHARLOTTE FORTEN, BORN IN 1837, was an African American teacher, mother and devout abolitionist who, in 1863, became the first northern "free woman of color" to travel to the South Carolina Sea Islands with the American Missionary Society to teach newly freed slaves to read and write. In comparison to other African Americans living in the nineteenth-century U.S., Charlotte had an exceptional degree of freedom, education, and opportunities, thanks to her family's wealth. However, she was by no means immune to the dire conditions of enslaved African Americans; indeed, the daily sight of groups of them bound by chains affected her greatly. Also, despite her intelligence and privileged status, she herself felt the sting of marginalization, as she had been ostracized by white students at the integrated school she attended. This constant exposure to injustice and inequality, as well as the lessons in social justice and advocacy she garnered from her abolitionist family and friends, made her vow to fight against inequality wherever and whenever she encountered it: "Oh, that I could do much towards bettering our condition," she writes in a January 1856 diary entry, continuing: "I will do all, all the very little that lies in my power, while life and strength last" ("PBS Online: Only a Teacher").

While teaching on the Sea Islands, the care and concern that Charlotte felt for her students inspired them, while they, in turn, inspired her with their unsurpassed capacity for learning and their determination to educate themselves in the face of the most difficult circumstances imaginable. The two years she spent amongst them, despite her exposure to disease and inadequate housing conditions and her fear of being attacked by disgruntled white townspeople, became the most memorable time of her life, as well as the inspiration for her unforgettable diaries, which are the only extant texts presenting a black woman's view of the Sea Island missionary project. As the following quotation suggests, Forten expected to warmly embrace (and be embraced by) her students, and she believed that her pedagogical efforts would promote social justice in the larger community:

> I shall dwell again among "mine own people." I shall gather my scholars about me, and see smiles of greeting break over their dusky faces. My heart sings a song of thanksgiving, at the thought that even I am permitted to do something for a long-abused race, and aid in promoting a higher, holier, and happier life on the Sea Islands. ("PBS Online: Only a Teacher")

Essentially, Forten equates teaching with what Patricia Hill Collins has famously called othermothering (Collins 178-219). Forten envisions living amongst people she considers family, envisions forming deep bonds of affection with "her" scholars as she strives to give them the knowledge and skills to attain greater happiness, virtue, and material well-being. Central to Forten's teacherly othermothering, which Nel Noddings would appropriately label a pedagogy based on an "ethics of care" (Smith), is the belief that she has a moral responsibility to join with others in a collective fight to promote justice for all oppressed and maligned peoples. As this essay demonstrates, the notion of teacher as othermother has been a constant in the African-American pedagogical tradition from the 1860s to the present.

This is not to say that female and male teachers of other ethnicities but similar philosophical mindsets and political agendas do not share any of the pedagogical beliefs and goals of most (though certainly not all) African-American teachers. However, African Americans as a people and African American women in particular share a unique cultural background that includes the convergence of slavery, sexism and classism (Beauboeuf-Lafontant 2002: 72), thus providing them with a particularly compelling reason to engage in pedagogical othermothering. By contrast, many non-African American women teachers would rather "deconstruct the maternal." For example, in a 1990 study that examined attitudes towards caring among women teachers of differing races and ethnicities, Kathleen Casey found that many female teachers who were not African American rejected the idea of being a mother figure in the classroom (Casey). These women viewed a motherly style of teaching as perpetuating and enabling paternal dominance and power over women and children and reinforcing a stereotypical and limiting role of woman as nurturer.

By contrast, the African American women teachers in Casey's study—because of African Americans' unique history of combating slavery and other institutional and systemic forms of subjugation—tended to embrace the association of teaching (and power) with mothering (Casey). For generations, othermothering, or caring for children other than one's own biological offspring, has been an effective and often essential survival strategy for African Americans, most of whom believe that an individual's fate is inextricably linked to that of his or her social group—and vice versa. Because race and class oppression continued to exist in educational as well as other settings long after emancipation (in some states educating freed slaves remained illegal, even punishable by death), othermothering became the primary method of educational and cultural transmission amongst African Americans, as well as their primary method of resisting racism, classism, sexism, and other forms of oppression (Case 26).

Lily Ann Granderson, acting with the care and concern of an othermother for those in her community to whom she was not biologically related, is an example of a teacher putting herself at extreme risk because she felt compelled to help her fellow slaves become literate. Born in 1816 as a slave, Granderson knew very well the severe punishment to be endured when rules were broken. She had secretly learned to read and write, and although she put herself in extreme jeopardy, she opened a school for slaves, where from midnight until two in the morning she helped other slaves become literate. She continued this practice for years until emancipation, at which point she then taught during daylight hours with the American Missionary Society (Haviland 300-301).

For these African American females, slavery and subjugation irrevocably shaped their self-perceptions as women and mothers. In the nineteenth-century, motherhood and femininity for upper-class white women was characterized by privilege, social status and morality, whereas black women were excluded from this genteel characterization and not even considered "true women." In contrast, motherhood for them was genuinely characterized by a mixture of love, bondage and loss (Littlefield 54). Dorothy Sterling contextualizes African American women's distinctive historical and cultural existence with these telling words: "To be a black woman in America was to live in the double jeopardy of belonging to the "inferior sex" of an "inferior race," yet they possessed a tenacity of spirit, a gift of endurance, a steadfastness of aspiration that helped a whole population to survive" (Sterling 9).

As Granderson and other early African American teachers realized, defining mothering as taking collective responsibility for others in the community could be very powerful. And the adversity these women faced had the effect of encouraging them to create new definitions of femininity and motherhood that addressed their unique needs and circumstances as black women; definitions that celebrated female strength and versatility instead of fragility and dependence.

Like earlier African American teachers, those of the late 1950s not only assisted their students in becoming literate, but also tirelessly and selflessly tried to give their students the knowledge and skills they would need to navigate a society that was slowly and often reluctantly becoming racially integrated. In 1954, African American teachers viewed the *Brown v. Board of Education* decision of the U.S. Supreme Court with equal amounts of excitement and trepidation, but overall their overall sentiment was that "we were Negroes first and teachers second" (Ramsey 1). By this they meant that their charge was to ensure the progress of their people, and that they would meet their obligations by preparing their students for whatever challenges awaited them within an integrated society. Janice Peterson, a high school student in 1954, fondly recalls the extraordinary measures her African American teacher took outside of school time to ensure that she and her fellow students were at least somewhat prepared to live in a "white world." She remembers how "our teacher arranged for us to travel to the closest big city that allowed black people to use the pool. She did this so that we would be prepared to save ourselves and others if there was trouble once our local pool was integrated" (Peterson).[1] Teachers who view their students through an othermothering lens see the student as a person with unique thoughts and needs and try to interact with that student without any preconditions or preconceived stereotypes or judgments. These teachers make a conscious effort to focus first on the humanity that connects us all as people; in effect, they view the student as part of us, not as one of "them." This sociological distinction has been thoughtfully explored in Lisa Delpit's groundbreaking book *Other People's Children*. Delpit, an expert in the field of culturally relevant education, examines how the majority, mainstream society often negatively labels minority children, which she argues, proves to be the origin of many of the problems that minority students face. Delpit contends that "the psychologists and the school administrators look at 'other people's children' and see damaged and dangerous caricatures of the vulnerable and impressionable beings before them. Distinctions, both subtle and overt between the majority member students, 'our children,' and minority children, 'other people's children,' abound" (Beauboeuf-Lafontant 2002: 74).

The root of the problem, according to Delpit, stems from the "culture of power"; the foundation upon which our society and, subsequently, our schools, are built. This power emanates from a tradition of European values and ideals that promote, as superior and correct, a particular style of communication, social behavior and intellectual capacity which the white, upper-class majority are socialized to adhere to and understand. Delpit describes students and parents who can effortlessly navigate within these parameters as possessing "cultural capital," in that they have the means and the ability to achieve within the dominant culture. Minority students and their parents, many of whom do not have such cultural capital, often experience a sense of marginalization and disconnection from the school setting, the very place where they should feel the most welcomed and accepted (Delpit 1988).

As a school librarian, I have personally witnessed the troubling effects of this phenomenon. A lively online discussion about parents and censorship came to an abrupt halt when one white librarian, who identified herself as working in an upper-middle class, predominantly white district, stated that those of us who worked in the urban, more racially diverse districts would not have to worry about our parents complaining if the books were inappropriate because "those" parents would not care, since "those" students and parents were more used to adolescent sexual behavior, violence and dysfunction than the students and parents in her district. I have found that this unconscious or conscious idea that "we and our children are good" and that "they and their children are bad" and that "those" students are a burden that "we" as a society must bear continues to pervade our society and its schools. I have encountered this distinction regarding the very students we, as educators, should be committed to nurturing and educating in an equal manner, and it makes me feel very unsettled and uncomfortable, whether the idea is formally spoken at faculty meetings or casually discussed in the teachers' lounge. As an African American educator and parent, I often wonder how my own children are viewed in their schools. I can only hope that they will be lucky enough to encounter teachers like the five with whom I recently conducted interviews—African American teachers for whom "the maternal serves as a relational compass for their teaching" (Beauboeuf-Lafontant 2002: 75).

Gail Anderson, a teacher of three years originally from Jamaica, initially experienced a sense of marginalization and "otherness" in the school system. She states that when she worked at an upper-class, predominantly white middle school for a two-year period, she never had a sense of belonging and didn't feel she "fit in with the staff or the students" (Anderson). She says that everyone was polite to her, but that they remained distant and she always felt like hired help. She transferred to an economically, racially and socially more diverse school and has never looked back: "Here, I have a purpose. The students here are not easy, but they need me. I care for them, work harder for them, and I give more of myself to them because I am determined to see them fulfill their promise" (Anderson).

Linda Ali, a new mother and a teacher for six years, is more explicit about her maternal approach to educating her students. Each September, Linda begins her annual Back to School Night parent presentation with the simple yet profound statement, "I am a mother." Linda explains that she makes this statement because it is her understanding of herself as a mother that guides her teaching philosophy. She laughs as she states that "I realize that some of my colleagues think it is unusual to share that particular information, but I feel that being a mother is such an integral part of my life and is so relevant to my profession that how could I not talk about it?" (Ali). Teachers like Linda are unapologetic about expressing their maternal sensibilities because they are certain that the warmth and energy that characterizes the mother-child relationship can encourage and enhance the educational experience when applied to the teacher-student relationship.

Regardless of gender, teachers who engage in pedagogical othermothering tend to view their students as "their kids" and interact with them as such. Ken Jones, a veteran teacher of many years, reflects with humor on the fact that the year he served as his own daughter's teacher, no one in the class knew or realized that she was his daughter until near the end of the school year, when her full name was read over the intercom for an award. This was a result of him teaching all of "his children" in the same manner, as he strongly believed in giving all of his students the same care and attention that he rendered to his own children. He never had any reason to single out his daughter, and the other students were shocked and surprised to learn of this father-daughter relationship (Jones).

Successful African American teachers often consciously develop personal, not just professional, relationships with their students that demonstrate their commitment to caring (Beauboeuf-Lafontant 1997: 2). Like Ken Jones, Karen Benson, a math teacher with two children, wants all children to have equal educational opportunities. She states, "I want what is best for my children and that is for them to learn. I take that same sentiment and apply it to my students because I want the same thing for them" (Benson). Karen makes a conscious effort to ensure that her ethnically and racially diverse students all know that she cares about each one of them. Every September she engages her new students in a getting-to-know-you activity during which she informs her students that she is a parent and one of eight siblings. She smiles as she recounts their typical reaction to her news: "They are always surprised and have many questions, as well as volunteer information about their own families." Karen states that, "I relay this information purposely because, even though I am a professional, I want them to know that they can relate to me because I share some of their families' characteristics. Communication in this manner allows us to begin to relate to each other as partners in achieving our shared education goals" (Benson).

Charlotte Forten's experiences so long ago with both discrimination and social injustices made her aware of her fundamental interdependence with other African Americans; she realized that until (relatively) privileged black persons like herself committed themselves to uplifting their own people, neither they, nor she, would ever be truly free. Many of today's African American teachers, who share Forten's experience of feeling both privileged and "other," also believe that it is their moral obligation and collective responsibility as educators to help their students become literate in the culture of power so that they can they can successfully take their place in society and the world. And they realize that to teach effectively, they must be ready to take on many roles and be willing to do more than simply impart facts and figures (Brown 4). Gail, a seventh grade literature teacher who was recently tenured after three years of teaching, laughs as she states that on any given day she can be "the teacher, the counselor, the mediator and yes, even occasionally the warden, but if that is what it takes to educate my students, I will" (Anderson).

The concern that these and many other African American teachers display for educating the whole child allows them to see themselves as "gate openers" rather than "gatekeepers"; they strive to ensure that their students, especially those of minority status, have access to all of the opportunities that should be available to them. African American educators also act as "boundary spanners"; because of their knowledge of mainstream school cultures and methods, they can effectively assist minority parents in asking the right questions of and communicating their concerns to white teachers and administrators. In essence, these African American teachers know how to speak the language of the educational system while simultaneously having familiarity with and firsthand experience of minority cultures and concerns (Brown 4).

The issues and problems surrounding education are pervasive, including high teacher attrition rates, lack of parental involvement, and the low reading level of many students (Hamil 1-9). Many propose as possible solutions longer school hours, merit pay for teachers, or the establishment of more charter schools; the idea of introducing more mothering and caring into the teacher-student relationship usually is not an idea found at the forefront of (or even broached during) these discussions. However, with teacher, student, and parent dissatisfaction at an all-time high, the importance of quality student-teacher relationships has garnered interest, with some researchers focusing on the efficacy of caring in our schools (Beauboeuf-Lafontant 2002: 71). Noddings, through her research on role of caring in pedagogy, has found that although caring obviously cannot fix everything wrong with the educational system, the idea of teachers gaining students' trust and committing themselves to learning about students' unique, individual personal situations, needs and talents could be influential in the development of stronger, more fruitful student-teacher relationships (Noddings).

Throughout slavery, emancipation, segregation and modern times, African American teachers have been at the forefront of this maternal approach to education. Their genuine sense of connection to and concern for their students infuses their pedagogy with passion and energy, and they often perceive teaching as a special calling or gift that they are obliged (and privileged) to share with others. For over a century and a half, such pedagogical othermothering has helped countless students maintain confidence in their intellectual abilities, as well as helped many students develop effective strategies for engaging in a life-long struggle to end racism and sexism. It is high time that these othermothering teachers—some of them male, and not all of them African American—be recognized and emulated.

[1]To preserve confidentiality and protect their privacy, all the teachers and students I interviewed have been given pseudonyms.

Works Cited

Ali, Linda. Personal interview. 24 January 2010.

Anderson, Gail. Personal interview. 11 January 2010.

Beauboeuf-Lafontant, Tamara. "A Womanist Experience of Caring: Understanding the Pedagogy of Exemplary Black Women Teachers." *Urban Review* 34.1 (2002): 71-86. Print.

Beauboeuf-Lafontant, Tamara. "I Teach You the Way I See Us: Concepts of Self and Teaching of African-American Women Teachers Committed to Social Justice." *Annual Meeting of the American Educational Research Association.* Chicago, March 24-28, 1997: 1-15. Print.

Benson, Karen. Personal interview. 5 May 2010.

Brown, Gilbert. "The Role of the African American Teacher: Why it's Essential in the School System." *Black Collegian Online* 2001: 1-5. Web. 8 Jan 2010.

Case, Karen. "African American Mothering in the Urban Elementary School." *Urban Review.* 29.1 (1997): 26. Print.

Casey, Kathleen. "Teacher as Mother: Curriculum Theorizing in the Life." *Cambridge Journal of Education* 20.3 (1990): 301. *Academic Search Premier.* EBSCO. Web. 3 Aug. 2010.

Collins, Patricia Hill. *Black Feminist Thought: Knowledge, Consciousness, and the Politics of Empowerment* . New York: Routledge, 2008. Print

Delpit, Lisa D. *Other People's Children: Cultural Conflict in the Classroom.* New York: New Press : Distributed by W.W. Norton, 2006.

Delpit, Lisa D. "The Silenced Dialogue: Power and Pedagogy in Educating Other People's Children" *Harvard Educational Review* 58.3 (1988): 280-298. Print.

Forten, Charlotte, Christy Steele, and Kerry Graves. *A Free Black Girl Before the Civil War: The Diary of Charlotte Forten, 1854 (Diaries, Letters, and Memoirs)*. Mankato, MN: Blue Earth Books, 1998. Print.

Hamil, Boyer, and Ashley Burnett. "Problems Facing American Education." *Focus on Colleges, Universities, and Schools*. 2.1 (2008): 1-9. Print.

Haviland, Laura S. *A Woman's Life-Work Labors and Experiences*. Charleston, SC: Biblio Bazaar, 2006. Print.

Jones, Ken. Personal interview. 7 February 2010

Littlefield, Marci. "Black Women, Mothering, and Protest in 19th Century American Society." *The Journal of Pan African Studies*. 2.1 (2007): 53-60. Print.

Noddings, Nel. "Caring in Education." *Encyclopedia of Informal Education* (2005): n. pag. Web. 24 April 2010.

"PBS Online: Only a Teacher: Schoolhouse Pioneers, Charlotte Forten (1837-1914)." *Public Broadcasting System*. n. pag Web. May 23, 2010.

Peterson, Janice. Personal interview. 29 January 2010.

Ramsey, Sonya. "We Will Be Ready Whenever They are: African American Teachers' Responses to the Brown Decision and Public School Integration in Nashville, Tennessee. 1954-1966." *Journal of African American History* 90.1/2 (2005): 29-51. Print.

Smith, M. K. "Nel Noddings, the Ethics of Care and Education." *The Encyclopedia of Informal Education* (2004): n. pag. Web. 8 March 2010.

Sterling, Dorothy. *We Are Your Sisters: Black Women in the Nineteenth Century*. New York: W. W. Norton and Company, 1984. Print.

Mothering Student Activists

Reflections on Maternal/Feminist Service-Learning Pedagogy

DEBORAH LEA BYRD

I AM A MOTHER AND A feminist, a white, heterosexual, (now) middle-class single woman who grew up in rural West Virginia. I do not leave those facets of my identity at home or in my office when I'm getting ready to interact with students; on the contrary, what scholars of intersectionality call my "positionality" accompanies me into the classroom, inevitably influencing (sometimes consciously, sometimes unconsciously) both what and how I teach. And since being a mother is certainly one of the most important aspects of my identity, one could argue that to a certain extent, my pedagogical foci, goals and strategies as a professor of English and Women's and Gender Studies are bound to be in some ways "maternal," bound to be influenced by the fact that I'm the non-biological mother of a biracial (white and African-American) tenth grader whom I adopted almost sixteen years ago. But when I'm at work—teaching at the small, private liberal arts college where I've been employed for close to thirty years—do I practice "maternal pedagogies" in any substantive sense—and if so, in what ways, in what contexts, and for what reasons? The essay that follows addresses these questions.

If I do engage in "mothering" when teaching U.S. college students, it would be mothering of a feminist sort, since being a feminist is as central to my identity as being a mother. And it would be the mothering of an actively anti-racist, anti-homophobic, socialist feminist who believes that a feminist should (both alone and working with others) seek to identify, object to, and eradicate all forms of injustice and oppression. But before I can determine if I practice feminist maternal pedagogies in my professional life, it seems important to identify how such pedagogies operate in my personal life, how they have manifested themselves in my ever-changing relationship with my "16 going on 21 year-old" son.

For me, to successfully engage in feminist maternal pedagogies within a family context means—in terms of "course content and goals"—that I have tried to teach my son how to recognize both subtle and obvious, both individualized and institutional forms of oppression and injustice, and that I have tried to inculcate in him a feminist desire to dislike and want to put an end to such discriminatory beliefs and behaviors, especially as they manifest themselves in individuals he knows or in institutions (such as school systems or sports leagues) of which he has firsthand knowledge. I also have tried to instill in him a curiosity about and appreciation for people of all sorts of beliefs and backgrounds, and I've tried to make him especially eager to support and form friendships with people who belong to groups that often are negatively stereotyped, whether they be kids with disabilities, children of color, classmates who are gay, or young people from low-income families. But the "what" of my feminist maternal pedagogy is much easier to specify than the "how"—as a mother, what is it that I do or say to try to make these lessons "stick"?

Like all teachers, I use a number of pedagogical strategies. When I had a lot of control over my son's life—and back when he loved nothing more than pleasing and doing things with Mom—I made sure that my son was exposed to lots of texts (children's books, television shows, theatrical performances, toys, games, dolls, puppet sets) that individually or collectively encouraged him to appreciate all different kinds of people and cultures. And I actively looked for opportunities to teach my son to see and be upset by instances of injustice—whether they occurred in books or in "real life"—as well as drew his attention to and urged him to applaud acts of kindness, fairness, and tolerance. Exposure to such texts and talks no doubt helps to account for the fact that at various times in his life, my son has chosen to do a book report on George Washington Carver, write an essay explaining why the U.S. should *not* celebrate Columbus Day, and argue in a research paper that the death penalty should be abolished due to the rampant racism within the U.S. legal and criminal justice systems.

But the most important component of my feminist maternal pedagogy, I have come to believe, is my decision to "walk the walk and not just talk the talk," a commitment that has given my son many opportunities to engage in "hands on," experiential learning and many occasions to practice and/or test the validity of the views and values I've promulgated in a more overtly didactic way. From the time I became a mother, I made a self-conscious effort to ensure that my son had regular, intimate contact with people of varying backgrounds. I was already living in an ethnically and racially diverse working-class neighborhood when I adopted my son, and I continued to seek out multicultural spaces for him as I selected a daycare, enrolled him in sports, and supervised study abroad programs in Greece. I took (and continue to take) my son to Passover Seders and Lebanese Heritage Days, and I have actively cultivated friendships with adults whose children are adopted, bi-racial, and/or of a different race than their parent(s). I have tried to lead by example, modeling for my son what it "looks like" to engage in a daily struggle to promote social justice and *showing* him how to build and sustain what bell hooks calls "beloved communities," communities comprised of culturally and physically diverse individuals who share a commitment to improving the world in which they live (264). I don't by any means intend to set myself up as a paragon of virtue; what I'm trying to emphasize is that to the extent that I've succeeded as a practitioner of feminist maternal pedagogy, I believe that it's because I've consciously placed my son in situations where he doesn't just read and talk and think about multiculturalism, but actually has regular, firsthand contact with "Others." My son's "inner circle" of friends is consistently comprised of a half dozen youth of varying races, ethnicities, and socio-economic backgrounds, and his concern for and loyalty to these friends sometimes make him an activist, such as when he confronts rich kids who speak negatively of, ignore, or condescend to their less wealthy peers.

If the central feature of my feminist maternal pedagogy on the home front is combining "discussion and mini-lectures" with experiential learning, how does this translate into my life as a teacher of undergraduate students? It means that in my view, I engage in feminist maternal pedagogy most effectively when teaching service-learning courses, courses in which students are required to interact with, learn about and from, and find ways to support individuals who belong to marginalized or oppressed groups. For me (but not necessarily for others), teaching in a "motherly" fashion has nothing to do with biology; I have no personal experience of bringing a fetus to term, giving birth, or breastfeeding. And it has nothing to do with traditional, patriarchal conceptions of nurturance, nothing to do with open displays of affection and concern for one's students. I do, of course, care about my students' well-being, sometimes very deeply, and my classroom demeanor is characterized by warmth, not aloofness. But for *this* feminist teacher, what is most maternal about my pedagogy is my desire to place my students in an environment in which they have regular contact with and can get to know individuals who are in one or more ways quite different from themselves, an environment in which my surrogate children have a chance to test, apply, or enact the feminist ideas they've been exposed to through assigned readings and class discussions.

The course in which I most fully engage in *my* brand of feminist maternal pedagogy is an upper-level Women's and Gender Studies service-learning seminar entitled "Single Motherhood in the Contemporary U.S.: Myths and Realities." This course focuses explicitly on motherhood as both an institution and a unique personal experience, with special attention to the challenges faced by teenage and low-income single mothers living in the contemporary U.S. In this interdisciplinary course, students view films and read personal narratives and scholarly writings on such topics as the history and ideological underpinnings of the U.S. welfare state, the various kinds of government programs available to the poor, the negative cultural stereotypes of pregnant teens and "welfare queens," the experiences of single mothers and their children within the criminal justice system, and the kinds of "Adverse Childhood Experiences" that increase the likelihood that a young woman will bear and keep a child as a teenager (for the latter, see Lipper 43-44).

About three weeks into the course, students begin spending time with and learning firsthand about the goals, challenges, accomplishments and unmet needs of two groups of women: pregnant and parenting teens at a large public high school, and single mothers living in subsidized housing facilities run by local non-profits. Except in unusual circumstances, students are expected to devote at least fifteen hours over the course of the semester to such service-learning experiences; most students interact directly with the mothers and mothers-to-be, but some spend time with the social service providers that in various ways support these primarily low-income women. In their reflective journal entries, which count 45 percent of the final course grade, students are asked to integrate what they've learned from course readings with knowledge gained "in the field"; then they are required to use this dual-sourced knowledge to individually or collectively design and implement activist projects. The projects vary greatly; they have included interactive sessions on ways to prepare for job interviews, handbooks describing the degree programs and financial aid opportunities at local community colleges, and "spa nights" at which the mothers receive written materials on stress management and positive parenting after they have been treated to dinner, a manicure, a yoga or belly-dancing lesson, and (of course) free childcare. Some projects the students have embarked on offer less direct but more long-term, structural support to our community's single mothers—indeed, to our community's low-income families in general. These projects, which are done in collaboration with local non-profit agencies and completed after students in two or three seminars have contributed to the effort, include a manual (both in English and Spanish) that lists free and low-cost health resources available to local residents, and a directory of area childcare facilities that (among other things) maps each facility's location in relation to public bus routes.

The first time I first taught the "Single Motherhood" course (fall 2005) I had six students; I have since taught the course four times, with enrollments ranging from 15 to 18 students. Before offering the seminar a second time, I decided to develop an "outcomes assessment" tool that I hoped would help me determine whether students were (1) truly more knowledgeable about the realities of single mothers' lives at the end of the semester, and (2) whether they were less prone to endorse some of the dominant culture's negative stereotypes about and misperceptions of teenage and low-income single mothers. In their reflective journals, most students *claim* that they've developed a more accurate and positive view of single mothers, but since the journal entries are graded and students know very well that I *want* to read such statements, I wondered how genuine such comments were. So I designed a survey (see Appendix 1) that I distribute on the first day of class—*before* I hand out the syllabus or say anything at all about course content, goals, or requirements. At the end of the semester, students complete the survey again; in both cases, they do so anonymously.

I should note at this point that my doctoral degree is in English literature; I have lots of experience identifying recurrent themes in student (and other) writing and selecting quotations that are typical—or particularly intriguing to discuss. However, my scholarly background does *not* include any formal training in the design and analysis of surveys; I have relied upon my colleagues in Psychology and a couple of student research assistants to help me analyze the data I've gathered.[1] What follows is a humanist's account of ways in which the two-pronged feminist maternal pedagogy she employs in her service-learning seminar seems to not only enhance her students' knowledge of and respect for teenage and low-income single mothers, but also helps her surrogate children develop or hone their skills as activists.[2]

***

The "before and after" survey contains a section eliciting demographic information, then asks students to respond to thirty-nine statements using a 5-point Likert scale, with 1 registering strong disagreement and 5 indicating strong agreement. Some of the statements measure how knowledgeable a student is; others measure the extent to which a student believes that the U.S. is a meritocracy (see McIntosh 358-60) or endorses false and demeaning stereotypes about the populations studied in the course. As Appendix 1 reveals, for two-thirds of the statements (26 of the 39) there was a statistically significant change in students' factual knowledge or in their perceptions of single mothers, including those on "welfare" (the word generally used in the U.S. as a synonym for cash assistance the government provides to impoverished individuals and families). Since student responses to questions on the survey did not vary in a statistically significant way from year to year, the likelihood that shifts in opinion are due to chance is very small).[3]

Greater Familiarity with "The Facts"

As is revealed by Appendix 1 (which notes the degree of statistically significant change in responses to each item) and Appendix 2 (which contains frequency bar graphs), my service-learning students did become more knowledgeable about many issues over the course of the semester. For example, after discussing course readings and interacting regularly with low-income mothers and social service providers, most students knew that it is *not* true that "The primary beneficiaries of most taxpayer/government social service programs are our country's most economically disadvantaged citizens" (item 1); they had become aware that such programs disproportionately benefit the middle class and wealthy (Gilens 15). Whereas student responses to item 1 had hovered in the middle of the spectrum at the beginning of the semester, with over 43 percent "somewhat" or "strongly" *agreeing* with the assertion, by the end of the semester more than 88 percent of the students *disagreed* with the claim, 32.7 of them "strongly."

Similarly, at the beginning of the semester only 41 percent of students disagreed with the frequently uttered but false claim that "It is fairly common for women on welfare to have additional children so that they can increase the amount of their monthly welfare payments" (item 7). By the end of the course, that number had risen to 76.5 percent, with 52.9 percent of the class (as opposed to an earlier 19.6 percent) strongly objecting to this statement. Most students had become aware of the reality: many states do not increase monthly payments by a single cent if a woman on welfare has another child, and as for those states that provide tiny increases, a Georgia welfare director says it all: "anyone who thinks that a woman goes through nine months of pregnancy, the pain of childbirth and 18 years of rearing a child for $45 more a month … has got to be a man" (qtd. in Moody 94).

During the course of the semester, an increasing number of students also became aware that although the U.S. government will pay (indeed is required to pay) foster parents for providing care to a child whose mother is in prison, the government generally does *not* offer cash assistance to relatives who provide such care (item 20; Ascione and Dixson 279). Initially, only 21.5 percent were aware of this sad state of affairs; four months later, 62 percent were "in the know." An increasing number of students also came to realize that quite a few teachers and guidance counselors actually discourage teen mothers from finishing high school or pursuing post-secondary education. At the beginning of the semester, close to 90 percent of the responses to item 29 were grouped in the middle of the scale, with only about 37 percent of the students believing that high school teachers and officials might discourage a young mom's educational ambitions. By the end of the course, almost 60 percent knew that this is often the case.

Other statements on the survey ask students to make value judgments about the welfare system—to indicate whether they think particular policies of the present or recent past are fair and reasonable. The data suggests that students find memorable the readings and the many discussions (both in the classroom and with single mothers) that focus on the so-called welfare "reform" that began in 1996 when the federal government passed the Personal Responsibility and Work Opportunity Reconciliation Act (PRWORA) and replaced Aid for Families with Dependent Children (AFDC) with Temporary Assistance to Needy Families (TANF). For example, students learn both from readings and from women who have been on welfare that under the supposedly improved system, single mothers have many fewer opportunities to pursue formal education—often the best route to economic self-sufficiency (Adair, "Fulfilling the Promise"); have to work longer and longer hours to "earn" the right to cash assistance, even when they have very young children (Handler 38); have their privacy invaded with increasing frequency (Madsen 144); and sometimes are punished quite harshly for minor, even unavoidable infractions of rules that don't make much sense in the first place (Owens-Manley).

As data in the appendices reveals, students were more critical of existing welfare policies at the end of the semester than when the course began. Initially, only a little over a third of the students disagreed with the notion that "Welfare recipients who are caught earning 'under the table' money or committing other kinds of fraud should be kicked off the welfare rolls, at least temporarily" (item 4). At the end of the semester, 77.6 percent of the students disagreed with this statement, and the percentage who disagreed "strongly" (36.7 percent) almost equaled the percentage of *all* those who initially disagreed (37.3 percent). Similarly, students became more critical of work requirements for women on welfare who have children under the age of three (item 14). The first day of class, 68.6 percent thought poor women with young children should not be forced to spend thirty hours or more in the paid labor force to be eligible for cash assistance; 92.2 percent of the students found the policy objectionable at the end of the semester.

The data gathered from the survey is consistent with reflective journal entries in which students claim that course readings and firsthand interaction with low-income single mothers made them more aware of the inadequacies of government-sponsored programs to support these women. Shannon writes that before taking the course,

> I didn't know that the welfare checks were not enough for someone to live on, let alone raise a family. I didn't know that once you were on welfare you, in a sense, lost some of your civil liberties like the right to privacy.... Most of the time women on welfare are damned if they do and damned if they don't. A welfare mom can't work late nights because she's neglecting her children but if she doesn't work late nights, then she's also neglecting her kids because then she can't feed and clothe them.

Jemirah makes a similar observation:

> I think the most important thing I learned is how convoluted the welfare system is and how hard some women battle each and every day to work through the ever-changing rules to make sure their

> children are fed and have shelter. I never realized how difficult it is to get public assistance, and didn't realize all the struggles people go through with case workers, filling out forms, etc. Learning all these things taught me to reject the stereotype that "people on welfare are lazy."

Whereas Shannon and Jemirah speak of changes in mindset, Aliyah is ready to take what she has learned and start working for social justice. "I'm both proud and humbled by my experience in this class," she writes at the end of the semester.

> I'm proud because I now have such an important tool at my disposal. I have the knowledge to encourage others to take a closer look at the experiences of single moms, especially those who live in poverty. I'm proud that I can rail against workfare and the state of welfare "reform." ...I'm also humbled that I have had very personal access into the lives of many women, through readings and in person, who shared so openly with the hope of simply being heard.... Because of those women, I can now speak and act with confidence, knowing that when we help each other, we all are better off. Now we just have to make it happen!

From Disapproval and Pity to Respect and Admiration

Quite a few students enter the service-learning seminar pitying teenage and low-income single mothers: "I subconsciously assumed that having only one parent was automatically a disadvantage for a child," an embarrassed Ellie confesses. Even more common is a belief that many women on welfare are either unmotivated to begin with, or become lazy and complacent after living (quite comfortably, students often assume) "on the dole." Several items on the survey are specifically designed to measure the extent to which students endorse such notions; in all cases, there was a statistically significant attitudinal shift, with students having a much more accurate and positive perception of the women they were learning about and from at the end of the semester. For example, over half (56.9 percent) of the students initially agreed that "For many recipients, welfare becomes a crutch and leads to the development of 'learned helplessness'"; by the end of the semester, only 11.7 percent agreed with this assertion (item 35). An equally dramatic shift is evident in responses to the statement "Most welfare recipients try very hard to find jobs that will allow them to become economically self-sufficient" (item12); the number in agreement with this assertion went from 58.9 percent to 96.1 percent. And when it came to the idea that the U.S. is a meritocracy in which "Almost anyone ... who works hard enough can eventually move out of poverty" (item 22), the number of students who believe that this is *not* the case rose significantly, from 72.5 percent to 94 percent.

As students learned from books and real people about the inadequacies of U.S. government-sponsored programs to help low-income single mothers attain economic self-sufficiency, they became even more supportive of increases in government welfare spending, even if it meant higher taxes for themselves. Because this is an upper-division Women's and Gender Studies courses that enrolls students who to a certain extent have already had "their consciousnesses raised," most students (60.8 percent) disagreed from the beginning with the statement "Too much taxpayer money is spent on welfare" (item 5). However, by the end of the course 96.1 percent of the students disagreed, 62.7 percent of them "strongly." Similarly, the number of students expressing a commitment to personally supporting impoverished single mothers increased. With item 9—"I would be willing to pay slightly higher taxes if the money went into the funds available for welfare recipients" [the majority of whom are single mothers]—student responses initially were clustered in the middle, with close to 90 percent selecting (and in almost equal numbers) either "neutral" or one of the two "somewhat" answers. Four months later, the 16 students (31.4 percent of the total) who had been unwilling to experience a small personal tax hike to help those needing cash assistance have magically disappeared. A few students (15.7 percent) remain neutral, but the remaining 84.3 percent are willing—at least on paper!—to support low-income single mothers with their hard-earned dollars, half of them enthusiastically. Again, survey data are in keeping with comments in students' reflective journals. For example, Donna decided to send a petition to all U.S. senators, explaining in a cover letter how important it is for them to raise the cutoff point for welfare eligibility at the same time they are raising the minimum wage. "The government needs to reassess the regulations and rules that have been set forth by TANF in order to fix and improve the system," Donna asserts. "The course has taught me that it is possible to make a difference.... I'm not going to stop until I get a response about someone taking positive action. This class has changed my views on welfare and has made me a bit of an activist, which I must say, I'm starting to enjoy!"

Student Assessments of Service-Learning Pedagogy

When asked at the end of the semester to write at some length about the relationship between and the relative value of the "experiential" and "traditional" components of the seminar, students claim that both elements were essential to the learning process. When it comes to assigned readings, they especially emphasize the value of the essays, books, and films we discuss *before* they have direct contact with teenage and low-income single mothers. Many students argue that had they not had some sense of what the lives of such women might be like before they met the women, they probably, in Kenia's words, would have been "totally unprepared and unsuited for the experience." On the other hand, many argue that getting to know the single mothers was what made the information they encountered in assigned readings especially meaningful and memorable. Jill writes:

> For me it was very important to have background knowledge and statistics and personal stories because then you go down to TSA [the transitional housing facility] having some idea about what these women deal with every single day ... because before I really had *no* idea. But it's the women at TSA who make the assigned stories and facts come alive. You don't get the full picture of what it's like to be a poor single mom unless you submerge yourself in these women's lives as much as possible.

Serena makes a similar comment, writing

> If I were to volunteer at TSA outside the context of this class, I would have absolutely no idea what the women who live there go through and probably not have as much respect for them as I do now. I put a great deal of effort into researching local college scholarships because I've read about other poor mothers who are discouraged from going back to school and I want the women *I've* come to know to succeed.

Or as Wendy remarks:

> All semester long we've been trying to understand poor and teen-aged single moms ... what makes them tick, why they are the way

> they are, and why we can't apply what *we* see as logical thinking to their lives.... Few of us could survive in the way that these moms have had to. So we learn not to belittle them; in fact, we celebrate their successes.

Marvin writes more specifically about how interactions with the single mothers have inspired him to engage in social justice work—and taught him the importance of persistence and collective action: "I think the service component is a great outlet for the frustration we feel reading the textual information," Marvin remarks. "However, it's kind of a double-edged sword ... the more work we do, the more work we see we have to do. Working to support the moms keeps us frustrated and challenged and doesn't make us think the little bit we are doing is just going to make the problems vanish in a week. It makes us see how important sustaining the effort is."

Sandra also credits experiential learning as the component of the course that most enlightened and motivated her; she confesses that:

> As much as I wish I could say I was more influenced by the numbers and the graphs and the figures, it's the personal accounts that have really brought issues home to me. I wanted to get to know the mothers we worked with not to compare myself and tell myself how lucky I was, but to educate myself, so that I could in turn educate others and be a better example in the way I talked about poverty, welfare, and single motherhood. Through their own sisterhood, these mothers taught me the importance of 'working together' when you're trying to address a problem. For welfare to be reformed, legislators and policy makers have to work *with* single mothers and people who are poor—not just throw rules, regulations, and arbitrary opportunities *at* them. So, besides learning how to carry an infant and chase a toddler at the same time, I learned one major thing from this course: never assume that just because a given course only occupies one semester on your transcript, the ideas and issues it has raised need to stay there.

A fair number of my "surrogate children" are pursuing social justice work as graduate students or in their professional lives; many of them email me with some regularity, sharing their accomplishments and challenges and/or sending me information about resources I might find useful when teaching my service-learning seminar. I may have nudged some of these students to make activism a central part of their lives, but others were probably headed in that direction before they were exposed to my particular brand of feminist maternal pedagogy. This pedagogy grows out of a conviction that the knowledge students gain from "doing feminism"—and equally importantly, subjecting that "doing" to intellectually rigorous analysis—is likely to be deep knowledge, knowledge that stays with students and guides and informs their future behavior.

I'll let Melissa, an extremely shy senior who took the "Single Motherhood" seminar a few months before entering the corporate world, have the last words on the deep learning that can result when students have a chance to learn *with* and *from*—not just *about*—individuals who are marginalized and oppressed. "I don't usually do this," Melissa writes,

> but I just wanted to tell you how your course has affected my life.... During Thanksgiving I felt tested as my family brought up the welfare system and made comments as naive as mine before I had taken the class. A woman was talking about a service project she was part of where they bought ... cribs and toys for low-income single mothers. In the midst of her story, a man interrupted with "I'm sorry, but those women should either close their legs or the government should make it a law that they are religious about taking their birth control." (Prof. Byrd, you know that I do not do well with speaking in large groups, but I was appalled and after a semester of learning what we had, I felt compelled to speak up). So to everyone's surprise, I went on a (about 20 minute) rant about how ridiculous a comment he had made and how a low income mother might not be able to afford birth control or make appointments for birth control since not many of them would have cars to get there and how unrealistic and sexist his comment was. He rebutted with "well, most of the women on welfare have as many babies as they can so that they can get money for each child." The conversations from our classes (especially the class where young moms in the Nurse-Family Partnership program came to speak with us) came rushing to my head. Last year I would have listened to this conversation and nodded in agreement. However, I just want you to know how much your class has changed my perspective on these issues. Because of the

> knowledge that I obtained, I felt confident enough to stand up to a man twice my age and speak my opinion.... I could tell the man was embarrassed and he said "well, I've never thought about it like that." THANKS AGAIN!"

Thank YOU, Melissa, for demonstrating the value of a feminist maternal pedagogy grounded in service-learning.

[1]I am especially indebted to Dr. Jamila Bookwala, Dr. Susan Basow, and Dr. Jeanine Pinto, who during the past year have generously shared with me their expertise in survey design and analysis. The survey data was organized and run by Nina Skretkowicz with the assistance Samantha Chalmers; both are students in the class of 2011 at Lafayette College. I'd also like to thank Dr. Mary Roth, Associate Provost of Lafayette College, for her office's financial support of this project.

[2]I use the word "seems" because I cannot prove definitively that the increased knowledge of and respect for teenage and low-income single mothers that is recorded in the outcomes assessment instrument is due solely or exclusively to these students having taken my service-learning seminar. Because I'm new to this kind of research, it didn't occur to me to establish a comparison or control group by having students not enrolled in the course also take the survey. However, the fact that the same trends occur all four years makes it highly likely that course readings and activities had a great deal to do with the statistically significant changes in students' responses to many of the questions.

[3]The statements for which there is no statistically significantly change in student responses tend to be of two kinds: (1) statements about topics that ended up receiving very little attention in readings and class discussion, and (2) factual information that students seemed to know before beginning the course.

Works Cited

Adair, Vivyan C. "Fulfilling the Promise of Higher Education." *Reclaiming Class: Women, Poverty, and the Promise of Higher Education in America.* Ed. Vivyan C. Adair and Sandra L. Dahberg. Philadelphia: Temple University Press, 2003. 240-65. Print.

Adair, Vivyan C. and Sandra L. Dahberg, eds. *Reclaiming Class: Women, Poverty, and the Promise of Higher Education in America.* Philadelphia: Temple University Press, 2003. Print.

Ascione, Wendy C. and Joyce Dixson. "Children and Their Incarcerated Mothers." *Women at the Margins: Neglect, Prunishment, and Resistance.* Ed. Josefina Figueira-McDonough and Rosemary C. Sarri. New York: Haworth Press, 2002. 271-93. Print.

Figueira-McDonough, Josefina and Rosemary C. Sarri, eds. *Women at the Margins: Neglect, Punishment, and Resistance.* New York: Haworth Press, 2002. Print.

Gilens, Martin. *Why Americans Hate Welfare: Race, Media, and the Politics of Anti-Poverty Policy.* Chicago: University of Chicago Press, 1999. Print.

Handler, Joel F. "Welfare Reform: Tightening the Screws." *Women at the Margins: Neglect, Prunishment, and Resistance.* Ed. Josefina Figueira-McDonough and Rosemary C. Sarri. New York: Haworth Press, 2002. 33-54. Print.

hooks, bell. *Killing Rage.* New York: Henry Holt, 1995. Print.

Lipper, Joanna. *Growing Up Fast.* New York: Picador, 2003. Print.

Ludtke, Melissa. *On Our Own: Unmarried Motherhood in America.* Berkeley: University of California Press, 1997. Print.

Madsen, Sandy Smith. "From Welfare to Academe: Welfare Reform as College-Educated Welfare Mothers Know It." *Reclaiming Class: Women, Poverty, and the Promise of Higher Education in America.* Eds. Vivyan C. Adair and Sandra L. Dahberg. Philadelphia: Temple University Press, 2003. 139-56. Print.

McIntosh, Peggy. "White Privilege: Unpacking the Invisible Knapsack." *Women: Images and Realities: A Multicultural Anthology.* 2nd ed. Ed. Amy Kesselman, Lily D. McNair, and Nancy Schniedewind. Mountain View, CA: Mayfield, 1999. 358-60. Print.

Moody, Jocelyn K. "To Be Young Pregnant, and Black: My Life as a Welfare Coed." *Reclaiming Class: Women, Poverty, and the Promise of Higher Education in America.* Ed. Vivyan C. Adair and Sandra L. Dahlberg. Philadelphia: Temple University Press, 2003. 85-96. Print.

Owens-Manley, Judith. "The Leper Keepers: Front-Line Workers and the Key to Education for Poor Women." *Reclaiming Class: Women, Poverty, and the Promise of Higher Education in America.* Ed. Vivyan C. Adair and Sandra L. Dahberg. Philadelphia: Temple University Press, 2003. 196-214. Print.

Appendix 1
Statements on the "Before" and "After" Survey

Note:
* means that the P < .05
** means that P < .01
*** means that P < .001

If no asterisks are attached to the statement, there was not a statistically significant change in students' responses from the beginning to the end of the semester.

1. The primary beneficiaries of most tax-payer/government social service programs are our country's economically disadvantaged citizens. (***)
2. Before the 60-month lifetime limit was established in 1996, many adults who went on welfare were not motivated to find paying jobs and remained on the welfare rolls for many years, even decades. (***)
3. Almost all of the girls who become mothers as teenagers are either ignorant about sex or careless about using adequate birth control methods.
4. Welfare recipients who are caught earning "under the table" money or committing other kinds of fraud should be kicked off the welfare rolls, at least temporarily. (***)
5. Too much taxpayer money is spent on welfare. (***)
6. When calculating the amount of federal financial aid a single parent can receive, financial aid officers should be able to take into account the amount of money the parent must spend on the children's food, clothing, and daycare. (*)
7. It is fairly common for women on welfare to have additional children so that they can increase the amount of their monthly welfare payments. (***)
8. About 25% of single parent families headed by women live in poverty. (*)

9. I would be willing to pay slightly higher taxes if it the money went into the fund available for welfare recipients. (***)
10. The U.S. leads all industrialized nations in the percentage of its citizens in jail, in prison, or on probation. (***)
11. The amount of cash assistance a welfare recipient receives is the amount that the government estimates is needed to move the family slightly above the poverty line.
12. Most welfare recipients try very hard to find jobs that will allow them to become economically self-sufficient. (***)
13. The teen pregnancy rate in the U.S. is about the same as that of other industrialized democracies.
14. Able-bodied women with children under the age of 3 should be required to work 30 or more hours a week in order to receive welfare payments. (***)
15. About half the women in the U.S. find themselves living in poverty after getting divorced.
16. The majority of welfare recipients are African-American. (**)
17. The percentage of females becoming mothers as teenagers has increased dramatically from 1950 to the present. (***)
18. Welfare recipients should be able to earn their right to be on welfare by taking high school, college, or job training courses rather than by working at a paying job. (***)
19. Any benefits that accrue from being a teenaged mom are almost always outweighed by the disadvantages of becoming a mother at a young age.
20. The government will provide childcare subsidies to relatives of female prisoners so that the women's children do not have to go into foster homes. (**)
21. Children are the primary beneficiaries of our welfare system.
22. Almost anyone in the U.S. who works hard enough can eventually move out of poverty. (***)
23. Most teen mothers come from low-income families.
24. Most welfare recipients are genuinely in need of financial help. (*)

25. The U.S. spends about the same amount of its Gross National Product on social services as do other industrialized democracies. (***)
26. White teenaged mothers graduate high school at a higher rate than black teen moms.
27. If one earns a salary while on welfare, the amount of one's earnings should be deducted from one's monthly welfare payments. (***)
28. Given that about a third of welfare agency employees once were on welfare themselves, it's not surprising that they tend to be knowledgeable about welfare regulations and very supportive of their clients. (***)
29. Most high school teachers and guidance counselors encourage teen mothers to finish high school, then pursue higher education or good job training programs. (**)
30. About 1 out of 20 (5%) of Pennsylvania residents live below the poverty line.
31. Many teen mothers were physically or sexually abused as children. (**)
32. A full-time day care worker earns a salary just slightly above the poverty line. (*)
33. Few welfare recipients have held full-time jobs before going on welfare. (**)
34. The males who father teenaged girls' children are generally teens themselves.
35. For many recipients, welfare becomes a crutch and leads to the development of "learned helplessness." (***)
36. Teenaged girls are becoming mothers at a much faster rate than U.S. females in any other age group.
37. When adjusted for inflation, the salaries of most U.S. workers have declined over the past thirty years. (*)
38. About 25% of America's poor are black.
39. When welfare recipients receive Section 8 vouchers for subsidized housing, they generally have to wait about a year before such housing becomes available. (*)

Appendix 2

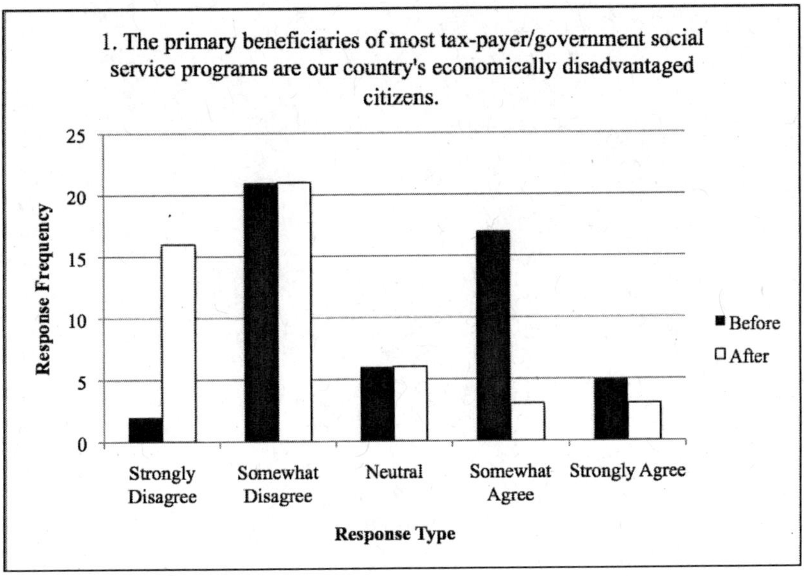
1. The primary beneficiaries of most tax-payer/government social service programs are our country's economically disadvantaged citizens.
Response Frequency
0
5
10
15
20
25
Strongly Disagree
Somewhat Disagree
Neutral
Somewhat Agree
Strongly Agree
Response Type
Before
After

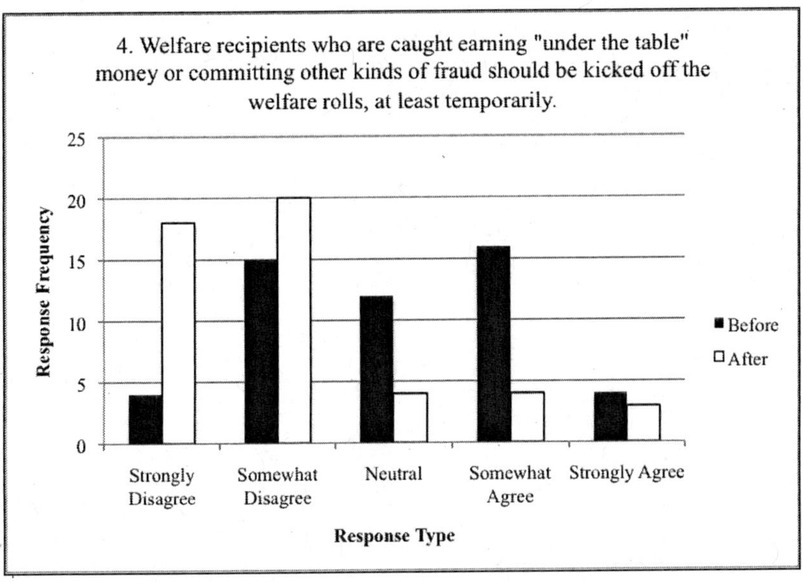
4. Welfare recipients who are caught earning "under the table" money or committing other kinds of fraud should be kicked off the welfare rolls, at least temporarily.
Response Frequency
0
5
10
15
20
25
Strongly Disagree
Somewhat Disagree
Neutral
Somewhat Agree
Strongly Agree
Response Type
Before
After

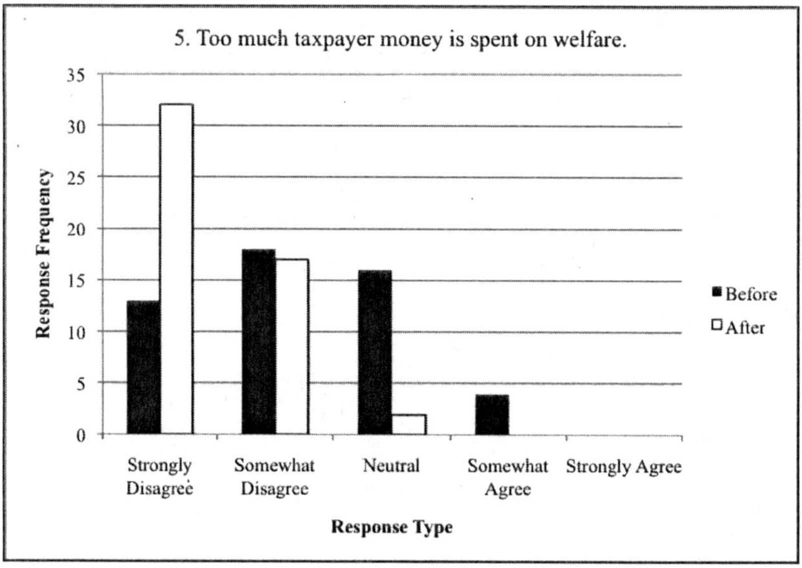
5. Too much taxpayer money is spent on welfare.
Response Frequency
35
30
25
20
15
10
5
0
Strongly Disagree
Somewhat Disagree
Neutral
Somewhat Agree
Strongly Agree
Response Type
Before
After

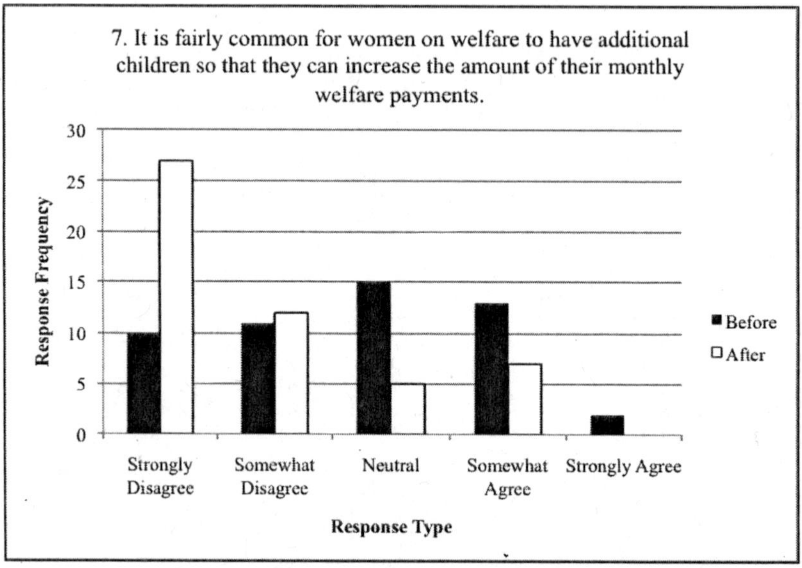
7. It is fairly common for women on welfare to have additional children so that they can increase the amount of their monthly welfare payments.
Response Frequency
30
25
20
15
10
5
0
Strongly Disagree
Somewhat Disagree
Neutral
Somewhat Agree
Strongly Agree
Response Type
Before
After

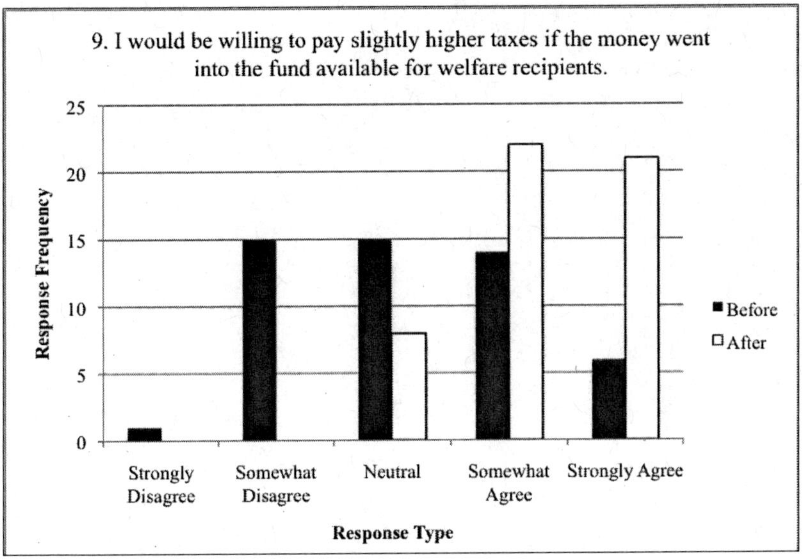
9. I would be willing to pay slightly higher taxes if the money went into the fund available for welfare recipients.
Response Frequency
25
20
15
10
5
0
Strongly Disagree
Somewhat Disagree
Neutral
Somewhat Agree
Strongly Agree
Response Type
Before
After

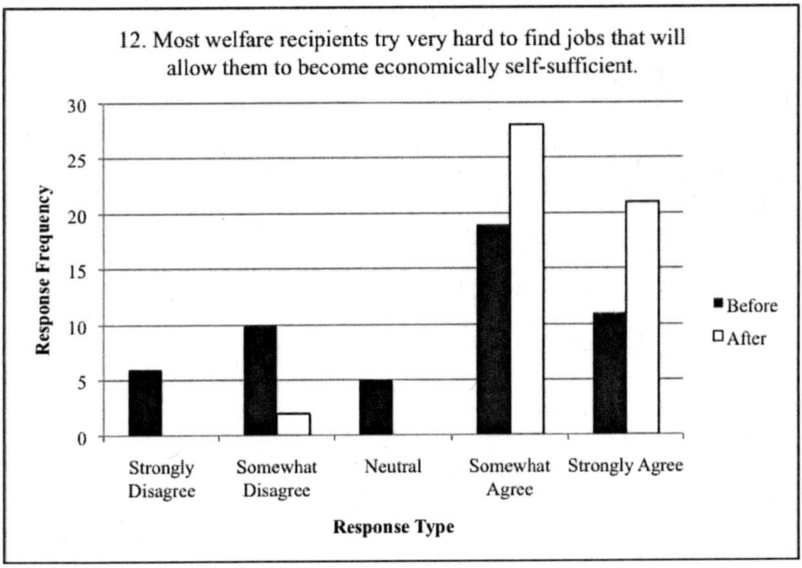
12. Most welfare recipients try very hard to find jobs that will allow them to become economically self-sufficient.
Response Frequency
30
25
20
15
10
5
0
Strongly Disagree
Somewhat Disagree
Neutral
Somewhat Agree
Strongly Agree
Response Type
Before
After

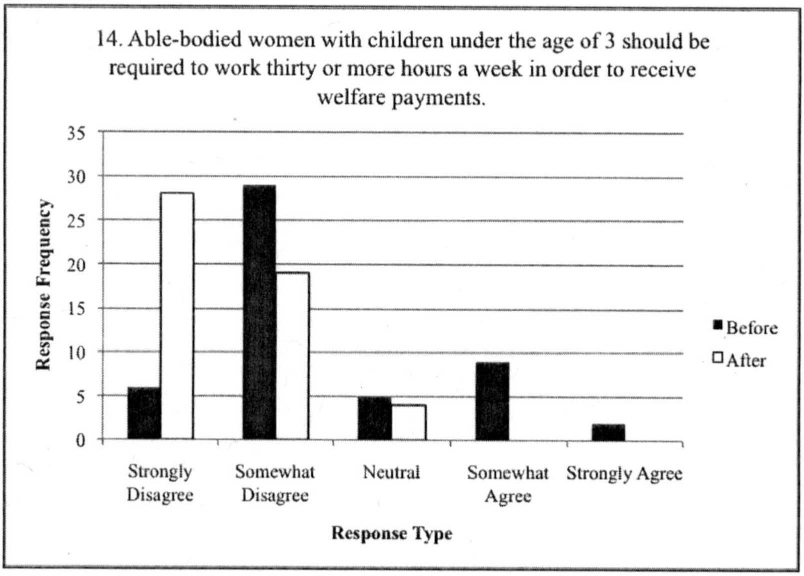
14. Able-bodied women with children under the age of 3 should be required to work thirty or more hours a week in order to receive welfare payments.
Response Frequency
35
30
25
20
15
10
5
0
Strongly Disagree
Somewhat Disagree
Neutral
Somewhat Agree
Strongly Agree
Response Type
Before
After

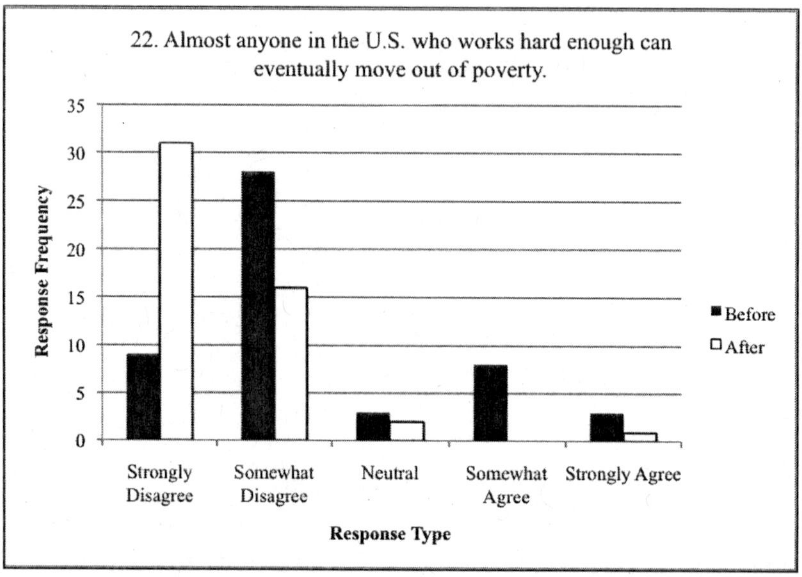
22. Almost anyone in the U.S. who works hard enough can eventually move out of poverty.
Response Frequency
35
30
25
20
15
10
5
0
Strongly Disagree
Somewhat Disagree
Neutral
Somewhat Agree
Strongly Agree
Response Type
Before
After

Mothering and Cancer

The Awakening of an Ecofeminist

HEIDI HUTNER

> The most alarming of all man's assaults upon the environment is the contamination of air, earth, rivers, and sea with dangerous and even lethal material.
>
> —Rachel Carson, *Silent Spring*

> Every time I look at you, I think, now I cannot die.
>
> —Sandra Steingraber, *Having Faith*

THE CANCER MEMOIR IS WELL known: Audre Lorde's *Cancer Diaries*, Sandra Steingraber's *Living Downstream*, Zillah Eisenstein's *Manmade Breast Cancers*, Susanne Antonetta's *Body Toxic*, and Terry Tempest Williams' *Refuge: An Unnatural History of Family and Place*, are brilliant examples of personal and feminist accounts of cancer, death and environmental degradation. These authors and narrators expose their histories as their bodies are exposed to the politics of a patriarchal world (medical, political, pharmaceutical, global, racist, heterosexist, technological). Each of these stories links cancer, feminism and disease in some way with the degradation of the environment.

The awakening of my eco-feminist consciousness occurs in the conjoining of my own cancer and mothering experiences. When I became pregnant, my concern about my own and my family's cancer history propelled me into paralytic fear. How could I protect my fetus from my own history, from my genes? In time, I began to think my cancer might be related to environmental degradation, and that my daughter's future and the future of all children would be (and is) imperiled and violated by toxic pollution. This shift from cancer orphan, to cancer patient, to mother, to environmental scholar and teacher, took place over many years. My story takes place both in and outside of the body, family, home, academia, the classroom, "nature," and the culture at large. The history of these assorted rivulets and tributaries all ultimately conjoin in an ocean of what I call an "ecological, feminist, and mothering awareness."

Let me begin here: I went back to college at age 25, after living several years in New York City as a struggling actress and singer. The pleasure I found in reading, writing and research was immense. I was a voracious reader and active personal journal writer, yet studying in a focused and scholarly way was new to me. Feminist and racial debates in my political science and anthropology classes were intellectually thrilling. My beloved professors and mentors guided and encouraged me to go to graduate school and become an English professor. I flew through and completed my undergraduate English degree, then immediately entered a doctoral in English program at the University of Washington.

In Seattle, I loved the bodies of fresh water, the tall evergreens, the mossy stone gardens, the flowers, the bike and walking paths, the many bookstores, the strong coffee, and the snow-peaked Mt. Rainier that emerged periodically above Red Square. The grey sultry days suited me just fine. My time at the University of Washington was intellectually intense, rigorous, and productive. In my first year at least, it was an exquisitely disciplined life—simple, focused, clear. It was a sublime balance of books, writing, and nature. Compared to living, studying and working in Manhattan (where I lived in a four-flight walk up, worked two jobs, and struggled to make ends meet, all the while studying for my BA), graduate school in the emerald city was a vacation. I could not believe they were *paying* me to read and write and teach, and to live in such beauty! In graduate school I found a "niche" in eighteenth-century studies, with a focus on women writers, colonial discourse, and race. Soon after the completion of my doctorate, I landed a tenure-track teaching position at Stony Brook University. My (academic) life appeared to be a great success.

However, several personal tragedies occurred during those years. At the end of my first year of graduate school, when I was twenty-nine, my father died from metastatic brain cancer related to two earlier melanoma diagnoses. One month after my father's death, my father-in-law passed away from colon cancer. A year or so later, my mother was diagnosed with lymphoma; she also had emphysema (from smoking), heart disease, and was frequently hospitalized for pneumonia. Five years after my father's death, my mother died from complications post-open heart surgery. Each of these deaths was traumatic beyond words. I had never known anyone close to me die, and to lose both of my parents at such a young age was devastating. Yet another blow came with my own cancer diagnosis one year after my mother's passing. My illness came at the tail end of my second round of job interviews and fly-backs for teaching positions.

Somewhere in between each of my parent's deaths, I married. In the early years of my marriage I wanted to have children immediately, but my (then) husband wanted to wait. My desire to be a mother consumed me. I did not need to hear the cultural, medical, and anti-feminist messages about the biological clock ticking. I heard the bell clanging loudly in my head every minute of the day. I was the kind of childless woman who passed a pregnant woman, baby carriage, or toddler, and wept. When friends became pregnant (everyone seemed to be getting pregnant), I would cry inconsolably. Losing my parents only made things worse—I wanted and needed to build my own family.

Then, at 35, I was diagnosed with the cancer—Hodgkin's Disease. The prospect of my never becoming pregnant because of the chemotherapy treatment I would undergo hit me very hard—more so than the prospect/possibility of dying. There was no time to extract eggs or freeze embryos. I was in the late stages of my disease and I had to begin treatment immediately. I made my husband promise that when the treatment was over, if I survived, we would have a baby. He agreed. I then went through six months of a grueling and debilitating chemotherapy treatment. It was, to put it mildly and succinctly, hell. I had 12 rounds of ABVD[1] every two weeks. The chemo knocked me out, and just as my body would begin to recover, the next cycle came around again. With each cycle, my body became weaker, more susceptible to the chemicals, and by the last month, I was barely able to walk. At the end of six months, I was declared cancer free. It was now time to heal.

A little over a year after my cancer diagnosis, the plan was for me to go back to work. I had accepted a tenure-track faculty position at SUNY Stony Brook (strangely, my diagnosis and job offer came simultaneously). Returning to the highly charged and competitive world of academia was scary after all I had been through. I was afraid to tell my new employers that I had been sick, for fear they would view me as unworthy or damaged. Teaching graduate seminars and large undergraduate courses for the first time would be challenging under any circumstances, but doing this so soon post-cancer was especially daunting for me. I was physically and emotionally frail.

Two years into my job at Stony Brook, at long last, I became pregnant. I hid the pregnancy from my colleagues and students for a long period of time. I feared their disapproval of my "motherhood"—as with the cancer, it seemed like anything corporeal would, in their eyes, mark me as less scholarly and lacking in commitment to "the profession." Like many women in the (academic) workplace, I feared that motherhood would diminish or mar my reputation. The general recommendation was to 'wait until you get tenure' to have a baby. I could not wait. I was old. I was a damaged cancer survivor.

Susan Griffin writes, "When we awaken, there is a child given to us. We are mothers. We feel a pain where the vulva has been cut. We are mothers. We feel the skin of the child is soft. The face to us in sleep is beautiful. The small body lying against our body is vulnerable. The cries move us.... We love this body, because we are a part of this body. We are mothers" (74). Now she was inside of me: a little fish swimming in my salty sea. Yet with that pleasure came fear about her future. I worried greatly, at first, about the genes she carried. All of her grandparents had had cancer, and only one lived through it (her paternal grandmother). Her mother was a cancer survivor. I felt guilty. What right did I have to give birth with my body, a polluted body, a damaged body that had coursed with chemicals? What right did I have to give birth to a child, when my life span was so unpredictable, when I might die *at any moment?* What right did I have to give birth to a child when I would pass along cancer genes?

How could I protect my fetus? This question sat heavily with me. At first, the only protection I could think of was my own diet during pregnancy and while nursing. So I ate only organic food, took loads of vitamins, and cut out anything processed or refined. This was not hard to do as I had changed my diet completely when I was diagnosed with cancer.

My mode of protecting my fetus through a healthy "diet" was, of course, a good one, but it was rooted (in part) in an ideology I now have trouble with. This belief system is one I came away with from New Age cancer healing approaches I had learned about from my father. My father believed that we bring cancer upon ourselves and that we hold the power to heal ourselves from any illness, be it physical or emotional. His philosophy was based in the self-healing models advocated by Louise Hay, Dr. Gerald Jampolsky, Dr. Bernard Seigal, and Norman Cousins. In the "I caused my cancer" and "I can fix my cancer by healing myself" movement, cancer functions as a private, individualized and personal issue. My problem with this belief system is that it often divides and isolates the patient and the illness from larger socio-political, economic, and environmental contexts, and lays the blame for cancer on the victim. Obviously, there are benefits to these self-help philosophies (better immediate health and well being), but I worry about the narrowness of this discourse and its potential to preclude social and political environmental activism. The laying of the responsibility for cancer (both getting and curing it) on the victim shifts the focus away from what more and more evidence shows us to be the likely cause of our cancer epidemic: toxics, chemicals, radiation, and other forms of pollution. In the view of many environmental cancer activists and scientists, *we* are sick because our environment is poisoned. Our environment is poisoned because we live in a capitalist and patriarchal system based on economic greed, domination, and the exploitation of nature (and many human beings) by a privileged few.

At some point, an alarm went off during my pregnancy, and something substantially shifted in my thinking about cancer and human health. I began to see the disease less as my own personal cross to bear and solve (something I could simply eat away), and more as a larger socio-political and ecological problem. This awakening happened one night while I was reading the book *A Civil Action.* What could be more terrifying to a pregnant female cancer survivor than a story about a cluster of children with leukemia in a town with contaminated water? At first I became terrified for my own unborn child: what if I lived in a cancer cluster like Woburn? What if, no matter how much organic broccoli I ate, the air, the soil, the water were so contaminated that this poison would enter my body anyway? What leaks and spills might be in my water and soil that remained hidden from public knowledge? My mind raced to my corporeal environmental history—what had I been exposed to during my life? Maybe my own cancer had been caused by toxic pollution?

I then read everything I could get my hands on at the time—*Silent Spring, Living Downstream, Our Stolen Future*. Later, after my daughter was born, Steingraber, whose daughter is about the same age as mine, published her book *Having Faith*. This book traces what happens to the fetus in the womb, when the mother's body is assaulted with environmental toxins and these toxins cross the placenta, and later pass from breast milk to the baby and child. I read ecofeminist theory and women's environmental history, such as Carolyn Merchant's *The Death of Nature*, and I came to understand that the exploitation of nature and the domination of women are "twin oppressions" (Warren x). Ecofeminist philosophers and historians (among others) helped me to see that cancer (and other diseases) and the degradation of the environment are integrally linked and that throughout our lives, even before we are fused as sperm and ova into embryos and fetuses, we are assaulted with toxics, chemicals, pollutants and radiation. Our bodies, all living bodies, are linked with the earth's ecosystem, and this ecosystem is polluted. Our earth is sick and so we are, too.

Cancer was the end of innocence for me, the end of safety or trust in my body, nature, life, and family. It was my exile from Eden, so to speak. My pregnancy was a moment of great change. I was happy, I was filled with life, but I was afraid: another being lived inside me. My death would be her death, and my illness would be her pain and suffering. A polluted earth would (and does) harm both of us, and all of us. *How can I protect my fetus?* This question led and leads me here. These problems drive me in my research, teaching, writing, and life. I want to be part of the 'waking up' from this fugue state of ecological unconsciousness. *A mother's womb is the earth's womb. My child is every child. I must care for my own biological child, as well as for all children, all people, all living creatures.*

The Awakening of an Ecofeminist And Mothering Consciousness in the Classroom—How It Begins:

Seven years after starting my job at Stony Brook, I received tenure. Needless to say, I breathed a tremendous sigh of relief. During my pre-tenure years, all of my scholarship and teaching had been focused on the eighteenth century—the field I had been hired to teach in. Tenure allowed me the opportunity to step back and consider my research and teaching future, to look beyond my original academic concentration to see what else might speak to me. Maybe it was time to tackle what had become so central to my life as a mother and cancer survivor: the relationship between cancer and environmental pollution? I had always been referred to in teaching observations as a "maternal" professor; now that maternal method would include bringing into the classroom a concern for the health and well-being of all living creatures.

My first attempt to shift directions was a six-week elective course on Ecofeminism that I taught in the summer of 2004. We discussed ecofeminist theoretical essays by Merchant, Warren, and Charlene Spretnak; work by Carson and Steingraber; films like *A Civil Action* and *Erin Brockavich;* and novels such as Jean Hegland's *Into the Forest*, Tempest Williams' *Refuge*, Barbara Kingsolver's *Animal Dreams*, and Jane Smiley's *A Thousand Acres*. My students (many of them first-generation college students from Long Island or New York City) had little knowledge of or interest in environmental issues before taking my class. They were shocked to hear about the connections between diseases like cancer and our poisoned earth, and many left the class frightened and despairing. Realizing that my students needed a sense of hope and strategies for confronting environmental problems, I created a semester-long course on Ecofeminism that gives students opportunities to both learn about and engage in environmental activism.

This course, which I teach yearly, draws heavily on what I've learned from both feminist and mothering theory—that "the personal is political, and the political is personal." I bring my own cancer and mothering history into the classroom, telling the story I have shared here—of my parents, of my own cancer, of my fears for my daughter. I talk about my concerns for our poisoned and degraded earth, and I name my friends, neighbors and family members who have died or who are ill and currently in cancer treatment. I talk about my birds and flower garden, and my sense of connection to the natural world. I ask my urban and suburban students to turn off their computers and cell phones and walk outside at night—to gaze at the moon and stars and listen to the sounds of nature in the dark. We take hikes in local preserves. We look at birds and plant life.

In effect, my maternal pedagogy is based on a deliberate blurring of boundaries: between the personal, the political, and the scholarly, between the environment(s) of classroom, home, natural world, and social/public space. And I am no longer the nameless professor who lectures impersonally at the blackboard—grading, judging, and imparting "higher" knowledge to empty minds. Instead, I am a cancer survivor, cancer orphan, mother, teacher, and feminist environmentalist with a passionate cause that comes from both direct personal experience and study. The destabilization of my traditional role as professor enables the students to position themselves differently as well. Students become active and highly engaged participants. They work in groups and grade and evaluate each other. They are touched by my stories, just as I/we become touched by theirs. When I enter the classroom, the chatter is so loud, the conversations so lively, that it is hard for me to interject and start the class in an official way.

Almost all the texts I assign in this cross-listed (English/Women's Studies) course address in some way the inter-connections between mothering and environmental degradation, as does the major course project.[2] Working in small groups, students conduct research on a prominent female environmentalist so they can better understand the varied ways in which women have engaged in environmental activism, and often as literal or metaphorical mothers. Through learning about activists like Winona LaDuke, Petra Kelly, Vandana Shiva, and Wangari Maathi, students become more aware of the global nature of environmental crises; they also learn that it is the world's women and children who are most negatively affected by environmental pollution and degradation—especially women and children of color and those living in poverty.[3] Most significantly, students learn that a female activist and her allies can effect enormous positive change when addressing issues of environmental injustice. Central to this group research project is urging students to find a creative and effective way of sharing their information with others; presentations have included elaborate story boards, short films, children's books, the creation of class blogs and websites, and tree-planting projects. In addition to doing class presentations for their peers, students share the results of their research at *Earthstock*, Stony Brook University's annual *Earth Day* event. By giving these presentations to both their classmates and the larger community, students become empowered environmental experts and activists, and our classroom family crosses into the public realm.

This group project also reinforces a central tenet of ecofeminist activism and ethics: that environmental healing can only come about in and through *community awareness and equitable interconnection with all living beings*. No successful environmental activist does her work alone, and true sustainability requires that we do away with the binaries of separation and division. Thus working with several peers as a team, students learn to practice an ecofeminist ethic of care. Stony Brook is a huge institution with large and often impersonal undergraduate classes. Many students live at home, commute to campus, and hold multiple jobs; as a result, their exposure to the campus community is quite limited. The group project creates a sense of community, as it demands that students connect with one another and find a way to integrate their assorted academic styles, schedules, approaches, cultures, and personal differences. It also forces students to be accountable to those around them. Through the process of working as a team, students discover how an ethic of care requires much negotiation, discussion, cooperation, and conciliation. Although occasionally tensions and disputes arise, the groups always find a way to work through these challenges to produce presentations that are impressive and inspirational.

Another significant assignment in this course is the environmental volunteer project. Working in groups, students must come up with an idea for, and then devote at least six hours to a volunteer project of their choosing. In my most recent class, one group of students worked on the *Campaign for Safe Cosmetics* (an anti-toxic body product campaign). Another group traveled to Washington, D.C. to attend Powershift, a clean energy and climate event sponsored by a coalition of fifty youth-led environmental and social justice groups. Perhaps the most notable result of this assignment was the creation of Stony Brook's organic garden by students in my first full-semester Ecofeminism class (subsequent classes have sustained the garden). Students tell me that working in the garden puts their bodies in touch with ideas encountered in class texts, fosters rich and complex conversations about course readings, and helps them grow closer to their classmates. Recently, I corresponded with Audra Vanderland, the student who spearheaded the creation of the organic garden. When I asked her what inspired her to build the organic garden, she replied:

> I think that when we read about the fact of the way things are being destroyed, it can seem really distant. When we think about the topsoil disappearing or water being polluted, it seems very far away, or out of our control.... By creating a garden, it brings all of those facts and stories into your life in a very real way. It becomes your soil that is being eroded, your seeds that are being hybridized. And yet, at the same time, you also can feel like you are, in a small way, fighting back.

Other students echo Audra's words: "I felt I was doing something good to heal the earth," writes one. Another notes that she "had great discussions about the novels while working with my class-mates, and I felt I was living out the words from our readings." A third student talks about gardening as a way of establishing a sense of community: "I became friends with new people, and I feel so connected to Stony Brook now. I'm a commuter and before this I never talked to anybody." As these comments reveal, volunteer projects like the creation of a community organic garden often bring about intense pedagogical engagement with course material and with one's peers. And, notably, a good deal of this experiential learning occurs without my being physically present; my students teach and learn from one another, and they then instruct me in essays and conversations about their projects.

It is always hard to say goodbye to my Ecofeminism students. Today, as students in my most recent class stop by my office to drop off their final assignments, they speak of how much their views of cancer, the environment, mothering, and activism have changed with the awakening of an ecofeminist consciousness. I urge them to stay in touch, to work in the garden as they wish, and to keep their bodies and skin safe from carcinogenic products. I remind them that my *Ecofeminist and Mothering Ruminations* blog is available for all to read. We also speak of our Stony Brook Ecofeminism Facebook page, which functions as a kind of ongoing virtual classroom. Through these forms of social networking, I am able to maintain long-term, mutually beneficial relationships with both current and former students. I also maintain long-term close relationships with many outside and beyond the classroom. This summer, for example, I will be traveling with several students from my spring class to a special sustainability conference—and so the classroom extends, again, beyond its traditional temporal and spatial limits.

Conclusions

I am a mother tree. My classroom is a garden, a web, an ocean, a womb—a place to think of the future—a place of hope, of precaution, of action, of waking up. Last year, I took five students to a feminist women's conference at the Omega Institute. At the end of the weekend, after a long hike, the young women gave me a precious gift: a statue of a tree/woman with her arms/branches raised high in a circle above her head. My students handed her to me and said, "This is you, Professor." Tears came to my eyes. I am honored to be the tree woman.

Some of the most profound experiences in my teaching of ecofeminism occur in the quiet moments when individual students share their own cancer stories with me. I have had many such moving moments, but there is one, in particular, that stands out. After one of my first ecofeminism classes, a young woman approached me and asked if we could speak privately. The two of us sat together outside under a blooming cherry blossom tree and, with her hands shaking, she held out a well-worn photograph. She tearfully explained that this was a picture of her mother, whom she lost several years prior to multiple myeloma (a cancer of the plasma cells). The young woman spoke softly and hesitantly to me: "I grew up in Brookhaven, right near the leaking nuclear reactor you told us about. Before this class, I had no idea about that tritium leak. None of us did. I couldn't understand why my mom died at such a young age, why so many of our neighbors died from cancer." My eyes filled with tears as she spoke. I ached for her loss—it is a loss I knew and know only too well. Then, with sad resignation, she said, "Now, I understand."

So I ache and write for the motherless girl, for the fish and the birds in the poisoned Gulf, for the rivers filled with PCBs, for the polar bears and penguins, for the forests, for the people of Japan and Fukishima and the irradiated land and sea, for the post-nuclear bomb test sites in the Nevada desert, for the children of Chernobyl, for the sick and dying soldiers and people and land poisoned with DU, for Carl, Miles, and Pinkney who have terminal cancers, for my friends Pamela and Amy just recovering from breast cancer, for the whales and dolphins, for the wolves, for the panthers, for Molly in remission from leukemia, for the spirit of my parents and many more lost (too early) loved ones, for the blind horses, and for our blue, blue planet.

As a mother, professor, writer, and cancer survivor, I dream that my work and the work of the many environmentalists and ecofeminists who inspire me will stir my students (and readers) to fight for our earth and for the lives of all living creatures. Many of my students take what they have learned in one semester and share it with many others. Some pursue careers in environmental law, environmental business, environmental activism, environmental health; some spread the word by sharing books, films, and environmental education. Some build their own gardens. My students are my seedlings. I hope to cast them, and these words, far and wide.

[1]ABVD is an acronym for the most common combination of chemotherapy drugs used to treat Hodgkin's Disease: Adriamycin, Bleomycin, Viznblastine, and Dacarbazine.

[2]In addition to those mentioned earlier, writers in the expanded version of the course include Paula Gunn Allen, Val Plummer, Linda Hogan, Octavia Butler, Margaret Atwood, Starhawk, Susanne Antonetta, Toni Morrison, Luci Topahonso, Mary Oliver, and Joy Harjo, as well as such films as

Homeland, Rachel's Daughters, Children of Men, and *Testament*.
[3]Other activists on which students have conducted research include Julia Butterfly Hill, Rachel Carson, and Lois Gibbs.

Works Cited

Carson, Rachel. *Silent Spring*. Boston and New York: Houghton Mifflin, 1962. Print.

Colborn, Theo, Diane Dumanoski, and John Peterson. *Our Stolen Future*. New York: Plume, 1997. Print.

Evans, Erina and Caroline Grant. *Mama PhD: Women Write about Motherhood and Academic Life*. New Jersey: Rutgers University Press, 2008. Print.

Griffin, Susan. *Woman and Nature: The Roaring Inside Her*. San Francisco: Sierra Club, 2000. Print.

Mason, Mary Ann and Eve Mason Ekman. *Mothers on the Fast Track: How a New Generation Can Balance Family and Careers*. New York: Oxford University Press, 2007. Print.

Merchant, Carolyn. *The Death of Nature: Women, Ecology, and the Scientific Revolution*. New York: Harper and Row, 1976. Print.

Merchant, Carolyn. *Radical Ecology: The Search for a Livable World*. New York: Routledge, 2005. Print.

Steingraber, Sandra. *Living Downstream*. New York: Vintage, 1988. Print.

Steingraber, Sandra. *Having Faith: An Ecologist's Journey to Motherhood*. New York: Berkeley Books, 2001. Print.

Warren, Karen J., ed. *Ecological Feminist Philosophies*. Bloomington: Indiana University Press, 1996. Print.

Williams, Terry Tempest. *Refuge: An Unnatural History of Family and Place*. New York: Vintage, 1991. Print.

5. Motherlines

Recording, Analyzing, and Transmitting Maternal Pedagogies

Reading Our Foremothers

Victorian and Eighteenth-Century Literary Mothers and Millennial Readers

KATHERINE ELLISON AND CYNTHIA HUFF

WITHIN THE FIRST TWENTY PAGES of Daniel Defoe's *Roxana* (1724), students are horrified: the as-yet unnamed protagonist, whose husband has left her penniless, decides that her maid must discharge her five children at the door of a relation and then "march off as fast as she cou'd" (19). If the relations cannot take them, the mother hopes that her children will be sent to Church-Wardens and provided for. How could any mother, no matter how poor, our students ask, send five small children away, especially without knowing for certain that they will be cared for? Even Roxana's grief over this decision does not gain student sympathy, perhaps because she describes in some detail the dire fate that may await her children. Roxana relates that she "was at first, sadly afflicted at the Thoughts of parting with my Children, and especially at that terrible thing, their being taken into the Parish-keeping . . . a hundred terrible things came into my Thoughts; *viz.* of Parish-Children being Starv'd at Nurse; of their being ruin'd, let grow crooked, lam'd, and the like, for want of being taken care of" (19). All of these possibilities "sunk my very Heart within me," Roxana narrates (19).

Our students are not swayed to pity Roxana because she fears for the safety of her children. Rather, they are even more disturbed that Roxana can imagine their starvation, illness, and corruption and still leave them and, just a few pages later, they are appalled that her feelings of fear and sadness seem so fleeting. Roxana announces that "my own Circumstances hardened my Heart against my own Flesh and Blood" and "I began to be reconcil'd to parting with them all, anyhow, and anywhere, that I might be freed from the dreadful Necessity of seeing them all perish" (19). The hardened mother Roxana becomes in Defoe's narrative only confirms most twenty-first-century students' conviction that Roxana is a horrible fictional mother, a villain who deserves absolutely no sympathy. Significantly, most students do not dwell on Roxana's certainty that she would have had the "dreadful" experience of "seeing them all perish" if she had chosen to keep her children with no means to support them.

That literature majors and non-majors alike at Illinois State University express such outrage over the "bad mothers" they encounter in eighteenth-century novels like *Roxana* is certainly a good sign that they are engaged with the readings. Yet the obstacle in teaching a number of novels from the period is that student pathos about mothering can become an obstacle to their gaining a critical understanding of how mothering functioned historically, ideologically, and narratively three hundred years ago. In fact, eighteenth-century fictional mothers catalyze in some students such strong feelings of anger and disgust that these students start hating an entire century of literature. At our predominantly middle-class, Caucasian, Midwestern university, it does not seem to matter whether students come from families in which they were parented by single mothers, single fathers, heterosexual couples, GLBT parents, or white, nonwhite or multiracial parents. While students of "othermothering" backgrounds are often more self-reflective and personally affected in their reactions, they, too, tend to immediately and unequivocally condemn Roxana and other "bad" mothers found in eighteenth-century texts.

Some of our students later take a course in nineteenth-century British literature, and these students respond quite differently—and much more positively—to the mothers they encounter in Victorian novels. Why? We argue that as they read both eighteenth- and nineteenth-century literary texts, most of today's students uncritically and unconsciously endorse the dominant Victorian discourse about mothers and mothering: the notion that mothering comes naturally to females and is enacted through the constant nurturing of others. Students read through this filter of the "angelic Victorian mother," we believe, because that paradigm continues to be perpetuated through the novel, a form with more political and social influence than today's students understand because of their impulse to de-politicize literature. One of our central pedagogical goals is to make visible to our students the fact that the concepts of good and bad mothering change over time and are constructed through the rhetorical complexities of both social and literary narratives.

As teachers of mothering in the context of these two centuries of literary history, we have three goals. Our first goal is to make students aware of their tendency to endorse the Western, nationally promoted notion of mothering that originated during the Victorian period and help them recognize the ubiquitous presence of this "ideal" in contemporary mainstream culture. As evidenced by responses to eighteenth-century narratives even by students who are not heterosexual, white, or middle class, millennials in our classrooms who are evaluating literary mothers generally employ a definition of "good" mothering that resembles a Victorian model of the "angelic woman" who selflessly devotes her life to her children and husband. In other words, we want to make our students aware of the danger of uncritically reading history and literature through a politically constructed domestic narrative that has little basis in the actual everyday lives of the women of a specific period and nation. Our second goal is to help students realize that mothering *has* a history often in conflict with the Victorian model. In other words, the iconic norm was not necessarily real—it may well have been a fantasy. We strive to teach students to resist *any* model of ideal mothering and to instead regard mothering as an act or state, as a dynamic cultural *narrative* constructed by a generation. And finally, our third goal is to help students see the extent to which the figure of mother (angelic or devilish) is a narrative pivot in the novel as a genre. For teachers of literature, the challenge is not just teaching millennial students that mothering has a history but showing them that its history is tangled in genre. In our classrooms, we provide examples of how the novel as a genre has itself always engaged in maternal pedagogy.

Crucial in the development of the novel form as it became a commercial force between the eighteenth and nineteenth centuries is the figure of the mother. The difference between eighteenth- and nineteenth-century depictions of mothering is not that "bad" mother characters prevail in the earlier period and "good" mothers a hundred years later, but that eighteenth-century and Victorian writers were operating within cultures with different political narratives of maternal responsibility. The Victorian ideal of the mother, familiar to students today, was of a caring, nurturing, unconditionally loving married woman at the center of a successful family and, even more importantly, a successful nation. Earlier eighteenth-century rhetoricians, in contrast, aligned motherhood with female irrationality and emotional instability and used this correlation to explain women's acts of political and social rebellion. The nineteenth-century novels that depict bad mothering are not as disturbing for millennial students because the offspring are still supported by a family or community that demonstrates the cohesive ideological structure that students, whether consciously or not, recognize and tend to embrace. Students worry about the fate of eighteenth-century children left on the doorstep and condemn the mothers who do not return for them because these texts do *not* suggest that nurturing comes naturally to women, nor do they imply that nurturing is widespread and highly valued by the culture. When they read novels written a hundred years later, however, they enter narrative worlds that suggest that children left on a doorstep might well be provided for and nurtured by persons who can serve as surrogates for the "bad" biological mother.

Roxana's motherhood is at once a reflection of and challenge to eighteenth-century theories of maternal irrationality and at the center of the work's generic identification as a novel, a new and inventive type of literary text with great marketability. Narratively, Roxana's abandonment of her children and thus the erasure of her position as mother essentially grants Roxana the liberty to engage in more romantic intrigues, but with the formal realism that Ian Watt famously declared the key to the novel's structure (Watt 32). With children in Roxana's personal history but without them intervening as constant narrative burdens, Roxana can travel the world, become romantically involved with many different kinds of men, and hoard her fortune. Without children, she can attempt to operate outside the oppressive regime of the patriarchy. Such a pursuit of independence, in our students' eyes, is in conflict with her maternity but the perfect recipe for a suspenseful, interactive novel, since they believe that once she is financially independent the first thing she should do is reclaim her children. To them she is selfish and irrational and should, in the end, be punished for putting herself first even though she does check on the wellbeing of her children from afar and even assists one of them anonymously. Students feel vindicated when Defoe brings one of the daughters, now grown, back into the narrative just as the reader assumes Roxana will live a happy life without maternal responsibility. Her daughter, Susan, suspects Roxana is her mother, and thus pursues Roxana until Roxana's loyal servant, Amy, murders Susan to protect Roxana's true identity. Julie Crane notes that "the unsettling account of Roxana's daughter's longing for her mother, for human affection, the need for parental acknowledgement, swamps the narrative" (24). Even though, in the end, Roxana's decision to give up her first five children turns out to have been a logical and not an irrational choice, and even though she later does try to provide anonymous support for at least two of them (Susan and one of her sons), millenial readers cannot understand why Roxana denies her daughter the affection and nurturance they believe is a child's natural right. That the drama ends in Susan's murder, which Roxana did not ask for and is furious about, is less baffling to students than her refusal to embrace Susan when she meets her.

Even when mothers do provide parental guidance in eighteenth-century novels, our students are disgusted by the nature of the instruction and think the mothers are selfish, which they easily equate with irrationality. When Eliza Haywood responded to Samuel Richardson's bestseller, *Pamela; or, Virtue Rewarded* (1740), by publishing *Anti-Pamela; or, Feign'd Innocence Detected* (1741), she inserts a mother in the narrative who, unlike Roxana, maintains a close relationship with her child. Haywood's dynamic mother-daughter duo of Ann and Syrena Tricksy shocks students in a new way. Ann teaches her daughter, Syrena, how to manipulate men to secure their fortunes and even how to induce an abortion by drinking a toxic herb. It takes several discussions for students to begin to realize that Ann Tricksy, like Roxana, is working within an oppressive culture in which women, particularly those in the working classes, must find entrepreneurial means to support themselves and control their own futures. Throughout the narrative, both women are demonized by students for the same behaviors that are viewed as typical, harmless, and even admirable when demonstrated by the male characters. Many of our students pity the men who fall prey to the Tricksys and cheer when the team is foiled in the end.

Novels about mothers like Roxana and Ann Tricksy sold copies not only because they were entertaining, but also because, on the surface, the fictional mothers' behavior seemed to reinforce contemporary scientific and psychological discourse about the impact pregnancy and motherhood had on the female mind. Students do not realize how effortlessly they begin to subscribe to this rhetoric as they discuss Roxana's motives and assert that she acts without reason. Ann Tricksy, too, seems to them at first to be crazy. They miss the fact that these two novels critique both patriarchal intervention in maternity and patriarchal definitions of the good mother; instead, students initially view these "monstrous" fictional mothers through the lens of "Victorian" definitions of proper mothering. But upon further discussion, our students come to realize that what bothers them most about these mothers it that they are *too* reasonable and rational;

they make their decisions based not on emotional impulse or a conscious desire to rebel but on a thoughtful, logical sense of what will be best for their children. Ann Tricksy does not *want* her daughter Syrena to become pregnant out of wedlock or to sleep with every man she meets; Ann offers Syrena a very clear life plan that she constantly revises as her daughter makes mistakes. Roxana's lack of emotion when she gives up her young children, and her decision not to find them later in life because she fears their retribution, disturbs them even as they admire her reasoning when she becomes wealthy by investing her money. A feminist analysis of these novels shows students how quickly they and other readers judge mothers, how they hold a woman's maternal responsibilities to a different standard of rationality than they do the woman's financial or political responsibilities, and how easily they repeat rhetoric that in theory they oppose.

Whereas many eighteenth-century novels test and challenge the prevailing scientific theories that pregnancy and maternity make women mad, many nineteenth-century novels contest the construction of woman as moral savior and as the centerpoint of the ethos of domesticity. The idea of the mother/woman as caring, compassionate, and morally corrective was a pervasive social value, a crucial trope in building what Benedict Arnold calls the imagined community—an imagined community not only of Victorian England but of the Western Anglophone empire as well. As Elizabeth Langland points out, popular and influential texts like Sarah Lewis' *Woman's Mission* (1839) and Coventry Patmore's *The Angel in the House* (1854-62) promoted an ideology in which women, and especially mothers, were deemed "the moral regenerator of mankind," possessing "a nature characterized by nurture, compassion, and a humanized community" (382).

But the Victorian novel did more than simply deliver sanitized versions of *The Angel in the House.* Such simplistic promotion would not appeal to a widening readership, especially to more and more women readers who could compare their own experiences with those of fictional women (see Altick). The elements of iconic motherhood—"nurture, compassion, and a humanized community"—were abstracted and disembodied in a national domestic ideology and could be resisted and represented in a variety of fictional modes and in characters who were not technically mothers or who might not even be women. Expecting characters in Victorian fiction who "stand for" easily recognizable cultural norms, millennial students are often challenged by the nuances of this persistent domestic ideology.

In an effort to answer why a Victorian ideological model of mothering so persistently molds student response, our next litmus case is *Wuthering Heights*, a Victorian novel popular with students in which biological mothers are notoriously absent and mothering is instead performed by surrogates. Beginning with the scene where Mr. Earnshaw brings home the dark orphan Heathcliff to live with his family, the role of biological mothers in the family economy is called into question. Nelly Dean relates the story of Heathcliff's introduction by Mr. Earnshaw to the Earnshaw family thus:

> We crowded round ... I had a peep at a dirty, ragged, black-haired child; big enough to walk and talk ... it only stared round, and repeated over and over again some gibberish that nobody could understand. I was frightened and Mrs. Earnshaw was ready to fling it out of doors: she did fly up—asking how he could fashion to bring that gipsy brat into the house, when they had their own bairns to feed, and fend for? What he meant to do with it, and whether he were mad? (Brontë 51)

Because Mrs. Earnshaw's reaction to Heathcliff excludes the interloper and thus is not properly "maternal," it is not surprising that she dies; she has to be excised from the narrative so that a re-imagining of the Victorian family can take place. The Victorian novel, with its emphasis on domesticity and the marriage plot, is a perfect vehicle for this reimagining as it functioned as a way to expand the concept of the family by making outsiders principal players in its narratives and thus re-envisioning mothering as an ideologically powerful and seemingly universal phenomenon. Initially, students have mixed responses to the child Heathcliff, pitying him because he is an orphan yet seeing him as usurping Mr. Earnshaw's affection for his biological children. Only after discussion do they understand that this pivotal scene helps Emily Brontë expand the concept of mothering to include surrogates.

Mrs. Earnshaw reacts to Heathcliff by naming him Other and concluding that her husband must be mad and economically irresponsible to bring "it" into the family circle. Although the faithful servant, Nelly Dean, initially echoes Mrs. Earnshaw's estimate of Heathcliff's danger, soon after this she nurtures him. By eliciting mothering from Nelly, Heathcliff works his way into the Earnshaw family, subverting any narrow biological definition of family as well as challenging prevailing conceptions of motherhood, lady, and gentleman—all shibboleths of Victorian culture that students need to be aware of.

Just as in eighteenth-century novels, in which mothers either give up their children, die prematurely before or at the beginning of the narrative, or like Ann Tricksy, offer maternal wisdom that is quickly ignored, it is axiomatic that numerous fictional Victorian children are biologically motherless. Catherine Earnshaw is no exception. Her biological mother is quickly replaced in the narrative world by her servant mother, Nelly Dean, who gives Catherine what advice she can even though Nelly can no more control Catherine than she can her other "wild child," Heathcliff. When Catherine returns from Thrushcross Grange her new social status separates her from Heathcliff, and Nelly tries to repair Heathcliff's self-esteem and self-presentation by weaving a story of his origins (67). In her role as Heathcliff's surrogate mother Nelly legitimates his place within the Earnshaw family, fosters Heathcliff's belief in himself as Catherine's rightful lover, and subverts any narrow definition of the British Victorian family by insinuating that the dark Other without discernible origins may have more value than a fair child whose line of succession can be validated. Nelly has done what mothers, biological or surrogate, are expected to do—save their children from embarrassment and low self-esteem.

In other portions of *Wuthering Heights*, Brontë lets us hear the voice of the othered child. In Heathcliff's story of revenge, the subaltern is allowed to speak and to expose cracks in any narrowly defined Victorian family edifice. Heathcliff's actions facilitate a devastating critique of a self-absorbed and insulated Victorian family, the Earnshaws: when he returns to Wuthering Heights, he goads the already dissipated patriarch, Hindley, into further self-destruction. Hindley's fall symbolizes the decay of a tight family structure that is bent on closing itself off from the outside world and is unable to envision and put into play alternative ways of familial living.

Heathcliff, by shattering a traditional, oedipal, paternalistic family model, paradoxically creates a new role for himself in relation to Catherine, a role some psychoanalytic critics see as maternal. The idea that the cold, hard Heathcliff, especially in his relationship to Catherine, could be viewed as a preoedipal, maternal alternative to the patriarchal family symbolized by Hindley is the hardest for our student readers to accept, at least initially, as it provides the most extreme case of alternative mothering in *Wuthering Heights*. Millennial students begin to see the caring side of Heathcliff only after they are exposed to psychoanalytic interpretations of Heathcliff as maternal, such as those of Michelle Massé and Philip Wion, who see, respectively, Catherine's relation with Heathcliff as evidencing her oedipal feelings toward her father, and Nelly as a mother figure when she provides food and drink but acting as a bad mother when she fails to do Catherine's bidding. Twenty-first century students often test these new perspectives by re-imagining the central scene in *Wuthering Heights* where Heathcliff overhears that Catherine intends to marry Edgar. When Catherine utters "Nelly, I *am* Heathcliff—he's always, always in my mind—as my own being—so don't talk of our separation again" (88), she succinctly identifies the preoedipal, maternal world she shares with Heathcliff before individuation and the law of the father replace the oneness between child and mother, since according to this psychoanalytic interpretation Heathcliff mothers Catherine in their preoedipal world. Nelly, in contradistinction to her usual role of nurturing mother, attempts to reason with Catherine in this scene by catechizing her love for Edgar and goading Catherine to consider marriage as a future commitment, not just a present desire. By doing so Nelly embodies reason and the law of the father, and thus is interpreted by Catherine as a bad mother. In other words, in serving as both good and bad mother in *Wuthering Heights*, Nelly locates rapidly shifting and conflicting role designations within the Victorian family economy, a historical situation that we need to make students aware of. In two very different ways, Brontë subverts the dominant view that a mother—or at least a good mother—is an always nurturing [and female] angel in the house who is biologically related to her child, thereby creating a more inclusive and far-reaching concept of motherhood that many millennial students come to embrace.

As Virginia Woolf so trenchantly reminds us, the idealization of the angel in the house was a Victorian fiction that trammeled flesh and blood women and was impossible to attain, or sustain, within the daily intricacies of family life. This, too, is the lesson of Emily Brontë's *Wuthering Heights*. There are no female angels in the houses of either Wuthering Heights or the Grange, no perfect fictional creatures whose function is to prop up a failed patriarchy. Instead, the novel shows us families in which the emperor has no clothes, where either the patriarchs have descended into debauchery (Hindley) or are ineffectual (Edgar).

However, novels like *Wuthering Heights*—in which biological mothers are replaced with nurturing surrogates—can reinforce as well as challenge patriarchal views. Although the novel dismantles the "ideal" nuclear family, it simultaneously reinforces the notion that all children have the right to a caring, nurturing mother figure, even if that figure is not a biological mother or even a female. Twenty-first century students, raised according to a Victorian ideology of nurturing motherhood and the Victorian invention of the cult of childhood, expect as their birthright caring mothering. If mothers, either biological or surrogate, are not omnipresent and all-caring then they must be replaced or dismissed; if mothers at times fail to be omnipresent and all-caring, then they are labeled bad. This basically sums up initial student reaction to *Wuthering Heights*, which at first students find to be a dark, depressing novel of a motherless family's dysfunctionality. After some discussion, though, students begin to see Nelly Dean as a mother figure because she cares for virtually every character in the novel. They have a harder time seeing Heathcliff as maternal because for them his desire for revenge overshadows any love he has for Catherine Earnshaw. Nudging students to see how Heathcliff's position as the subaltern affects his actions helps them consider him as more complex and even caring.

Our challenge is to teach students that mothering is a historically embedded concept and that their idea of motherhood as caring is a powerful ideology that informs their reading and is narratively—particularly through the novel form—and culturally reinforced daily. This involves calling into question the idea of mothering as *natural* by interrogating the concept of nature as itself culturally constructed. It also involves juxtaposing eighteenth-century associations of mothering with irrationality and unreasonableness to nineteenth-century associations of mothering with compassion and moral certitude. Teaching these cultural constructions not only causes students to question the potent ideology of the caring mother but also nudges them toward understanding that all concepts have a history and that to better understand their own generation's cultural assumptions about motherhood, they need to be aware of that history, its social and cultural location, and the tenacious persistence of Victorian definitions of the "good" mother. "I wanted to examine motherhood," Adrienne Rich writes in her "Introduction" to the second edition of *Of Woman Born: Motherhood as Experience and Institution*, "in a social context, as embedded in a political institution" (ix). We ask our students to take the same journey, to see in the literary mothers—good, bad, or absent—of eighteenth- and nineteenth-century novels the complexities and contestations of motherhood, recognizing these characters as pieces of what Rich calls "this immense half-buried mosaic in the shape of a woman's face" (17).

Works Cited

Altick, Richard D. *The English Common Reader: A Social History of the Mass Reading Public, 1800-1900.* Chicago: University of Chicago Press, 1957. Print.

Brontë, Emily. *Wuthering Heights.* Ed. Linda H. Peterson. 2nd ed. Boston: Bedford/St. Martin's, 2003. Print.

Burke, Meghan L. "Making Mother Obsolete: Eliza Fenwick's *Secresy* and the Masculine Appropriation of Maternity" *Eighteenth-Century Fiction* 21.3 (Spring 2009): 357-384. Print.

Crane, Julie. "Defoe's *Roxana*: The Making and Unmaking of a Heroine." *Modern Language Review* 102 (2007): 11-25. Print.

Davis, Lennard J. *Factual Fictions: The Origins of the English Novel.* Philadelphia: University of Pennsylvania Press, 1983. Print.

Defoe, Daniel. *Roxana: The Fortunate Mistress.* 1724. Ed. John Mullan. Oxford: Oxford University Press, 2008. Print.

Haywood, Eliza. *Anti-Pamela; or, Feign'd Innocence Detected* in *Anti-Pamela; or, Feign'd Innocence Detected by Eliza Haywood and Shamela by Henry Fielding.* Ed. Catherine Ingrassia. Toronto: Broadview, 2004. 51-227. Print.

Haywood, Eliza. *Fantomina* (1725). *Popular Fiction by Women 1660-1730.* Ed. Paula R. Backscheider and John J. Richetti. Oxford: Oxford University Press, 1996. 227-248. Print.

Langland, Elizabeth. "Patriarchal Ideology and Marginal Motherhood in Victorian Novels by Women." *Studies in the Novel* 19.3 (1987): 381-94. Print.

Massé, Michelle A. "'He's More Myself Than I Am': Narcissism and Gender in *Wuthering Heights.*" *Psychoanalyses/Feminisms.* Ed. Peter L. Rudnytsky and Andrew M. Gordon. Albany: State University of New York Press, 2000. 135-153. Print.

Rich, Adrienne. *Of Woman Born: Motherhood as Experience and Institution.* New York: Norton, 1986. Print.

Todd, Dennis. *Imagining Monsters: Miscreations of the Self in Eighteenth-*

Century England. Chicago: University of Chicago Press, 1995. Print.

Watt, Ian. *The Rise of the Novel: Studies in Defoe, Richardson, and Fielding.* Berkeley: University of California Press, 1957. Print.

Wion, Philip K. "The Absent Mother in Emily Brönte's *Wuthering Heights.*" *American Imago: Studies in Psychoanalysis and Culture* 42.2 (1985): 143-164. Print.

Aboriginal Single Mother Students

Teaching the Next Generation(s) by Example

MARLENE POMRENKE

> It can be done. We have to think about the seven generations ahead of us. Once we find that pride within ourselves we find our will and ability to succeed.
>
> —Research Participant

MOTHERHOOD, AS A SINGLE OR lone mother, represents an enormous undertaking. Without the support of a co-parent, or strong support system, the many roles of parenting can present challenges and stressful family situations. Single mothers are still often viewed as a marginalized population in Canadian society. However, family structures have changed over the last three decades, with a growing proportion of mothers taking on sole responsibility for raising their children. According to the Census, in 2006 15.9 per cent of families in Canada were headed by "lone parents"—the term the government uses when referring to a female parent who has one or more children living with her (Statistics Canada). If statistics gathered in Winnipeg, Manitoba are typical of the country as a whole, the number of Canadian lone-parent families appears to be growing, while the number of two-parent families is declining (Silver). The most recent government statistics state that Manitoba has 42,930 lone-parent families (Statistics Canada). Even though many lone parents/single mothers fulfill their parenting responsibilities while attending school and/or working full- or part-time in the paid labor force, they and their families tend to experience more poverty and economic disadvantages than two-parent families. Aboriginal single mothers often have additional barriers to overcome, including higher than usual rates of unemployment and poverty, feelings of isolation, social discrimination, and a lack of preparation for the post-secondary education system. This chapter identifies the factors that motivate one particular group of Aboriginal single mothers to attend, stay in, or return to school, as well as draws attention to the resources that the student mothers believe to be key to their success. The chapter concludes with a discussion of pedagogical strategies these mothers employ to communicate with their children what they have learned about overcoming the barriers faced by many Aboriginal single mother students.

To help address socio-economic inequities, Aboriginal people have attempted to increase their level of education over the years. Yet university education completion rates amongst Aboriginal peoples remain low (Hull; Mendelson). Furthermore, by comparison with non-Aboriginal single mothers, Aboriginal single mothers have significantly lower rates of enrollment and completion at university (Multest). This may help explain the economic gap evidenced by the average income of Aboriginal women, which is approximately 72 percent of that earned by non-Aboriginal women (Indian and Northern Affairs, Canada).

Employing a resilience framework offers a meaningful way to understand how people adapt to stressful life situations. Resilience is defined as the capacity to navigate towards health-sustaining, culturally relevant resources during times of psychological or environmental adversity (Ungar). Jo Boyden and Gillian Mann also suggest that resilience is negotiated discursively, as it is influenced by the culture and context in which it is formed. Therefore, to fully engage the concept of resilience, issues concerning culture and gender need to be addressed, as we consider various external and internal support systems for Aboriginal single mothers.

Pedagogy is another term that needs to be viewed through a cultural lens when considering how Aboriginal single mothers in university use support mechanisms. This is particularly important as the history of forced residential schooling continues to have an impact on First Nation and Aboriginal people's experiences with and pursuit of education. Past injustices, caused by systemic racism and forced assimilation, have made it difficult for Aboriginal people to be part of mainstream post-secondary institutions (Spence, White, and Maxim).

It is in the context of culture, gender, and resiliency that I conducted a study exploring how Aboriginal single mothers utilize various resources to succeed as students in a university setting, then pass this knowledge on to their children. I discovered that the factor that most motivated these women to enroll in or return to post-secondary educational programs was their desire, as mothers, to make short and long-term improvements in their children's lives. The study demonstrated that to be successful university students, Aboriginal single mothers must discover and utilize a variety of both external and internal resources. Finally (and most importantly for the purposes of this collection), I discovered that these Aboriginal single mother students had a strong desire to not only impress upon their children the importance of obtaining post-secondary education, but also to teach their children about resources the children could use when following in their mother's footsteps. In their role as teachers, the mothers employed two major pedagogical strategies: they served as role models, teaching by example, and they honestly and openly discussed with their children the difficulties of meeting the ambitious goals they had set for themselves. The results of this study enhance our understanding and appreciation of the coping strategies and strengths of Aboriginal single mother students, as well as provide us with a picture of how they transform family norms by modeling—and discussing with their children—the road to a better life.

Research Process

The research study sought to answer questions related to how Aboriginal single mothers cope with the multiple demands of parenting, university studies, employment/economic needs and other daily tasks. Issues connected to gender, motherhood and cultural diversity were also explored. It became apparent throughout the research process that many of these women exhibited a great deal of courage and fortitude, often in the face of great adversity.

Over a five-month period, between March and July of 2009, twenty women attending the University of Manitoba, the University of Winnipeg, and Red River College participated in face-to-face interviews. Six of these women also took part in a focus group at a later date, two months after the interviews were completed. The participants were all mothers raising their biological children and ranged in age from 19 to 38. The children's ages ranged from infancy to young adulthood. Most of the women were completing undergraduate degrees in social work, education, business, or the arts. Two women were students in the faculty of law and another was beginning her graduate degree in a different faculty. One woman had completed an arts degree at an earlier life stage, and was currently enrolled at a community college completing her early childhood education diploma. Thirteen out of the twenty women were either the first in their family to attend university, or the first to graduate from a post-secondary institution. The majority of these women received no child support. They financed themselves through social assistance, the ACCESS program (a university-sponsored program through the University of Manitoba offering financial, academic and personal support), part-time employment, student loans and/or bursaries, Band financing, and/or savings from previous employment. If a woman has Aboriginal status she may qualify to receive financial aid from her Band. However, some of the women spoke about funds not being available to them through this source due to scarce resources on the reserve or their post-secondary education not being seen by the Council members of the Band as a priority.

Qualitative research, specifically the grounded theory approach, focuses on understanding the research participants' interpretation of experiences (Creswell). In my research I used a grounded theory methodology, which relies heavily on interviews with participants to provide information gained within a naturalistic setting, in this case, the family and community. Open-ended questions were used as a way of exploring the research questions. The questions ranged from obtaining information about demographics, childcare and financial arrangements to discussing the impact of gender, culture, support systems and career planning.

Grounded theory also relies on bits of data being organized based on commonalities, similarities, interrelatedness and connectedness (Kirby et al.). Data analysis consisted of finding recurrent themes or issues in the data and subsequently developing or refining a theory about each phenomenon. The major themes arising in this study include lack of financial support, limited involvement by the fathers, the importance of social support networks, and the participants' desire to improve life circumstances as a way to provide a better socio-economic climate for their children.

The final component of data collection was obtained through the facilitation of a focus group, which had two functions. Focus groups generally provide a form of member-checking, a way to ensure reliability in the study. Member-checking ensures that previously collected data is organized and understood as the participants intended through previous discussion from individual interviews. Focus groups also allow for clarification and for the collection of additional information. The information acquired through this focus group brought additional insight into the above-mentioned themes. As well, a critical piece of information was gained with respect to 'outsider-insider' research (Dwyer and Buckle). Focus group members discussed the impact of research on Aboriginal Peoples conducted by non-Aboriginal researchers. They were pleased that this issue was examined and hopeful that the outcomes of this research could bring changes in how policy was implemented in this area. However, the trust in non-Aboriginal researchers was limited due to not having the same lived experiences.

The phrase "paradigm model" is used in conjunction with grounded theory methodology (Strauss and Corbin). John Creswell defines this model as a "coding paradigm" or "logic diagram" that visually portrays the organization of the data. In this study, the "Context," i.e., broad conditions that influence the strategies (Aboriginal single mothers pursuing post-secondary studies) influence the "Causal conditions," i.e., categories of conditions (Family challenges) that influence the phenomenon with specific "Action/Interaction Strategies," (External and Internal support systems). Finally, a central category is identified and the "Phenomenon" (Strengths of these mothers) is revealed. An illustration of this coding paradigm appears later in this essay.

External Resources

The mothers spoke about external resources that had aided them, either as an impetus to begin their university studies and/or to help them complete their degree. As one woman stated, "Without my supports I wouldn't still be in university." External support systems for these women included community groups and/or agencies, study groups/student peers, Aboriginal ceremonies, counselors from ACCESS programs, mentors, Aboriginal parent support groups, food banks, an Aboriginal Student Centre, instructors and/or faculty advisors, family members, friends, daycare staff and children's teachers, Elders, tutors, and a "Higher Power." These resources provided mothers with support on a number of levels. At times practical support, in the form of caregiving of the children by roommates and/or family members, allowed mothers to find time to complete school work. For example, a grandmother moved in with one mother and her children during the final year of studies in order to provide the woman with respite from childcare responsibilities. Other external resources, such as Elders and faculty advisors, provided guidance, while friends, counselors, and parent support groups offered emotional support. These support systems helped the women deal with the stresses inherent in being part of academe, and showed them how to apply their new-found coping mechanisms to other parts of their lives. For example, single-parent support groups helped some of these women find resources, such as daycare or respite care, and provided valuable emotional support, particularly to those parenting children with behavioral or emotional challenges.

Internal Resources

Building and/or finding internal resources or interpersonal strengths (Anderson, Cowger and Snively) motivated mothers to begin their university studies and/or complete them. Self-efficacy and an internal drive to succeed appeared to be the most prevalent ways of coping that were utilized by these women. The following statements provide examples:

> I just keep thinking I know I can do this, I tell myself that and it is easy. I do a lot of self-talk.

> Just try and don't give up on what you want. Find that motivation and determination to get through it all.

Integrating internal and external support systems helped these mothers to find strengths from within as well as from outside. For example, one mother stated, "I find my motivation to succeed from inside myself. Then I talk to other classmates and they give me suggestions and feedback, which helps out a lot." Another woman stated, "Use whatever resources are available from within and don't be afraid to ask for help."

Culture-based ideals were also identified as motivators. Some were seen as challenges while others offered ways to understand how to utilize strengths. One woman stated, "Pride in Aboriginal culture gives me strength. I know getting an education will break the cycle of poverty." Finding the internal and external resources to surmount cultural barriers was sometimes difficult for these mothers. One mother stated,

> At university even the way English is spoken is different from res.... I didn't have the study skills necessary to do the work, they are not taught at the res.... You have to learn to discipline yourself. I also had to find resources through the Learning Assistance Centre at the University to help me figure out how to write papers. It's a

> balance of making sure you can still have a social life, spend time with your family and complete your schoolwork.

Other women talked about the importance of guidance from Elders and how they use Aboriginal teachings. One woman stated, "I speak with an Elder who works at the University on a regular basis. He shows me ways to use my gifts."

Resiliency: Navigating Towards Resources and Finding Strengths

While this study focused on the experiences, views and goals of Aboriginal single mothers, it also reflects the inherent resilience of these women. Understanding the external and internal resources utilized by these women moves us towards understanding the interrelationship of these concepts. An example of this is seen in the following narrative from one of the mothers:

> It's recognizing how much we have to endure as single parents of Aboriginal descent to take that step and better ourselves. It's a much different road than a non-Aboriginal person; we do things different, I don't think we are less than, we just came from a different system so therefore we face more challenges. I think that we try to adapt to a non-Aboriginal mainstream society and it's a bit more difficult for us. So there are a lot of things that we will experience along the way and we may try a few times, like for myself this is my third time trying university and it takes a lot of growth, it takes a lot of confidence because not only are we a marginalized group we are Aboriginal women. This leaves us with more walls to climb. We hope we can be known as the women that are keeping the home fires burning and building our families into something different and better. We need to use our determination and outside supports to help us find our way.

Lerner and Benson discuss the relationship of positive coping skills and resilience in conjunction with finding both internal and external resources. These women showed how their ability to access both internal and external resources helped to sustain their motivation to succeed in their post-secondary studies and thereby improve their family's future. Processing the data in the form of a paradigm (as seen on page 191) allows us to visualize how these women are transformed by their role as both mother and university student and, in turn, transform their extended family norms as a result of these experiences.

Family has always been implicitly and explicitly recognized as a critical social unit for the mediation of cultural beliefs and practices (McCubbin et al). This research provides data conducive to inductive theory-building, linking external and internal resources to cultural support systems and identifying ways in which these families respond to and cope with life's traumas and transitions. A proposition or hypothesis integrating the categories outlined in the coding paradigm suggests the following. Strong external and internal support systems allow Aboriginal single mothers pursuing post-secondary education to utilize their resilient attributes. Improving their children's short- and long-term futures is the women's major motivation to succeed. Their internal resiliency (as manifested, for example, in determination and self-efficacy) shows their children the value and importance of post-secondary education, and their honest discussions of the challenges they face teaches the children about obstacles they themselves may face—and ways to overcome these obstacles.

Discussion: Maternal Pedagogies Practiced by these Aboriginal Single Mothers

The results of this study suggest that these women used their role as mothers to transform the way in which their family may face the future. As one woman stated,

> Going back to school felt like it would be a good way to provide financial security for my children. So in the beginning my children were the main reason why I had to make better choices, but, in the end as I start to come closer to graduation I realize that the education is for all of us, we will all benefit from it.

Finding the courage to change family norms associated with poverty, substance abuse, and societal conflict challenged these women to build and utilize internal and external resources to complete their university studies. Accessing their internal resilient attributes of self-efficacy and self-confidence allowed them to enroll in a post-secondary institution and

Coding Paradigm

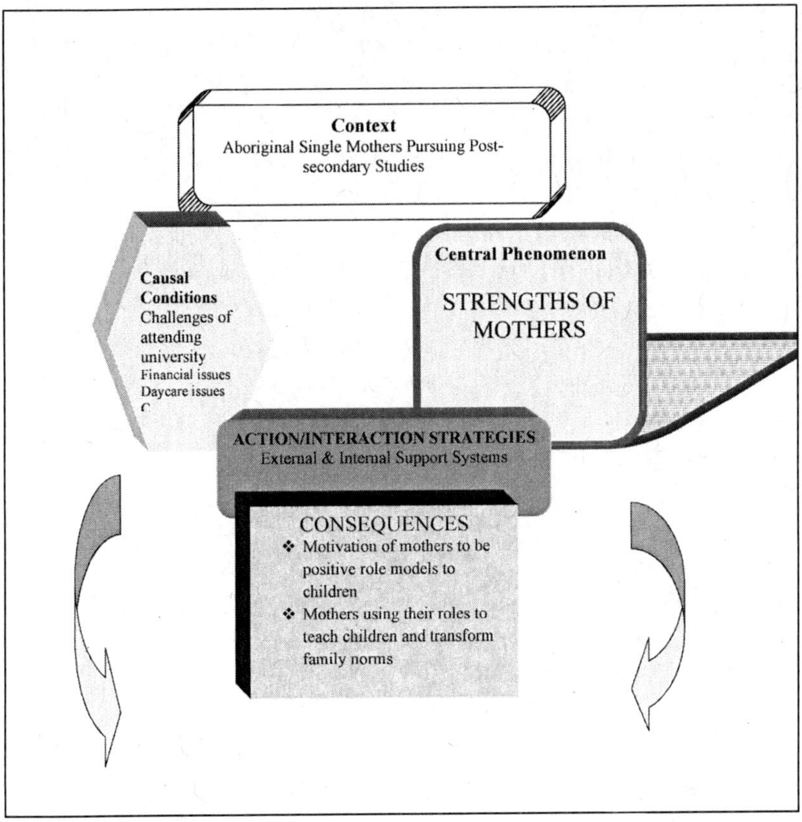

continue with their educational journey. Teaching their children alternative ways of viewing the world further energized and validated their efforts to complete their university education. As one woman stated, "In order for my children to succeed, I need to succeed."

Pedagogy appears to be both inherent and transformative to both the mothers and the children. One of the mothers stated, "The main reason I chose to enter into post-secondary studies was to be able to make better choices and show my children how we will benefit from these choices." Many of the mothers spoke of entering into post-secondary studies because they wanted to be better role models for their children. They actively chose different paths from other family members to teach their children how to change patterns and move towards a different way of life. One woman talked about how she spoke with her children about the need to make changes, why it was important and how the next generations could benefit. As one mother stated, "The main reason I want to go to university is to have a good life for me and my son. I want to show him that we can change our life circumstances. He is proud of me. I hope that, one day, he will remember this pride and use it to make his life better."

The mothers used various ways of role modeling and teaching to show their children how education can help them to take some control of their lives. One mother stated,

> I know my son is little but I want to be a good role model for him. I want him to see that I am trying even if it takes a long time. I want him to be the same way, so he won't drop out of high school. I want him to attend university. So, the main reason I came back to school is for him. I feel I am teaching him how we can make changes.

The mothers transmitted knowledge in a number of different ways. For example, the external and internal resources used by these women showed children how their mothers managed the addition of university studies to their lives. Some learned time management skills and showed their children that by establishing schedules everyone could still spend time together. Many used role modeling and discussion of family goals as a way for children to understand the importance of a university education, i.e. completing post-secondary studies could lead to fulfilling employment and a better income. These women are teachers, healers and nurturers, and actively influence their children and those in their extended family. As many of these women were first in their families to enter into university, they showed their children how to make positive changes in the family system, allowing the children to witness the power of change and self-determination. They opened up new vistas to their children, showing them new paths. Through their use of formal and non-formal education processes these women serve as role models, in their capacities as caregivers and relatives, through their work for organizations, and as teachers, healers, community workers and leaders. Information gained from this study is supported by Kim Anderson's research with Aboriginal women:

> Aboriginal women must now come to terms with family structures

> where there is often no male presence.... Uncles and grandfathers, biological or not, have a place in working with mothers and their children. They can fulfill the role of helper and bring men's teachings to single-mother households. (209).

Some of the women spoke of first learning about Aboriginal traditions at the time they entered university. They were excited and began to understand how colonization and racism had hindered them and other family members. Others spoke about how their Aboriginal heritage was their primary motivator helping to empower them towards achieving their goals. They taught their children about their heritage through the use of smudging, taking family members to Aboriginal ceremonies, and talking about Aboriginal traditions. One woman states,

> When I first introduced my oldest one to the culture she was just like, 'Mom, can Creator see this? Mom, can Creator see that?' She badly wanted to go into sweat lodges and like in my culture Aboriginal people see that as very spiritual ... my daughter is really gifted in the Aboriginal sense and I want to continue to teach her and guide her.

Another way of using maternal pedagogy is to draw on family members to be part of the decision-making process. The mothers were able to use this way of transmitting knowledge about life transitions. For example, one mother stated,

> Going to university is a family thing. You need to include your kids in the experience as much as you can so they understand it. It will help them feel and see how challenging it is. I talk with them about it. I say how going to school and having kids isn't the worst thing but it is tough and if you have a choice I would tell you not to choose it, go to school first and wait, because you can feel inadequate as a parent trying to balance everything. It will help them to understand how to make choices when they get older.

Another woman reflects on how important it is to talk to her children about both the struggles and the rewards of gaining a university education:

"I tell them they are not alone, they should continue with their education after grade twelve, it will be hard for them, but if they can find help through their 'Higher Power' they will be able to do it. Getting a university education means they can be the teachers for our Peoples."

Reflections

Throughout my data collection it was apparent that the women had a great deal of inner determination and worked hard to use their strengths to navigate towards a place of emotional health and fulfillment. As Jack Pransky states, "There can be no greater strength that exists automatically and naturally within each and every human being" (Pransky and McMillan 240). This value statement guided my research study.

Barriers these mothers encountered must also be addressed. These include financial, cultural and caregiving issues. Post-secondary educational institutions and educators need to find ways to offer ongoing outreach and encouragement to non-traditional students. Providing external resources in the form of counselors, mentors, academic advisors and support groups are crucial. These women can then act as mentors and advocates to others like themselves. As Susan Bernheimer notes,

> These are women who can stand on the shoulders of their past and reach out with understanding and experience to help children, parents, and other students who feel alone in our world.... It will be through their stories that our field can expand in new ways to become truly vital and effective. (23-24)

It was a privilege to meet with the women who agreed to partake in this study. Through their generous collaboration, I was able to explore and gain an understanding of their motivations for pursuing university studies, despite the complications of added financial, emotional, cultural and physical challenges in their lives. A significant finding of this study suggests that their motivation to succeed is driven by their role as mothers. They want a better life for their children. They also want to be good role models and teachers. As one woman stated,

> There are days I wake up and before I open my eyes, I question, Can I do this one more day? Then I open my eyes, go into the

shower, and wake up my daughter. Looking at her gives me the courage and motivation to get through that day.

Works Cited

Anderson, Kim. *A Recognition of Being: Reconstructing Native Womanhood.* Toronto: Sumach Press, 2000. Print.

Anderson, Kim, Charles Cowger, and Carol Snively. "Assessing Strengths: Identifying Acts of Resistance to Violence and Oppression." *The Strengths Perspective in Social Work Practice.* Ed. Dennis Saleebey. 5th ed. Boston: Pearson Education, 2009. 181-219. Print.

Bernheimer, Susan. *New Possibilities for Early Childhood Education: Stories from our Nontraditional Students.* New York: Peter Lang, 2003. Print.

Boyden, Jo and G. Gillian Mann. "Children's Risk, Resilience, and Coping in Extreme Situations." *Handbook for Working with Children and Youth: Pathways to Resilience Across Cultures and Contexts.* Ed. Michael Ungar. Thousand Oaks, CA: Sage Publications, 2005. 3-26. Print.

Creswell, John. *Qualitative Inquiry and Research Design: Choosing among Five Traditions.* Thousand Oaks, CA: Sage Publications, 1998. Print.

Dwyer, Sonya Corbin and Jennifer Buckle. "The Space Between: On Being an Insider-Outsider in Qualitative Research." *International Journal of Qualitative Methods* 8.1 (2009): 54-63. Print.

Hull, Jeremy. *Post-secondary Education and Labour Market Outcomes, Canada, 2001.* Ottawa: Strategic Research and Analysis Directorate, Indian and Northern Affairs Canada, 2009. Web.

Indian and Northern Affairs, Canada. 2001. Web. Retrieved 26 August 2008

Kirby, Sandra, Lorraine Greaves, and Colleen Reid. *Experience Research Social Change: Methods Beyond the Mainstream.* 2nd ed. Toronto: Broadview Press, 2006. Print.

Lerner, Richard M. and Peter C. Benson. *Developmental Assets and Asset-Building Communities: Implications for Research, Policy and Practice.* New York: Kluwer Academic/Plenum Publishers, 2003. Print.

McCubbin, Hamilton, Elizabeth Thompson, Anne Thompson, and Julie Fromer. *Resiliency in Native American and Immigrant Families.* Thousand Oaks, CA: Sage, 1998. Print.

Mendelson, Michael. *Aboriginal Peoples and Post-Secondary Education in*

Canada. Ottawa: Calendon Institute of Social Policy, 2006. Web.

Multest, R. A. and Associates. Ltd. *Best Practices in Increasing Aboriginal Post-Secondary Enrollment Rates.* Ottawa: The Council of Ministers for Education, 2002. Print.

Pransky, Jack and Diane McMillan. "Exploring the True Nature of Internal Resilience." *The Strengths Perspective in Social Work Practice.* Ed. Dennis Saleebey. New York: Longman, 1992. 240-261. Print.

Silver, Jim. *Solutions that Work: Fighting Poverty in Winnipeg.* Manitoba: Fernwood, 2002. Print.

Spence, Nicholas, Jerry White, and Paul Maxim. "Modeling Educational Success of First Nations in Canada: Community Level Perspectives." *Canadian Ethnic Studies* 39.1/2 (2007): 145-167. Print.

Statistics Canada. *Profile of Census Divisions and Subdivisions in Manitoba: 2006 Census.* Ottawa: Statistics Canada Catalogue no. 95-551-XPB 2009. Print.

Strauss, Anselm and Juliet Corbin. *Basics of Qualitative Research.* Thousand Oaks, CA: Sage, 1990. Print.

Ungar, Michael. "Resilience Across Cultures." *British Journal of Social Work* 38.2 (2008): 218-235. Print.

Feminist Maternal Pedagogies

Inside and Outside the Classroom

FIONA JOY GREEN

> Good teaching requires conspicuous thought and [is] not just about content delivery. It necessitates reflection on practising in intentional ways that are effective for learning to take place, beyond or outside of the expectations of others. (O'Reilly 2009: 7-8)

FEMINIST, MOTHER AND TEACHER ARE identities and positions that I cherish and live daily. Since my earliest recollection, and long before I was introduced to the language and practice of feminism as a university student in my early twenties, I have implicitly lived a feminist politic. I have been a teacher for more than three decades, first as a swim instructor from my mid-teens to my mid-thirties, and more recently as a university professor beginning in my late 20s to my recent 50th birthday. The year before I began teaching at the post-secondary level, I became a mother with the birth of my now 22-year-old son.

The timing and intersection of these paths has ensured that my teaching over the past two decades, both as a mother outside the classroom with my son and as a professor inside the classroom with my students, has been infused with feminism. The convergence of these identities and experiences also means that my post-secondary teaching has heavily influenced my mothering, and that my research has focused on the dynamic interconnections among feminism, mothering, teaching and activism.

During a larger research project addressing the interplay of feminism and mothering in the lives a small group of self-identified feminist mothers who purposely mother in ways that are informed by and embody their feminism, I recognized the practice of four core elements of feminist pedagogy identified below (Green 2009).[1] The purpose of this chapter is to begin developing a theory of feminist maternal pedagogies that takes into account some of the similarities and complexities of feminist mothering and teaching both within and beyond the classroom. I begin by briefly outlining these four elements, then provide a single example from my earlier research to demonstrate how a specific feminist mother enacts each belief in her motherwork. Since that earlier work, I have come to recognize the significant role of compassion in maternal feminist pedagogy, which I address in the second section of this chapter. I conclude by suggesting the need to include feminist maternal pedagogies into feminist motherlines and their potential usefulness for future generations of mothers, children, teachers, students, scholars and theorists.

Due to limitations of space, I have left to others in this and other collections the important and relevant discussion of the role maternal thinking, as theorized by Sara Ruddick, plays in feminist maternal pedagogies (see Andre; Ferris; Green 2003; Nathanson; O'Reilly 2009; O'Reilly and Ruddick; Porter; and Satz; and Watt—found in this collection). I must also note that while I focus primarily on the interaction of feminist mothers with their own children, much of what I argue is applicable to various forms of othermothering, for example, in instances when the students are not one's children and/or when the teacher/parent is male or transgendered.

What is Feminist Pedagogy?

Feminist educators have a passion for their teaching, and are driven by a vision of "a world which is not yet." They work differently, depending where and what they teach and what their politics are. They interrogate their teaching practices from a variety of perspectives (Manicom 365).

Feminist pedagogy is the art, practice, science and/or act of teaching that is informed by a feminist worldview that: 1) recognizes various forms of domination and oppression and the ways in which they intersect within people's lives, including the systematic oppression of women; 2) believes in the need and possibility of change; 3) favors the sharing of power, privilege, property and opportunities; and 4) understands the need for empowerment and collective organizing to bring about social change (Briskin; hooks 1988 and 1994; Spelman; Washington; Webb et. al). By definition, feminist pedagogy challenges what is seen to be the obvious, the natural, the accepted, and the unquestioned (Briskin 31). By raising thought-provoking questions, feminist educators guide themselves and others through the process of critical thinking, scrutinizing and analyzing their own and other people's ideas as well as contesting the assumptions informing specific ideas and actions (Bunch 1987; hooks 1988; Ropers-Huilman; Shrewsbury; Webb et al.; Zimmerman et al.).

Feminist Pedagogical Practices within the Context of Feminist Mothering

1) Strategies for Teaching about Systemic Oppression

Thinking critically entails refusing to accept the givens, making connections between facts and ideas that have been left unconnected and constantly retesting assumptions and hypotheses against lived experiences. (Rich 28)

Because feminist mothers are aware of the prevalence of patriarchy, sexism and misogyny in their own and in their children's lives, they purposefully motivate their children to think systematically and analytically about the world, particularly in relation to gender. They speak directly with them about the specific ways in which people are treated differently and how females are habitually devalued, discriminated against and oppressed. They engage their children in conversations about society and encourage them to observe and think critically about the power dynamics among people. They show them how limited conceptions of gender can be confronted and changed through examples of positive representations of females and alternative characterizations of males.

I draw from an interview with Francis, a heterosexual lone mother of a nine-year-old son, to demonstrate how a feminist mother might teach her child about gender discrimination. In this case, 45-year-old Francis spends time talking with her young son about the ways girls and boys are viewed when she engages him in the activity of counting the number of characters in his childhood storybooks. Together they discover males are more frequently represented than females, and talk about how people may think that a greater number of boys and men in books may mean that they are more important than girls and women. As they change the pronouns and gender of characters they create alternative, and at times, more equitable stories. In her parenting, Francis often uses this strategy of re-telling stories, as when she shares an alternative vision of Hanukkah with her son and his peers during a visit to his grade four classroom. Instead of limiting her narrative of Hanukkah to the experiences of men, as is routinely done, she includes the participation of women to illustrate how they also have contributed to the survival of Jewish people and how "history" also includes "herstory." In her revision of the traditional Hanukkah story, Francis teaches her son and his peers how both systemic sexism and systemic anti-Semitism operate, demonstrating how the intersectionality of oppressions can be taught to young students.

2) The Need for and Possibility of Social Change

Like many feminist classroom teachers, these feminist mothers teach their children how to recognize and critique the oppression of girls and women and how diversity, while not always prominent, is present and available as an alternative to mainstream thinking and presentations of reality. They speak candidly about and offer alternatives to narrow gender and sexual stereotypes, showing alternative and diverse ways of being in the world. They also demonstrate, as some feminist teachers do, how people can complicate, contest and revise dominant ways of looking at and thinking about women and men. For example, 36-year-old Kim speaks openly and frankly with her two- and six-year-old sons about the multiple ways people create families, and together with her common-law partner and their father, they spend time with the family's single and queer friends in same-sex partnerships.

Feminist teachers, whether inside or outside the classroom, encourage critical reflection on what is presented as truth and reality by encouraging their students/children to identify the meanings others have attached to gender, then examine the implications of those constructions (Bunch 1979; Green; hooks, 1988, 2000a; Ropers-Huilman 105). Also inherent in a feminist worldview and feminist teaching is the need for and possibility of social change. As feminist theorist and human rights activist Charlotte Bunch argues, feminism is concerned with putting an immediate end to women's oppression through active change; she notes that without an active and workable strategy, such as providing alternative models of understanding and participating in the world, change is unlikely.

Feminist mothers, too, are critical of patriarchal social structures and society, and actively work toward social change. The above example of Kim providing alternatives to ideas about who can love who and what constitutes a family illustrates how feminist mothers are committed to and active in creating social change. Another example of working for social change by recognizing and sustaining non-oppressive alternatives can be seen in the motherwork of 45-year-old lone mother Carol, who actively supports the growth and development of her children by equally encouraging, rather than trying to change, the unique characteristics of her compassionate 10-year-old son and her competitive 13-year-old daughter.

3) Promoting Egalitarian Relationships that Foster Collaborative Learning

Feminist commitment to social change is also evident in how mothers promote egalitarian relationships with their children that foster collaborative learning, empowerment, and self-governance. Yet, feminist mothers also acknowledge that they hold the dominant position within a power structure and that completely egalitarian relationships with their children/students are impossible. To suggest otherwise grossly oversimplifies their task and leaves unaddressed the contradictions faced by both feminist mothers/teachers and their children/students (Currie 353; Webb et. al.).

Just as Briskin, Currie, Ferris, hooks and Webb et. al. reflect upon and critique their own wielding of power as teachers who are part of a hierarchical educational system, so feminist mothers are aware of the power dynamics informing their relationships with their children. And like feminist teachers who seek to re-shape the classroom into a space that is shared by students and teachers, feminist mothers also construct collaborative pedagogical encounters, where cooperation and sharing are fundamental and where the positions, experiences and knowledge of both mothers and children are taken into account and honored.

Feminist teachers and feminist mothers often share a similar experience of being idealized while simultaneously having their authority disregarded or contested. Since feminist teachers recognize that "power can't be washed away" (Martindale 330) and that one of the tasks of feminist pedagogy is to "challenge the normative" (Briskin and Coulter 252), both feminist teachers and mothers recognize their location and relationship within their social context and accept the limitations of their personal ability to shape their environments—while simultaneously taking up the challenge of creating relationships and environments that foster collective ways of learning, teaching, and knowing.

Recognizing and troubling relations of dominance requires self-reflection and interrogation of both one's own position and the position of others in relation to power and authority. It also entails using various strategies, which may include those of midwife by providing a supportive environment for others to speak, of translator by helping people understand each other, or of interpreter by contesting dominant and oppressive ideologies and practices (Manicom 380; Zimmerman et. al.).

Since feminists condemn the unjust use of opportunities, power and privilege and are critical of relationships based on an imbalance of power, feminist teachers and mothers model the importance of egalitarian relationships by acknowledging the power differential in their daily interactions between themselves and others. Like feminist teachers, feminist mothers attempt to foster relationships with their children that are neither intimidating nor domineering; they strive to relate to their children in ways that are not based on the (ab)use of their authority and power as adults and parents. Rather than exercise absolute control over children, they strive for relationships based on respect, responsibility and accountability, while acknowledging that the relationship can never be truly egalitarian.

In not wanting to dominate her children, 50-year-old May encouraged her two bi-racial daughters from the time they were very young to talk with her about their lives, as well as contribute to open and honest discussions. They speak candidly with May, especially when they are experiencing hardships or challenges, because they have learned they can openly share their thoughts, ideas and experiences with her without fear of judgment. Like other feminist teachers, such as bell hooks (1994), May works from the premise that she can learn from everyone, including her daughters, and sees her children's knowledge and questions as resources for collaborative and collective learning. For instance, when her daughters question her thinking, May seriously reflects on her "own reasoning, motives and presumptions" and talks with them about their differing perspectives and what they learn from each other. By participating in relationships based on honesty, respect and accountability rather than on domination and subordination, May and her children practice a relationship that differs from the standard parent/child relationship and one that is similar to the way feminist teachers challenge the patriarchal teacher/student relationship (Briskin; Ferris; hooks 1994, 2000a; Larson, Luke; Maher 1986, 2008; Markowitz; Russell; Spelman; Washington; Webb et. al.; Zimmerman et. al.).

In the process of discussing their own thoughts along with the various points of view introduced by others, be they their mothers, teachers or others, children and students learn that there are numerous ways of interpreting and being in the world. They realize that people do not always agree and that associations can be based on egalitarianism rather than on relations of domination and submission (hooks 1994). Together they redesign conventional power dynamics by using strategies that help them be "theorists of their own lives by interrogating and analyzing their own experience" (Weiler 34).

3) Fostering Empowerment and Collective Action

> Classrooms exist in different contexts, and those contexts profoundly affect the possibility of empowerment. (Litner, Rossiter and Taylor 301)

Feminist mothers respectfully encourage their children to engage in difficult discussions where their thinking is challenged, where they are introduced to alternative points of view, and where they develop a sense of autonomy and mutuality. Rather than dictate their children's thoughts, mothers acknowledge the experiences and knowledge of their children and encourage them to talk about their own understandings and experiences.

Shar, a 60-year-old mother, uses this approach (which she first developed raising her now three 30-something-year-old children and two preteenaged grandchildren) in her current interactions with the children in her home-based childcare. Rather than telling the children to be quiet, ignoring what they are saying, or disregarding what they are asking, as many parents and adults do, she listens attentively and encourages them to recognize and articulate what they need. As she talks with them about their concerns, ideas and dreams, Shar attempts to make "deep connections with children by acknowledging the experiences they have" and urges them to articulate what they are thinking and to make decisions based on what they know. By showing them that "their thoughts and their feelings matter," she fosters their capacity to think, reason and learn that they are significant in a world where their realities are often denied and where adults overpower children. They also learn that their contributions are important and credible, how to think critically about their own knowledge, and to be responsible for their thoughts and actions. Giving a voice to children who are often silenced helps them to learn to be empowered people who can identify and articulate their values and their needs.

Feminist theorist Carolyn Shrewsbury notes a central goal of feminist pedagogy is to increase the power of all without limiting the power of some. Children of feminist mothers, like students of feminist teachers, are empowered in relationships where they make their own decisions based on their own reasoning and are held accountable for those actions. Empowerment and self-governance are learned within these compassionate relationships through conversations about their own and other's concepts and ideas. They learn to respectively consider and critique various perspectives and understandings, learn they are independent, self-governing people and that their decision-making and behaviors are powerful.

Tammy, a 37-year-old mother of two children between the ages of five and ten, shared with me an example of how she encourages her children to think for themselves and tries to support their values and decisions, even when they may conflict with those of people in authority. She told me how astonished she was to hear about a program at her children's school that gave "pink slips" to students for inappropriate behavior and "late slips" for being late to class and how she reminded her children about making choices and the responsibility that accompanies this action. While explaining her thinking to them about the implementation of the "pink slip" program she said:

> What really matters is what you were doing, whether it was appropriate or inappropriate, not how the teacher saw it or how the principal saw it. If you knew what you were doing was for a logical reason, and it was working towards a constructive end, I don't mind if you get a pink slip. It's a piece of paper, who cares?

Clearly there are times when the actions and choices of a child may be dangerous or hurtful to themselves or to others. When this occurs, feminist mothers often speak with their children of poor decisions they themselves have made and the harmful consequences of those choices. As they directly discuss the consequences of their children's regrettable decisions, they often encourage the children to empathize with another person's situation/feelings or to talk about how they currently are feeling about their own poor choices. They also remind their children that the power that accompanies decision-making entails taking responsibility for those actions, and that their actions generally affect others around them.

Whether a person is a child, student, teacher or mother, they develop a sense of their own agency in the world and discover how they can think actively about their own and others' interests and needs through their connections with others. Rather than rejecting authority per se, this model of collaborative feminist teaching names the power differential between folks, aims to equip people with the ability to acknowledge and use wisely the power they have "by virtue of their class, race or gender," and seeks to develop an appreciation for and engagement in collective learning and actions (Briskin 14). This approach draws attention to the agency of each individual and assists children/students in naming power relations within relationships rather than assuming, masking, or denying them. It also highlights an individual's capacity and responsibility to act as a change agent and as a leader in the world, both inside and outside the classroom (Briskin 15-16; Larson).

Paula, a 40-year-old separated mother of three children, provides a specific example of how people learn to act as empowered change agents within a community. She recounts how her eleven-year-old daughter successfully challenged the policy of "boys only" soccer teams at her former school, which was located in a rural Manitoba community. Instead of taking a lead role in challenging this sexist practice, Paula supported her daughter's wishes and agency, cheering from the sidelines as her daughter tapped into the power of collective action, something that Paula had frequently modeled for her daughter by being an active member of many community organizations. Paula quietly and proudly watched her daughter organize her friends and other parents to collectively convince the school authorities to change the practice of "boys only" soccer because it was unjust.

The Role of Compassion and Love in Feminist Mothering and Teaching

> Compassion is one of the most important facilitators for social change. (Cole 35)

Although few scholars have directly addressed compassion and love in their discourse on the principles and practice of feminist pedagogies, some feminist thinkers have considered the importance of love and compassion in their writings on political activism and libratory education (Cole; Frye; Green 2003; hooks 2002; Noddings 1984, 2002; Rose; Ruddick; Zimmerman et al.). For instance, feminist theorist Marilyn Frye articulates the need for a "science of the loving eye" which allows for and demands a plurality of experiences and subjective knowledge, presupposes embodied knowledge and independence, and "knows the complexity of the other as something which will forever present new things to be known" (76). Rather than blindly adhering or submitting to the ideas and ideals of others and ourselves, the loving eye allows for critical reflection and the creation of new meanings for us and for others. Feminist critic and scholar bell hooks has written a trilogy in which she posits an ethic of love that insists "we make choices based on a belief [in] honesty, openness and personal integrity" (88) and argues that in restoring love to its rightful place at the centre of our lives, we are more able to nurture and sustain the well-being of individuals and "give care, be responsible, show respect and indicate a willingness to learn" (94).

Love and compassion are central to the practice of feminist maternal pedagogies practiced by feminist mothers in their relationships with their children and to feminist pedagogies fostered by many feminist teachers in their relationships with students. Clearly, feminist mothers Francis, Kim, May, Shar, Tammy and Paula practice "the science of the loving eye" and "an ethic of love" in their interactions with their children. Feminist teachers also engage in the "the science of the loving eye" and an ethic of care when they honor their students' knowledge and realities, appreciate where their feelings and stories are coming from, and "nurture the unfolding, expanding material spirit" within each human being (Ruddick 57).

Through this research and my analysis of the pedagogical goals and strategies of self-identified feminist mothers with their children, I realize that I have largely overlooked the important role of love and compassion in this pedagogical dynamic. And I wonder if feminists who are teaching those who are not their children might enhance the learning experience and process for their students and for themselves by also being more openly affectionate and compassionate. While I recognize that there may be a danger of playing into stereotypes of the feminine/maternal/biological female by encouraging teaching based on an ethics of care, a loving eye, or attentive love, I argue that compassionate and loving pedagogical approaches can be practiced by all teachers, regardless of gender or parenting identities. And like Jane Ward, I argue that female teachers who have a "masculine" teaching style can, and often do, practice compassionate and loving pedagogies, although their ethics of care might be performed differently than those whose teaching style is more openly nurturing and traditionally "maternal."

Toward a Theory of Feminist Maternal Pedagogies

In previous works I have addressed the importance of feminist motherlines in providing a space and place for feminist mothers to record and share their knowledge/s and experiences of feminist mothering (Green 2006, 2008). I argue that feminist motherlines acknowledge the many struggles that accompany the embodied experiences, realities and knowledge/s of feminist mothering; contain invaluable lessons, memories and support for feminist mothers; and ensure a recorded legacy of feminist mothering and motherwork for others. I see the development, practice and discussion of various feminist maternal pedagogies as part of this motherline and as essential to ensuring that the difficult, yet rewarding and complex, work of feminist mothering practices remains documented, communal, and a political praxis.

Even though the final three essays in this anthology have been specifically allocated to this concluding section on Motherlines, I believe all of the essays in this compilation contribute to such a project. By making visible and documenting the variety and complexity of maternal pedagogical theory and practices, we can continue to learn about and teach important lessons regarding this topic, as well as ensure that critical analyses and personal accounts of maternal pedagogies are available to future generations of mothers, children, teachers, students, scholars and theorists. This collection is the first step towards recording and preserving our knowledge of a wide variety of maternal pedagogies that are practiced both within and outside the classroom.

I am grateful to Deborah Byrd for her insightful reading and input on the draft of this chapter.

[1]Over a two-year period (from 1996 to 1998), I interviewed 16 self-identified feminist mothers who were living in Winnipeg, Manitoba. Their ages ranged from 25 to 50 years. All were temporarily able-bodied birth mothers raising biological children, with two also raising non-biological children. Half of the women were raising children alone and the other half were raising children in partnerships. Six mothers identified themselves as single, two as lesbian, one as bisexual, eleven as heterosexual, and two did not identify their sexuality. Eleven women were born in Canada,

two in the U.S., two in England, and one in Colombia, South America. One woman identifies as African, one as Metis, and two as Jewish. Two women have Colombian/European ancestry, two are of Jewish/European descent, and seven have mixed European heritage. Four women identify themselves as poor and the other twelve consider themselves to be middle-class. All mothers have a post-secondary education.

Works Cited

Andre, Judith. "The Virtue of Honoring Oneself." *Maternal Thinking: Philosophy, Politics, Practice*. Ed. Andrea O'Reilly. Toronto: Demeter Press, 2009. 79-90. Print.

Briskin, Linda. *Feminist Pedagogy: Teaching and Learning Liberation*. Ottawa: Canadian Research Institute for the Advancement of Women, 1992. Print.

Briskin, Linda and Rebecca Coulter. "Feminist Pedagogy: Challenging the Normative." *Canadian Journal of Education* 17 (1992): 247-263. Print.

Bunch, Charlotte. "Not By Degrees: Feminist Theory and Education." *Quest: A Feminist Quarterly* 5.1 (1979): 240-253. Print.

Bunch, Charlotte. *Passionate Politics: Feminist Theory in Action*. New York: St. Martin's, 1987. Print.

Cole, Susan. 2010. "Women Reunite! A Radcliffe Radical Reflects on her Women's Collective Days." *Herizons: Women's News and Feminist Views*. 23.4 (2010): 30-35. Print.

Cully, Margo and Catherine Portuges, ed. *Gendered Subjects: The Dynamics of Feminist Teaching*. Boston: Routledge and Kegan Paul, 1985. Print.

Currie, Dawn. "Subject-ivity in the Classroom: Feminism Meets Academe." *Canadian Journal of Education* 17.3 (1992): 341-364. Print.

Ellsworth, Elizabeth. "Why Doesn't this Feel Empowering? Working Through the Repressive Myths of Critical Pedagogy." *Feminism and Critical Pedagogy*. Ed. Carmen Luke and Jennifer Gore. New York: Routledge, 1992. 90-119. Print.

Ferris, Denise. "The Mother in Mr. Chipps: Educating Artists and Maternal Thinking." *Maternal Thinking: Philosophy, Politics, Practice*. Ed. Andrea O'Reilly. Toronto: Demeter Press, 2009. 120-130. Print.

Frye, Marilyn. "In and Out of Harm's Way: Arrogance and Love." *The Politics of Reality: Essays in Feminist Theory*. New York: The Crossing Press, 1983. 52-83. Print.

Green, Fiona Joy. *Feminist Mothering in Theory and Practice, 1985-1995: A Study in Transformative Politics*. New York: Edwin Mellen, 2009. Print.

Green, Fiona Joy. "Feminist Motherline: Embodied Knowledge/s of Feminist Mothering." *Feminist Mothering*. Ed. Andrea O'Reilly. New York: SUNY Press, 2008. 161-176. Print.

Green, Fiona Joy. "Developing a Feminist Motherline: Reflections on a Decade of Feminist Parenting." *Journal of the Association for Research on Mothering* 8.2 (2006): 17-20. Print.

Green, Fiona Joy. "What's Love Got To Do With It? A Personal Reflection on the Role of Maternal Love in Feminist Teaching." *Journal of the Association for Research on Mothering* 5.2 (2003): 47-56. Print.

hooks, bell. *All About Love: New Visions*. New York: Perennial, 2000. Print.

hooks, bell. *Feminism is for Everybody*. Boston: South End Press, 2000a. Print.

hooks, bell. *Communion: The Female Search for Love*. New York: Perennial, 2002. Print.

hooks, bell. *Salvation: Black People and Love*. New York: Perennial, 2001. Print.

hooks, bell. *Talking Back: Thinking Feminist, Thinking Black*. Toronto: Between the Lines, 1988. Print.

hooks, bell. *Teaching to Transgress: Education as the Practice of Freedom*. Boston: South End Press, 1994. Print.

Hughes, Kate Prichard. "Education for Liberation? Two Australian Contexts." *Gender in Popular Education: Methods for Empowerment*. Ed. Shirley Walters and Linzi Manicom, London: Zed Books, 1996. 102-117. Print.

Larson, Laura. "The Necessity of Feminist Pedagogy in a Climate of Political Backlash. *Equity and Excellence in Education* 38.2 (2005): 135-144.

Luke, Carmen. *Feminisms and Pedagogies of Everyday Life*. Albany: State University of New York Press, 1996. Print.

Litner, Blumal, Amy Rossiter, and Marilyn Taylor. " The Equitable Inclusion of Women in Higher Education: Some Consequences for Teaching." *Canadian Journal of Education*17.3 (1992): 286-302. Print.

Maher, Frances. "Classroom Pedagogy and the New Scholarship of Women." *Gendered Subjects: the Dynamics of Feminist Teaching*. Eds. Margo Culley and Catherine Portuges. London: Routledge Kegan Paul, 1985. 29-48. Print.

Maher, Frinde. "Twisted Privileges: Terms of Inclusion in Feminist Teaching." *Radical Teacher* 83 (2008): 5-9

Manicom, Ann. "Feminist Pedagogy: Transformation, Standpoints, and Politics." *Canadian Journal of Education* 17.3 (1992): 365-389. Print.

Markowitz, Linda. "Unmasking Moral Dichotomies: Can Feminist Pedagogy Overcome Student Resistance?" *Gender and Education* 17.1 (2005): 39-55, 17.

Martindale, Kathleen. "Theorizing Autobiography and Materialist Feminist Pedagogy." *Canadian Journal of Education* 17 (1992): 321-339. Print.

Morgan, Kathryn Pauly. "The Perils and Paradoxes of Feminist Pedagogy." *A Reader in Feminist Ethics.* Ed. Debra Shogan. Toronto: Canadian Scholars Press, 1993. 393-405. Print.

Nathanson, Janice. "Maternal Activism: How Feminist Is It?" *Feminist Mothering.* 243-256. Print.

Noddings, Nel. *Caring: A Feminine Approach to Ethics and Moral Education.* Berkeley: University of California Press, 1984. Print.

Noddings, Nel. *Starting at Home: Caring and Social Policy.* Berkeley: University of California Press, 2002. Print.

O'Reilly, Andrea, ed. *Feminist Mothering.* New York: State University of New York Press, 2008. Print.

O'Reilly, Andrea, ed. *Maternal Thinking: Philosophy, Politics, Practice.* Toronto: Demeter Press, 2009. Print.

O'Reilly, Andrea and Sara Ruddick. "A Conversation About Maternal Thinking." *Maternal Thinking: Philosophy, Politics, Practice.* Ed. Andrea O'Reilly. Toronto: Demeter Press, 2009. 14-38. Print.

Porter, Marie. "Sara Ruddick's 'Motherwork': Personal Perceptions to Academic Analysis." *Maternal Thinking: Philosophy, Politics, Practice.* Ed. Andrea O'Reilly. Toronto: Demeter Press, 2009. 191-203. Print.

Rich, Adrienne. *Of Woman Born: Motherhood as Experience and Institution.* London: Virago, 1986. Print.

Ropers-Huilman, Becky, ed. *Feminist Teaching in Theory and Practice: Situating Power and Knowledge in Poststructural Classrooms.* New York: Teachers College Press, 1998. Print.

Rose, Hilary. *Love, Power and Knowledge: Towards a Feminist Transformation of the Sciences.* Cambridge: Polity Press, 1994. Print.

Ruddick, Sara. *Maternal Thinking: Toward a Politics of Peace.* Boston: Beacon, 1989. Print.

Russell, Michele. "Black-Eyed Blues Connections: Teaching Black Women."

Gendered Subjects: The Dynamics of Feminist Teaching. Eds. Margo Cully and Catherine Portuges. Boston: Routledge and Kegan Paul, 1985. 155-168. Print.

Satz, Martha. "The Baffled Mother: Maternal Puzzlement in Narrative, in Pedagogy in Academia." *Maternal Pedagogies: In and Out of the Classroom*. Eds. Deborah Lea Byrd and Fiona Joy Green. Toronto: Demeter Press. 2011. 91-101. Print.

Shrewsbury, Carolyn. "What is Feminist Pedagogy?" *Women's Studies Quarterly* 15.3and 4 (1987): 6-14. Print.

Spelman, Elizabeth. "Combating the Marginalization of Black Women in the Classroom." *Gendered Subjects: The Dynamics of Feminist Teaching*. Eds. Margo Cully and Catherine Portuges. Boston: Routledge and Kegan Paul, 1985. 240-244. Print.

Ward, Jane. "Queer Pedagogies and the Specter of the Maternal." *Maternal Pedagogies: In and Outside the Classroom*. Eds. Deborah Lea Byrd and Fiona Joy Green. Toronto. Demeter Press. 21-29. Print.

Washington, Mary. "How Racial Differences Helped Us Discover Our Common Ground." *Gendered Subjects: The Dynamics of Feminist Teaching*. Eds. Margo Cully and Catherine Portuges. Boston: Routledge and Kegan Paul, 1985. 221-229. Print.

Watt, Jennifer. "Re-Searching Mommy: Narrating my Inquiry of Maternal Pedagogies." *Maternal Pedagogies: In and Out of the Classroom*. Eds. Deborah Lea Byrd and Fiona Joy Green. Toronto: Demeter Press, 2011. 53-65. Print.

Webb, Lynne, Myria Allen and Kandi Walker. "Feminist Pedagogy: Identifying Basic Principles." *Academic Exchange Quarterly*. 6 (2002): 67-72.

Weiler, Katherine. "Freire and a Feminist Pedagogy of Difference." *Debates and Issues in Feminist Research and Pedagogy*. Ed. Janet Holland, Maud Blair and Sue Sheldon. Philadelphia: Open University Press, 1995. 23-44. Print.

Zimmerman, Lynn, Laura McQueen and Gwendolyn Guy. "Connections, Interconnections, and Disconnections: The Impact of Race, Class and Gender in the University Classroom." *Journal of Theory Construction and Testing* 11.1 (2007): 16-21. Print.

Notes on Contributors

Margaret Auguste is a School Media Specialist at a New Jersey Middle School, obtained her Master's in Psychology at Pepperdine University and has contributed to the anthologies *Hair Power, Skin Revolution.* She is currently writing the forthcoming book, *The Voice of Youth Advocates Guide to Censorship* and her work also appears in the *Faces of World Cultures, Teacher Librarian,* and *School Library Journal.*

Lynne Bond is Professor of Psychology at the University of Vermont and a founding member of its Women and Gender Studies Program. Her scholarship focuses on women's ways of knowing in contexts of community, family, and peer interaction, as well as on strategies for optimizing human development in community contexts.

Deborah Lea Byrd is Associate Professor of English and Women's and Gender Studies at Lafayette College. She is co-author of *Teaching Against the Isms; Feminist Pedagogy Across the Disciplines* and has published articles on service-learning pedagogy, mentoring programs for teen moms, and writers such as Tennyson, Joyce, Fowles, and the Brownings. Debbie also collaborates with local non-profits on community-based research projects designed to support and empower low-income families.

Karen I. Case is Associate Professor of Educational Leadership at the University of Hartford, where she cofounded a Doctoral Program in Educational Leadership. Her research is concerned with the creation of curriculum modifications for disenfranchised students. Currently, she is investigating the role of community-based research in doctoral program reform.

Katherine Ellison is Associate Professor of Eighteenth-Century Literature at Illinois State University and co-edits *Digital Defoe*. She is author of *Fatal News: Reading and Information Overload in Early Eighteenth-Century Literature* (2006) and articles in *Eighteenth-Century Fiction*, *Book History*, *Educational Research*, and *AEQ*. She has three sons aged five, four, and one.

Fiona Joy Green, feminist mother, Associate Professor and Chair of the Department of Women's and Gender Studies at the University of Winnipeg, is the author of *Practicing Feminist Mothering* (Arbeiter Ring Publishing, 2011) and numerous articles addressing feminist mothering and representations of mothers on reality TV. Within the context of teaching a feminist practicum course, she works collaboratively with students and feminist community-based organizations to foster feminist pedagogical practices within and outside the classroom.

Elisabeth Harrison is a Ph.D. student in Critical Disability Studies at York University in Toronto. Her undergraduate and Master's degrees are in Women's Studies. She is a psychiatric survivor, and her research interests include the psychiatrisation of women and queer people, representations of disability in media, and fat studies.

Tabitha R. Holmes, Ph.D., is an Assistant Professor of Psychology at the State University of New York, New Paltz. Her scholarship and teaching focus on how individuals develop within diverse ecological contexts. She also studies how individuals' belief systems help shape interactions between family members.

Cynthia Huff, English Studies Professor at Illinois State University, has authored *British Womens' Diaries*, edited *Women's Life Writing and Imagined Communities* and co-edited with Suzanne Bunkers *Inscribing the Daily: Critical Essays on Women's Diaries*. She is currently working on a book project, tentatively titled *Family Fictions*.

Heidi Hutner, is Associate Professor of English at SUNY Stony Brook, the author of *Colonial Women* (Oxford University Press, 2003), *Polluting Mama: Ecofeminism, Film, and Literature* (Demeter forthcoming) and editor of *Rereading Aphra Behn* (University of Virginia Press, 1993). She is writing a memoir on cancer, toxics, nuclear activism, and mothering. She is a mother and cancer survivor.

Margaret MacDonald is an Associate Professor in the Faculty of Education at Simon Fraser University. Her research interests include Mothering, Intergenerational Programs, Pedagogical Documentation, and Curriculum Development in early childhood education. She is currently working on a longitudinal project investigating Halq'eméylem language revitalization within the Stó:lō community.

Adwoa Ntozake Onuora is a doctoral candidate in the Department of Sociology and Equity Studies in Education at OISE/University of Toronto. Her areas of specialization are African and Black feminist theories, feminist pedagogy, cultural Studies and Afro-indigenous knowledge production. Her doctoral dissertation examines African-Canadian women's maternal pedagogies through arts-informed methodology.

Marlene Pomrenke received her doctorate in Social Work at the University of Manitoba (2006), and currently works at the Student Counselling and Career Centre with Student Affairs at the University of Manitoba as an Assistant Professor. Her research interests include mothering, attachment issues, resilience, and issues faced by post-secondary students.

Victoria Proulx-Schirduan, Ed.D, is an educational consultant, has taught at the elementary, middle school, high school, and college level for the past 18 years, and has counseled individuals with ADHD in private practice. Her research, presentations, and publications are in the area of attention deficit hyper activity disorder and multiple intelligences theory.

Martha Satz teaches at Southern Methodist University, exploiting her background in philosophy and literature to publish essays on such diverse topics as Jane Austen and genetics and the disability community. The adoptive mother of two bi-racial children (African American and white), now adults, she has written frequently about this experience.

Rebecca L. Upton holds the Edward Myers Dolan chair in Sociology and Anthropology at DePauw University. She has researched and written on infertility and HIV/AIDS in northern Botswana, on the impact of a second child in the American dual earning middle class and the intersections of qualitative and quantitative methodologies.

Samantha Walsh is a Ph.D. student in Sociology and Equity Studies at the University of Toronto. Her research, rooted in narrative, addresses the lived experience of disabled people and social policy work. She received her MA in critical disability studies from York University, and her BA in sociology from University of Guelph.

Jane Ward is Associate Professor of Women's Studies at the University of California Riverside. She is the author of *Respectably Queer* (Vanderbilt University Press, 2008), and several articles on queer politics, the social construction of heterosexuality, and the failure of diversity programs. She teaches courses in feminist and queer studies.

Jennifer Watt, emerging expert in loose teeth and racecars (thanks to daughter Else, age seven and son Sebastien, age five), is in the midst of her doctoral studies in "Education for Transformative Teaching, Learning, and Leading" at the University of Manitoba.

Index

Note: This index does not include pseudonyms used to protect the identities of interview subjects.

N